LOGICAL REASONING

Class 5

with **Chapter-wise Previous 5 Year** (2018 - 2022) Questions

In the interest of student community

Circulation of softcopy of Book(s) in pdf or other equivalent format(s) through any social media channels, emails, etc. or any other channels through mobiles, laptops or desktops is a criminal offence. Anybody circulating, downloading, storing, softcopy of the Book on his device(s) is in breach of the Copyright Act. Further Photocopying of this book or any of its material is also illegal. Do not download or forward in case you come across any such softcopy material.

DISHA Publications Inc.

45, 2nd Floor, Maharishi Dayanand Marg,
Corner Market, Malviya Nagar, new Delhi -110017
Tel: 49842349/ 49842350

© Copyright DISHA Publication Inc.

All Rights Reserved. No part of this publication may be reproduced in any form without prior permission of the publisher. The author and the publisher do not take any legal responsibility for any errors or misrepresentations that might have crept in.
We have tried and made our best efforts to provide accurate up-to-date information in this book.

Typeset By

DISHA DTP Team

Buying books from DISHA

Just Got A Lot More Rewarding!!!

We at DISHA Publication, value your feedback immensely and to show our apperciation of our reviewers, we have launched a review contest.

To participate in this reward scheme, just follow these quick and simple steps:
- Write a review of the product you purchase on Amazon/Flipkart.
- Take a screenshot/photo of your review.
- Mail it to *disha-rewards@aiets.co.in*, along with all your details.

Each month, selected reviewers will win exciting gifts from DISHA Publication. Note that the rewards for each month will be declared in the first week of next month on our website.

https://bit.ly/review-reward-disha.

Write To Us At
feedback_disha@aiets.co.in

Preface

We are pleased to launch the 2nd edition of **Olympiad Champs Logical Reasoning Class 5** which is the first of its kind book on Olympiad in many ways.

The Unique Selling Proposition of this new edition is the inclusion of past year questions till 2022 of different Olympiad exams held in schools.

The book is aimed at achieving not only success but deep rooted learning in children. It is prepared on content based on National Curriculum Framework prescribed by NCERT. All the text books, syllabi and teaching practices within the education programme in India must follow NCF. Hence, Olympiad Champs become an ideal book not only for the Olympiad Exams but also for strengthening the concepts for Class 5.

There is an exhaustive range of thought provoking questions in MCQ format to test the student's knowledge thoroughly. The questions are designed so as to test the knowledge, comprehension, evaluation, analytical and application skills. Solutions and explanations are provided for all questions. The questions are divided into two levels - Level 1 and Level 2. The first level, Level 1, is the beginner's level which comprises of questions like fillers, analogy and odd one out. When the child covers Level 1, it means his basic knowledge about the subject is clear and now it is ready for Level 2. The second level is the advanced level. Level 2 comprises of techniques like matching, chronological sequencing, picture, passage and feature based, statement correct/ incorrect, integer based, puzzle, grid based, crossword, venn diagram, table/ chart based and much more.

The first concern which each parent faces is how to make their children read a book especially when it is based on academics. Keeping this in mind interesting facts, real life examples, historical preview, short cut to problem solving, charts, diagrams, illustrations and poems are added. In addition to this, we have introduced comic strip which increases the readability quotient and make the reading experience for the children more exciting.

With the vision to remove all the misconception a child may have pertaining to the subject, to relate his knowledge to the real world and to develop a deeper understanding of the subject this book will cater all the requirements of the students who are going to appear in Olympiads.

While preparing this book, some errors might have crept in. We request our readers to identify those errors and send it across on **feedback_disha@aiets.co.in**.

We wish you all the best for your Olympiads and happy reading.......

Team Disha

For feedback : feedback_disha@aiets.co.in.

CONTENTS

1. **Analogy and Classification** — 1-17
2. **Patterns** — 18-41
3. **Alphabet Test** — 42-56
4. **Coding-Decoding** — 57-71
5. **Blood Relations** — 72-85
6. **Direction Sense Test** — 86-113
7. **Number, Ranking & Time Sequence Test** — 114-130
8. **Arithmetical Reasoning** — 131-147
9. **Logical Venn Diagram** — 148-167
10. **Problem Solving** — 168-183
11. **Estimation** — 184-199
12. **Geometrical Shapes** — 200-223
13. **Mirror and Water Image** — 224-242
14. **Embedded Figures** — 243-255
15. **Visual Reasoning** — 256-274

Unlock your child's **HIDDEN GENIUS!** with

Scan code to gain **FREE access** to "**Olympiad Champs**", a unique page dedicated to prepare students of class 1-8 to ace all National Level Olympiad Exams.

Current Affairs Updates, Mock Tests, Past Papers, Quizzes, Interesting, Fun Facts, Parenting Articles & Free Courses

10 Principles to CRACK ANY EXAM

1. Chase consistency, not intensity.

Doing intensive study makes your day. But it also exhausts you in the long run, leading to lesser output and added pressure. Toppers always focus on doing consistent work daily, for consistency is far more valuable than intensity. Remember consistent study of 4 hours every day is more important and powerful than studying 12 hours a day and then not studying at all for next 2 days.

2. Go beyond the surface.

Most students only see a few reasons (teacher, coaching, books, etc) behind Toppers' success, which is only the tip of the iceberg. What they donot see is Toppers Mindset, self belief, habits and discipline and that is where the real problem is.

3. Focus on giving your best, not chasing the best.

We want the best coaching, the best teacher, best batch and the best books but we are not ready to give our BEST. Success comes only when we are ready to give our best. We must focus on giving our best than chasing excuses to cover up our failures.

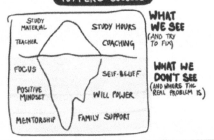

4. Clarity of concept is the key

Concept clarity is critical. If you cannot solve a question, you must go back to the theory and thoroughly examine the concept instead of referring to the solutions. Remember question is one of the chehra(face) of the concept. When toppers get stuck in a problem, they go back and refer the theory(read the concept again and again on which the question is based)

5. Every failure should be a lesson learned.

Most students do not learn from their failures and repeat their mistakes. Toppers also face failures, but they learn from mistakes and elevate themselves. Making mistakes and learning from them is the key to success.

6. Choosing the quality of resources is more important than quantity.

More than 90% of the questions in most books are the same as their substitutes. Instead of practicing from four books and failing to complete them, it is best to prepare from two books and complete them with thorough revisions.

7. Difficult things become easy by taking it one day at a time.

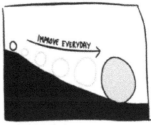

The best way to take any preparation forward is by taking it one day at a time. It makes the impossible possible by taking small steps every day.

Starting a difficult subject. No worries. Keep on working session by session, day by day and week by week and one day you will become unstoppable force.

8. Everything is easy

Before starting everything looks difficult. Once you take a first step, it slowly starts looking easy and over a period of time you become master in the activity. This is toppers secret to become master in any subject.

9. Nobody is gifted

We think toppers are god gifted. We think toppers have high IQ. We think toppers are special/lucky. But the truth is every topper was once an average student (no body is born topper). What makes them different is their consistent and focused efforts

10. Believe in your journey and success will come to you.

There is never a straight path to success; hard work & patience is required for the results to show up. Keep on working hard without thinking too much about the results and success will come to you eventually.

The above doodles have been taken from book, **"Stop being a Maggu"**. Stop being a Maggu is story of 3 aspirants **Abhyas** (the maggu), **Lakshya** (the born topper), and **Chunky** (the romeo) where their dreams are met with failures, external hurdles, & internal conflicts – leading to an extraordinary journey of realising untapped potential & remarkable transformation.

Buy Your Copy Today

MRP : ₹ 249/-
Must read for all students

CHAPTER 1

Analogy and Classification

OBJECTIVES

- Students will be able to study the similar patterns.
- They will be able to sort out objects on the basis of similarity.
- Classification based questions list the abilities of the students to observe the differences and similarities among objects or things.
- Students will learn assorting the items of a given group on the basis of certain common quality.

INTRODUCTION

Analogy

In 'analogy', a pair of figures/letters/words/numbers is provided and a similar relationship is followed by another pair of figures/letters/words/numbers. This is also known as 'Similarity' or 'Matching pairs'.

Types of Analogy

1. **Word Analogy**

    In word analogy, a group of three words is given, followed by four alternatives. The student is required to choose the alternative, which is similar to the given group of words.

Example 1:

Astronomy : Stars : : Geology : ?

   (a) Sky   (b) Geometry   (c) Science   (d) Earth

Ans. (d)

Explanation : Astronomy is the branch of science which deals with celestial objects such as moon, planets, stars, galaxies etc. While Geology is the science which deals with the physical and substance of the earth, their History and the processes which act on them.

Example 2:

Flower is related to Petal, in the same way as Book is related to .... ?

   (a) Pages   (b) Content   (c) Author   (d) Library

Ans. (a)

Explanation : Flower is made of Petals. Similarly, Book is made of Pages.

2. **Letter Analogy**

In letter analogy, a group of letters is given, followed by four alternatives. The student is required to choose the alternative, which is similar to the given group of letters.

Example 3:

Complete the second pair in the same way as first pair.

                AT is to CV, as LR is to

   (a) MS   (b) NT   (c) KQ   (d) RL

Ans. (b)

Explanation: As,   A T   Similarly,   L R

             +2↓ +2↓   +2↓ +2↓

              C V   N T

So, NT will complete the second pair.

Example 4:

COME is related to EOMC, in the same way HOME is related to

   (a) EMOH   (b) IPNF   (c) EOMH   (d) FNPI

Ans. (c)

Explanation: As,   C O M E   Similarly,   H O M E

             E O M C   E O M H

So, HOME is related to EOMH.

3. **Number Analogy**

In number analogy, a group of numbers is given, followed by four alternatives. The student is required to choose the alternative, which is similar to the given group of numbers.

Example 5:

63 is related to 3, in the same way as 96 is related to...............?

   (a) 15   (b) 3   (c) 9   (d) 5

Ans. (d)

Explanation: As, $63 = 6 + 3 = 9$ and $9 \div 3 = 3$

             Similarly, $96 = 9 + 6 = 15$ and $15 \div 3 = 5$

So, 96 is related to 5.

   4. **Mixed Analogy**

      In mixed analogy, a group of combination of numbers/letters/words is given, followed by four alternatives. The student is required to choose the alternative, which is similar to the given group of combination of numbers/letters/words.

Example 6:

A : 1 : : C : ?

   (a) 2   (b) 4   (c) 6   (d) 9

Ans. (d)

Explanation: As, $A \rightarrow (1)^2 = 1$ (the positional value of A is 1)

             Similarly, $C \rightarrow (3)^2 = 9$ (the positional value of C is 3).

So, C is related to 9.

   5. **Figure Analogy**

      In figure analogy, a group of figures is given, followed by four alternatives. The student is required to choose the alternative, which is similar to the given group of figures.

Example 7:

Which figure will complete the second pair in the same way as first pair.

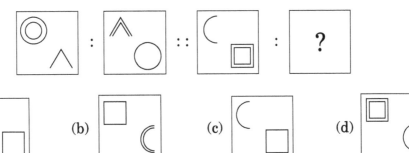

Ans. (b)

Explanation : Each one of the upper elements is replaced by an element similar to the lower element(s) and each of the lower elements is replaced by an element similar to the upper element(s).

CLASSIFICATION

Classification means 'to assort the items of a given group on the basis of a certain common quality they possess and then spot the stranger or 'odd one out'. These questions are based on words, letters and numerals. In these types of problems, we consider the defining quality of particular things. In these questions, four elements or parts are given, out of which one doesn't belong to the group. You are required to find the 'odd one'.

Questions on Classification Types

These are the types of questions which we shall consider in classification:

Type I: Choosing the Odd Word

In these types of problems, some words are given which belong to real world. They have some common features except the odd one. You are required to find the 'odd one out'.

DIRECTIONS (Examples 1-3):

In each of the following questions, four words have been given, out of which three are alike in some manner while the fourth one is different. Choose the odd one.

1. (a) Sparrow (b) Kingfisher (c) Nightingale (d) Bat

Ans. (d)

Explanation : Except Bat, all others are birds.

2. (a) Wave (b) Current (c) Tide (d) Storm

Ans. (c)

Explanation : Except Tide, all other terms are related to both air and water. But tide is a regular rise and fall in the level of sea, caused by the attraction of moon and sun.

3. (a) Mustard (b) Onion (c) Olive (d) Sesame

Ans. (b)

Explanation: All except onion are used for extracting oil.

Type II: Choosing the Odd Pair of Words

In these types of problems, different pairs are classified on the basis of some common features/properties like names, places, uses, situations, origin, etc.

DIRECTIONS (Examples 4 to 5)

In each of the following questions, four pairs of words are given, out of which three pairs bear a certain common relationship. Choose the pair in which the words are differently related.

4. (a) Gold : Ornaments (b) Cloth : Garments
   (c) Leather : Footwear (d) Earthen pots : Clay

Ans. (d)

Explanation: Except pair (d), in all other pairs, the first is the raw material which is used to make the second.

5. (a) Petrol : Car (b) Ink : Pen
   (c) Garbage : Dustbin (d) Lead : Pencil

Ans. (c)

Explanation: Except pair (c), in all other pairs, first is required by the second for its functioning.

Type III: Choosing the Odd Letter/Letters Group

In these types of problems, some groups of letters are given. One out of them is different and this is to be chosen by the student as the answer.

DIRECTIONS (Example 6): Choose the group of letters which is different from others.

6. (a) H (b) Q (c) T (d) Z

Ans. (b)

Explanation: All other letters except (b), occupy the even-numbered positions in the English alphabets.

Type IV: Choosing the Odd Numbers/Pair of Numbers

In these types of problems, certain numbers/pair of numbers are given, out of which except one, all have common characteristics and hence are alike. The 'different one' is to be chosen as the answer.

DIRECTIONS (Example 7): Choose the one which is different from the rest three.

7. (a) 57 (b) 87 (c) 131 (d) 133

Ans. (c)

Explanation: Except 131, all other numbers are non-prime (composite) numbers.

Type V: Choosing the odd picture/figure

In these types of problems, some groups of pictures/figures is given. One out of them is different and this is to be chosen by the candidate as the answer.

Example 8:

Choose the one which is different from the others.

Ans. (c)

Explanation : Except figure (c), in all other figures, the inner design consists of less number of sides than that of the outer design.

LEVEL-1

1. Odometer is to mileage as compass is to .... ?
   (a) Hiking   (b) Needle   (c) Direction   (d) Speed
2. Window is to pan as book is to .... ?
   (a) Novel   (b) Page   (c) Cover   (d) Glass
3. Find the odd one out.
   (a) 242   (b) 512   (c) 701   (d) 660
4. Reptile is to lizard as flower is to .... ?
   (a) Petal   (b) Daisy   (c) Steam   (d) Bulb
5. Play is to actor as concert is to .... ?
   (a) Symphony   (b) Piano   (c) Musician   (d) Percussion
6. Asthma : Lungs : : Conjunctivitis :
   (a) Bones   (b) Teeth   (c) Eyes   (d) Blood
7. Choose the odd one out.
   (a) BDG   (b) LNQ   (c) RST   (d) WYB
8. Find the odd one out.
   (a) Lake   (b) Rain   (c) Well   (d) River
9. Which shape or pattern completes the second pair in the same way as the first?
10. Which shape or pattern completes the second pair in the same way as the first?

11. Choose the one which is different from the others.

    (a) 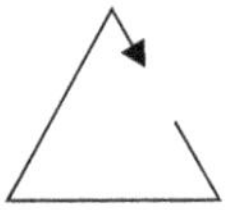 (b) 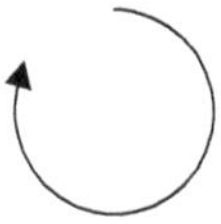 (c) 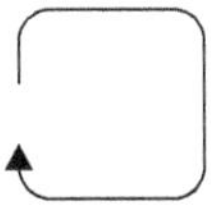 (d)

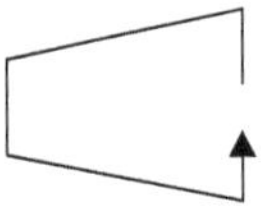

12. Find the number that will replace the question mark(?).

    6 is to 42 as 8 is to ___?

    (a) 64 (b) 56 (c) 72 (d) 48

13. Identify the relationship of the first pair and then find the missing term in the second pair.

    CDH : HCD :: KPQ : ?

    (a) QPK (b) LQR (c) QKP (d) RQL

14. Choose the one which is different from the others.

    (a) 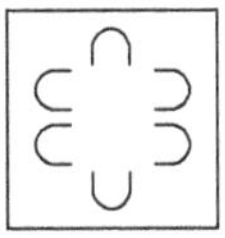 (b) 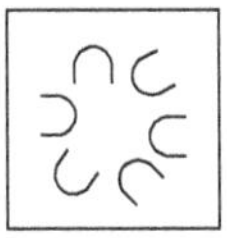 (c)  (d)

15. Find the figure which will complete the second pair following the same rule that first pair follow.

    (a)  (b)  (c)  (d)

16. Four different lockers are shown below. Each locker represents a combination of a letter and a number. Choose the one which represents different combination from others.

    (a) 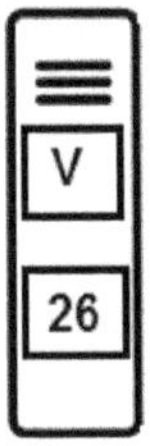 V, 26 (b) 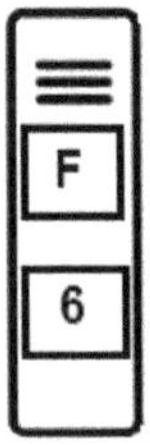 F, 6 (c) 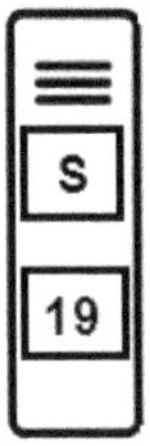 S, 19 (d) 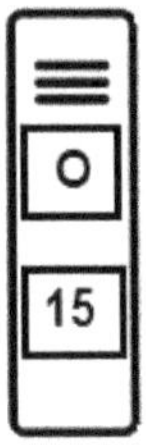 O, 15

17. Find the term which is different from the others.

    (a) Pomegranate (b) Apple (c) Honey (d) Brinjal

18. Choose the odd one out.

    (a) 421 (b) 835 (c) 725 (d) 945

19. Find the missing term in the second pair.

    5 : 525 :: 7 : ?

    (a) 725 (b) 727 (c) 575 (d) 755

20. Which inversion is different from the others?

   (a)   (b)   (c)   (d)

21. Which shape or pattern completes the second pair in the same way as the first?

   (a)   (b)   (c)   (d)

DIRECTIONS (Qs. 22 – 30): Identify the relation between each of the given pair on either side of : : and find the missing term.

22. Fear : Threat : : Anger : ?
    (a) Panic   (b) Compulsion   (c) Provocation   (d) Force
23. PEARL : JRAƎP : : SEAL : ?
    (a) LAƎS   (b) JAƎS   (c) ꙅEAJ   (d) ꙅEAL
24. 21 : 3 : : 574 : ?
    (a) 23   (b) 82   (c) 97   (d) 113
25. 1 : 1 : : 25 : ?
    (a) 26   (b) 125   (c) 240   (d) 625
26. 6 : 36 : : 4 : ?
    (a) 25   (b) 20   (c) 16   (d) 18
27. AG : FL : : EK : ?
    (a) LR   (b) JP   (c) PV   (d) SY
28. Fox : Cunning : :
    (a) Cat : Playful   (b) Horse : Runner   (c) Vixen : Cute   (d) Ant : Industrious
29. Choose the odd one out.
    (a) Axe   (b) Knife   (c) Hammer   (d) Scissors
30. ADE : FGJ : : KNO : ?
    (a) PQR   (b) PQT   (c) RQP   (d) TPR
31. Identify the relationship of the first pair and then find the missing term in the second pair.

    M I : O G :: C I : ?

    (a) AJ   (b) EI   (c) EN   (d) EG
32. Identify the relationship of the first pair and then find the missing term in the second pair.

    1 , 2 , 3 : 2 , 3 , 4 :: 3 , 4 , 5 : ?

    (a) 2, 3, 4   (b) 4, 5, 6   (c) 5, 4, 3   (d) 4, 4, 5
33. Find the odd one out.
    (a) Small   (b) Huge   (c) Heavy   (d) Big
34. Choose the odd one out.

    (a)   (b)

(c) 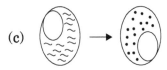   (d)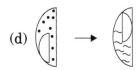

35. Which shape or pattern completes the second pair in the same way as the first?

(a)   (b)   (c)   (d)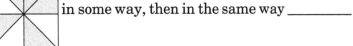

36. If [figure] is related to [figure] in some way, then in the same way _____ is related to [figure]. **(2018)**

(a) 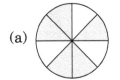   (b) 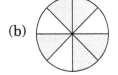   (c) 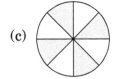   (d)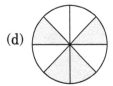

37. There is a certain relationship between the pair of terms on the either side of ::. Establish the relationship of the left pair and find the missing term.

SOF : UQH :: IMO : ?   **(2020)**

(a) KQO   (b) JOQ   (c) KOQ   (d) GKM

38. What will come in place of the question mark(?)?   **(2022)**
Bull : Bellow :: Monkey : _?_
(a) Roar   (b) Bray   (c) Mew   (d) Chatter

LEVEL-2

1. Cube is related to square in the same way as square is related to ....?
   (a) Line   (b) Triangle   (c) Point   (d) Plane
2. Choose the odd number.

   43, 53, 63, 73, 83

   (a) 43   (b) 53   (c) 63   (d) 83

3. Clock : Time : : Thermometer : ?
   (a) Heat (b) Temperature (c) Energy (d) Radiation
4. Mountain : Valley : : Genius : ?
   (a) Brain (b) Intelligence (c) Think (d) Idiot
5. Identify the one which is different from others?
   324, 244, 136, 352, 514
   (a) 324 (b) 244 (c) 136 (d) 514
6. Young is related to old in the same way as wide is related to .... ?
   (a) Insufficient (b) Narrow (c) Big (d) Long
7. MIKE : NJLF : : HAND : ?
   (a) NDAH (b) GZMC (c) GBOE (d) IBOE
8. DELITE : ETILED : : FLOWER : ?
   (a) FWORE (b) LFWOER (c) REWOLF (d) OLFREW
9. YELLOW : ZDMKPV : : BLUE : ?
   (a) AMTD (b) CKVD (c) CMVF (d) AKTD
10. [figure] : [figure] : : [figure] : ?
    (a) [figure] (b) [figure] (c) [figure] (d) [figure]
11. [figure] : [figure] : : [figure] : ?
    (a) [figure] (b) [figure] (c) [figure] (d) [figure]
12. [figure] : [figure] : : [figure] : ?
    (a) [figure] (b) [figure] (c) [figure] (d) [figure]
13. [figure] : [figure] : : [figure] : ?
    (a) [figure] (b) [figure] (c) [figure] (d) [figure]
14. [figure] : [figure] : : [figure] : ?
    (a) [figure] (b) [figure] (c) [figure] (d) [figure]

15. 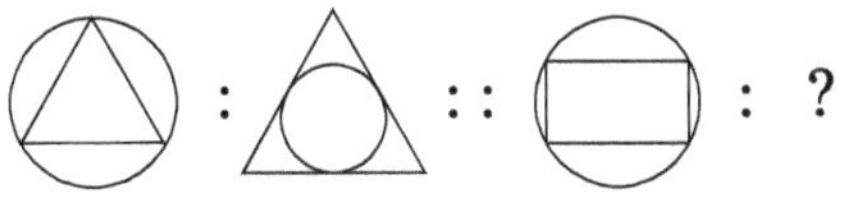

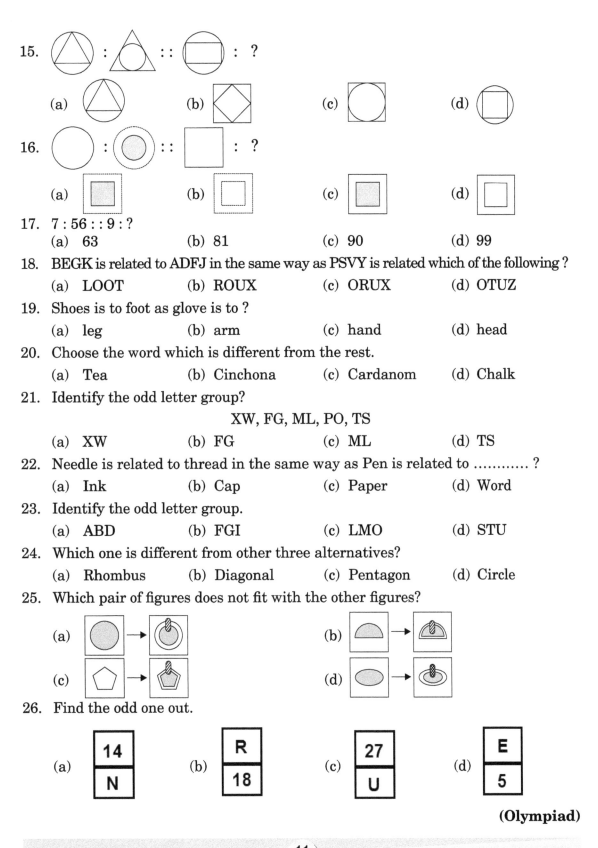

(a) 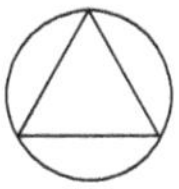 (b)  (c) 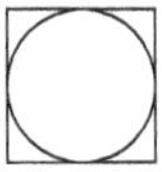 (d) 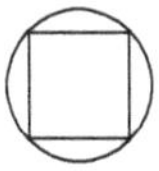

16. 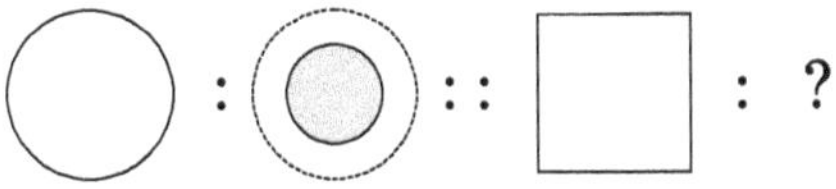

(a)  (b)  (c) 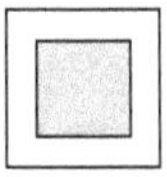 (d) 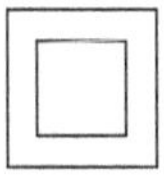

17. 7 : 56 : : 9 : ?

(a) 63 (b) 81 (c) 90 (d) 99

18. BEGK is related to ADFJ in the same way as PSVY is related which of the following ?

(a) LOOT (b) ROUX (c) ORUX (d) OTUZ

19. Shoes is to foot as glove is to ?

(a) leg (b) arm (c) hand (d) head

20. Choose the word which is different from the rest.

(a) Tea (b) Cinchona (c) Cardanom (d) Chalk

21. Identify the odd letter group?

XW, FG, ML, PO, TS

(a) XW (b) FG (c) ML (d) TS

22. Needle is related to thread in the same way as Pen is related to .... ?

(a) Ink (b) Cap (c) Paper (d) Word

23. Identify the odd letter group.

(a) ABD (b) FGI (c) LMO (d) STU

24. Which one is different from other three alternatives?

(a) Rhombus (b) Diagonal (c) Pentagon (d) Circle

25. Which pair of figures does not fit with the other figures?

(a) 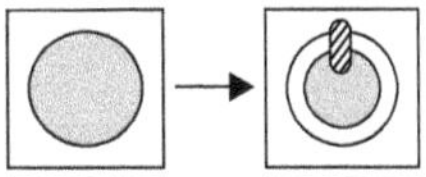

(b) 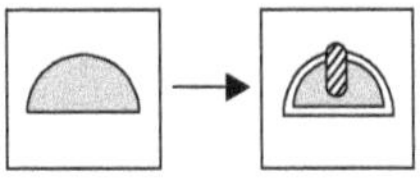

(c) 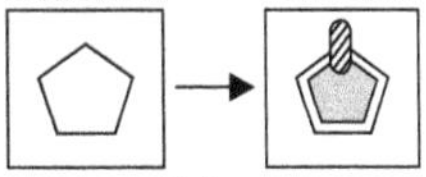

(d) 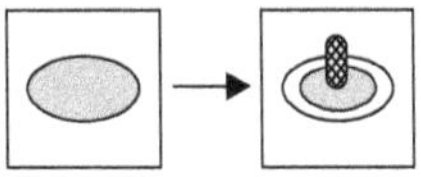

26. Find the odd one out.

(a) 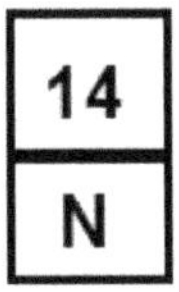

(b) 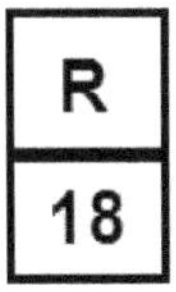

(c) 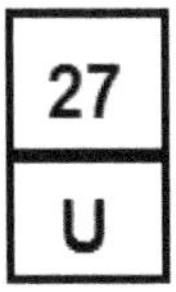

(d) 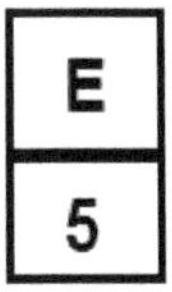

(Olympiad)

27. Find the wrong term in the given series.

X1M W2N V3O U4Q T5Q

(a) W2N (b) V3O (c) U4Q (d) Y5Q

(Olympiad)

28. Which is the missing figure?

(a) (b) (c) (d)

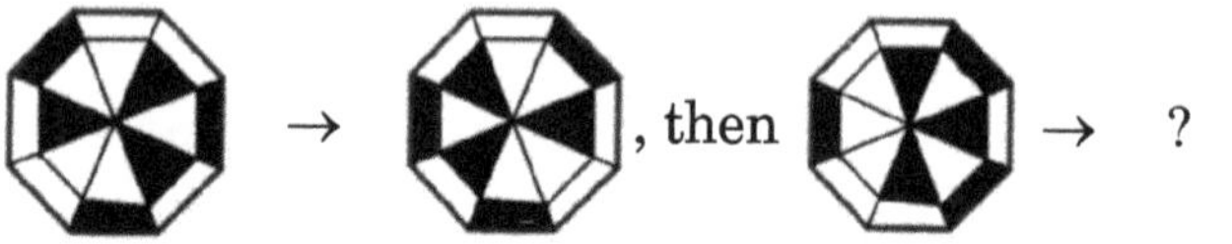

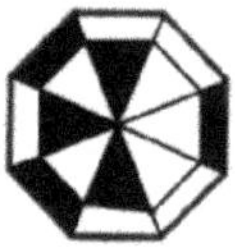

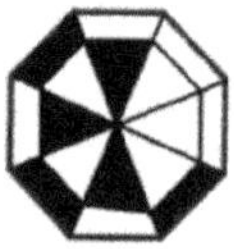

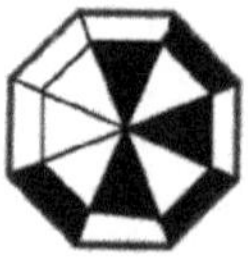

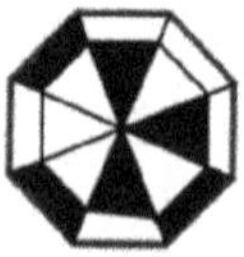

(Olympiad)

29. Fig.(i) and (ii) are related in a particular manner. Establish the same relationship between fig. (iii) and (iv) by choosing a figure from the given options.

(i) (ii) (iii) (iv)

(a) (b) (c) (d)

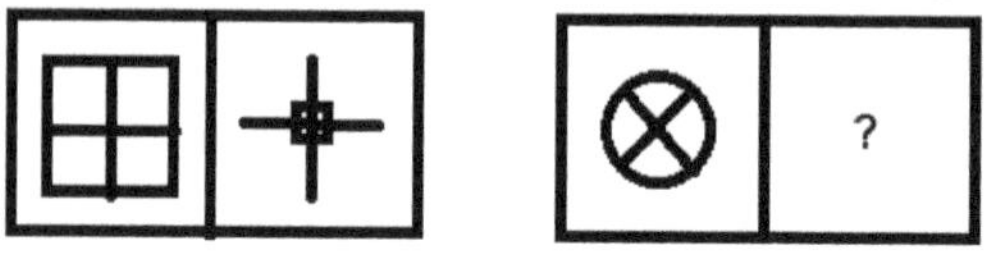

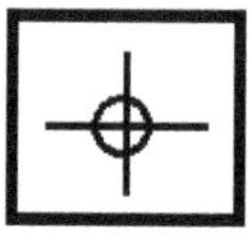

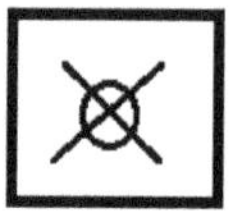

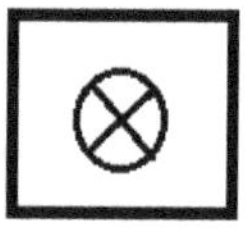

(Olympiad)

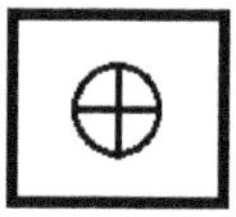

30. There is a certain relationship between fig. (i) & (ii). Identify the relationship and establish the same relation between figure (iii) & (iv), by selecting the figure from the given options which will replace the (?) in fig.(iv).

(i) (ii) (iii) (iv)

(a) (b) (c) (d)

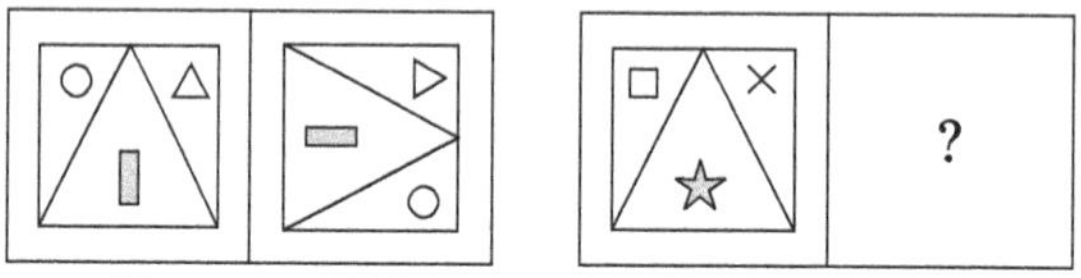

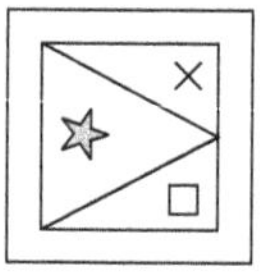

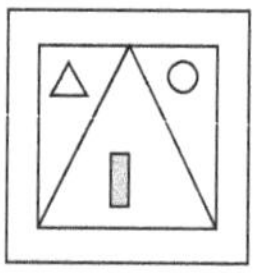

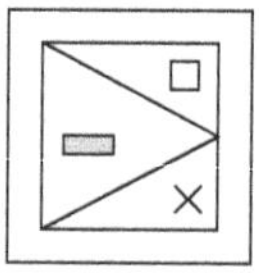

(Olympiad)

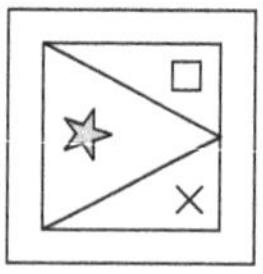

31. There is a definite relationship between fig. (i) and (ii). Establish the same relationship between fig.(iii) and (iv) by selecting a figure from the options which will replace the (?) in fig. (iv).

(i) (ii) (iii) (iv)

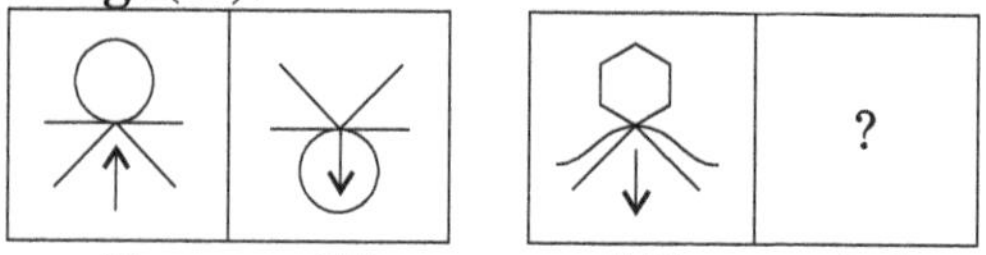

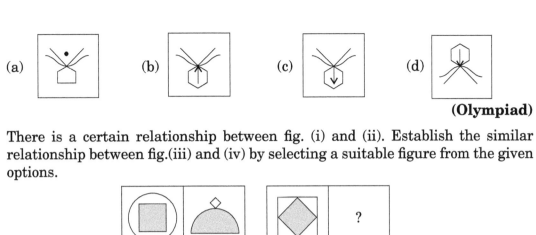

32. There is a certain relationship between fig. (i) and (ii). Establish the similar relationship between fig.(iii) and (iv) by selecting a suitable figure from the given options.

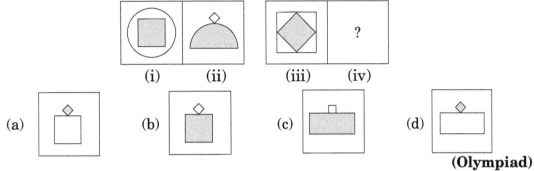

33. Find the figure which is different from the others.

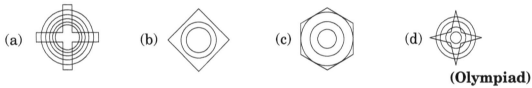

34. Find the odd one out.

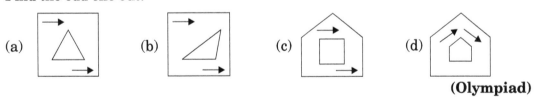

35. There is a definite relationship between fig. (i) and (ii). Establish the same relationship between fig.(iii) and (iv) by selecting a figure from the options which will replace the (?) in fig. (iv).

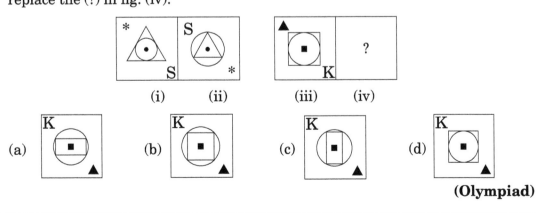

(Olympiad)

36. Find the missing number, if same rule is followed in all the three figures. **(2020)**

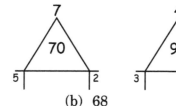

(a) 72   (b) 68   (c) 84   (d) 78

Answers and Explanation

Level-1

1. **(c)** An Odometer is an instrument used to measure mileage. Similarly, a compass is an instrument used to determine direction.
2. **(b)** A window is made up of panes and book is made up of pages.
3. **(d)** As, 2 + 4 + 2 = 8, 5 + 1 + 2 = 8 and 7 + 0 + 1 = 8. But, 6 + 6 + 0 = 12.
4. **(b)** A lizard is a type of reptile and a daisy is a type of flower.
5. **(c)** An actor performs in play where as a musician performs at a concert.
6. **(c)** Asthma is a lung disease. Similarly, conjunctivitis is a eye diseases.
7. **(c)** As, B D G, L N Q
             +2 +3   +2 +3
   and
   W Y B but, R S T
   +2 +3   +1 +1
   So, option (c) is odd one out.
8. **(b)** Except (b) all others are water bodies.
9. **(b)** Shapes are gelling vertically inverted.
10. **(b)** First shape (□) becomes the outermost, second shape (△) becomes the innermost and third shape (○) takes the middle place.
11. **(d)** Except (d) all others are opened up clockwise.
12. **(b)** As, 6 × 7 = 42
    Similarly, 8 × 7 = 56.
13. **(c)** As,
      1 2 3   3 1 2
      C D H : H C D

    Similarly,

      1 2 3   3 1 2
      K P Q : Q K P

    So, option (c) is correct.
14. **(a)**
    all curves are inverted inward.
15. **(d)** Second shape becomes large and merges first shape in itself after in verting.
16. **(a)** Here, all lockers consists of a letter and its positional value (in English alphabetical order), whereas locker in option (a) consists of letter 'V' whose positional value is '22' not '26'. So, it is odd one out.

17. **(c)** All except honey are produced by plant or tree. But honey is produced by bee.
18. **(a)** As, 8 – 3 = 5, 7 – 2 = 5 and 9 – 4 = 5 but, 4 – 2 ≠ 1.
19. **(b)** As, 5 : 5 2 5 ⟶ New number
    Similarly,
    7 : 7 2 7 ⟶ New number
20. **(d)**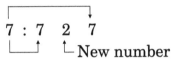
21. **(a)**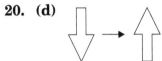
22. **(c)** First arises form the second.
23. **(b)** Second is the mirror image of the first.
24. **(b)** The relationship is
    21 ÷ 7 = 3
    574 ÷ 7 = 82.
25. **(d)** The relationship is $X : x^2$
    1 × 1 = 1
    25 × 25 = 625.
26. **(c)** Second is the square of the first number.
27. **(b)** Each letter of the first group is moved five steps forward to obtain the corresponding letter of the second group.
28. **(d)** Fox is considered to be cunning. Similarly, ant is considered to be industrious creature.
29. **(c)** Except Hammer, all others are used to cut.
30. **(b)** The rule followed is
    $$\overset{+3}{A\ D\ E} : \overset{+3}{F\ G\ J}$$
    with +5 and +5
    So, if we follow the same rule
    $$\overset{+3}{K\ N\ O} : \overset{+3}{P\ Q\ T}$$
    with +5 and +5
31. **(d)** As, M I
    +2↓ –2↓
    O   G
    Similarly,
    C   I
    +2↓ –2↓
    E   G
32. **(b)** As, 1   2   3
    +1↓ +1↓ +1↓
    2   3   4
    Similarly,
    3   4   5
    +1↓ +1↓ +1↓
    4   5   6
33. **(c)** Except Heavy, all others are used to denote the size.
34. **(d)**
35. **(d)** Figure has been rotated 180° anticlockwise.
36. **(b)**
37. **(c)**
    S O F   I M O
    +2↓ +2↓ +2↓   +2↓ +2↓ +2↓
    U P H   K O Q
38. **(d)**

Level-2

1. **(a)** Cube comprises square on all of its surfaces. In the same way, square comprises line on all of its sides.
2. **(c)** Each of the number except 63, is a prime number.
3. **(b)** First is an instrument to measure second.

4. **(d)** The word in each pair are antonyms of each other.

5. **(a)** Sum of the each digits in each number is 10.
$244 = 2 + 4 + 4 = 10$
$136 = 1 + 3 + 6 = 10$
$352 = 3 + 5 + 2 = 10$
$514 = 5 + 1 + 4 = 10$
$\boxed{324 = 3 + 2 + 4 = 9} \rightarrow$ odd

6. **(b)** Both are the antonyms of each other.

7. **(d)** As, MIKE is to NJLF; Plus/alphabet
$M \xrightarrow{+1} N \quad H \xrightarrow{+1} I$
$I \xrightarrow{+1} J \quad A \xrightarrow{+1} B$
$K \xrightarrow{+1} L \quad N \xrightarrow{+1} O$
$E \xrightarrow{+1} F \quad D \xrightarrow{+1} E$

8. **(c)** Reverse the letter to get the current form.

9. **(b)** As, Similarly
$Y \xrightarrow{+1} Z \quad B \xrightarrow{+1} C$
$E \xrightarrow{-1} D \quad L \xrightarrow{-1} K$
$L \xrightarrow{+1} M \quad U \xrightarrow{+1} V$
$L \xrightarrow{-1} K \quad E \xrightarrow{-1} D$
$O \xrightarrow{+1} P$
$W \xrightarrow{-1} V$

10. **(d)** Second element becomes enlarge and first element becomes its inner figure after inverting down.

11. **(a)** Shaded space becomes unshaded and unshaded becomes shaded.

12. **(a)** Second is the mirror image of first one.

13. **(a)** Second is the mirror image of first one and inner figure becomes dotted.

14. **(b)** ⌐○⌐

15. **(c)** Inner element becomes the outer element and outer element becomes the inner element.

16. **(a)** Element becomes dotted in second figure and same small element is added in the dotted element.

17. **(c)** The relationship is $x : x(x + 1)$
$7(7 + 1) = 56 \Rightarrow 7 \times 8 = 56$
$9(9 + 1) = 90 \Rightarrow 9 \times 10 = 90$

18. **(c)** Clearly, each letter of the first pair is moved one step backward to obtain the corresponding letter of the second pair
$B \xrightarrow{-1} A \quad P \xrightarrow{-1} O$
$E \xrightarrow{-1} D \quad S \xrightarrow{-1} R$
$G \xrightarrow{-1} F \quad V \xrightarrow{-1} U$
$K \xrightarrow{-1} J \quad Y \xrightarrow{-1} X$

19. **(c)** A shoe is worn on a foot. A glove is worn on a hand.

20. **(d)** All the things are obtained from crops except chalk.

21. **(b)** Except (b) all other groups contains two consecutive letters in reverse order.

22. **(a)** Second is required for the working of the first.

23. **(d)**
(a) $A \xrightarrow{+1} B \xrightarrow{+2} D$
(b) $F \xrightarrow{+1} G \xrightarrow{+2} I$
(c) $L \xrightarrow{+1} M \xrightarrow{+2} O$
(d) $S \xrightarrow{+1} T \xrightarrow{+1} U$
Odd one out.

24. **(d)** Except circle all other are made from straight lines.

25. **(d)** Shaded design is different.

26. **(c)** Here, all blocks consists of a letter and its positional value (in English alphabetical order), whereas block in option (c) consists of letter 'U' whose positional value is '21' not '27'.

27. (c) The pattern is as follows:
$$X \xrightarrow{-1} W \xrightarrow{-1} V \xrightarrow{-1} U \xrightarrow{-1} T$$
$$1 \xrightarrow{+1} 2 \xrightarrow{+1} 3 \xrightarrow{+1} 4 \xrightarrow{+1} 5$$
$$M \xrightarrow{+1} N \xrightarrow{+1} O \xrightarrow{+1} \text{\textcircled{Q}} \xrightarrow{+1} Q$$
There should be P in place of Q.

28. (a) Second is the mirror image of the first one.

29. (b)

30. (a) Figure is rotating 90° clockwise and inner unshaded elements interchange their places after rotation.

31. (b) Upper shape becomes the lower shape and viceversa. Arrow reverses its directions.

32. (c) Outer figure becomes half and inner figure sets at the mid-top of outer figure after being smaller.

33. (a)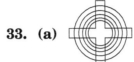

34. (d)

35. (b) Middle figure becomes the outer figure and outer figure becomes the middle figure signs at the corners interchange diagonally.

36. (a) 5 × 2 × 7 = 70; 3 × 8 × 4 = 96. Similarly, 4 × 3 × 6 = 72

CHAPTER 2

Patterns

OBJECTIVES
- Students will learn to develop and extend patterns.
- Students will learn to discover how patterns arise in a variety of mathematical and everyday contexts, and to establish the rules which govern them.

INTRODUCTION

Patterns are
- repeated designs or recurring sequences.
- an ordered set of letters, words, numbers, shapes or other mathematical objects, arranged according to a particular rule.

Type I: To find the missing term or next term (number or letter)
- Identify the rule followed in rest of the given terms using mathematical operation: addition, subtraction, multiplication, division, skip counting and reverse counting.
- Identify the order of alphabetical series either from A to Z or Z to A.
- Skipping letters.

Type II: To find the missing part in the figure pattern.
- Complete the figure pattern by drawing its incomplete part in the pattern.

Example 1:

In the number pattern below, what are the values of A and B respectively?

4	A	16	25	36	B

(a) 9, 49 (b) 49, 9 (c) 9, 64 (d) 81, 49

Ans. (a)

Explanation: Pattern followed in the above series is

$2 \times 2 = 4$, $3 \times 3 = 9$, $4 \times 4 = 16$, $5 \times 5 = 25$,
$6 \times 6 = 36$, $7 \times 7 = 49$

Example 2:

Which is the missing square?

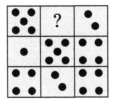

(a) [image] (b) [image] (c) [image] (d) [image]

Ans. (b)

Explanation: Sum of circles in each row or column is 10.

Example 3:

Which one will replace the question mark?

5	6	30
6	7	42
9	?	36

(a) 2   (b) 3   (c) 4   (d) 5

Ans. (c)

Explanation : As, $5 \times 6 = 30$
and $4 \times 7 = 42$
Similarly, $9 \times ? = 36$
$? = \dfrac{36}{9}$
$? = 4$

Example 4:

Find the missing pair of letters in the series.

CD   FG   IJ   ?   OP

(a) KL   (b) LM   (c) KM   (d) MN

Ans. (b)

Explanation : The pattern is as follows:

Example 5:

Which figure will replace the question mark in the figure pattern below?

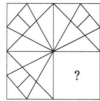

(a) (b) (c) (d)

Ans. (d)

Explanation :

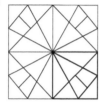

Example 6:

Which figure will replace the question mark in the series?

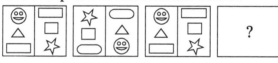

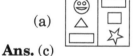   

(a) (b) (c) (d)

Ans. (c)

Explanation : The figure repeats itself after two steps.

LEVEL-1

1. Which number will replace the question mark in the number pattern given below?

    (a) 71   (b) 75   (c) 80   (d) 81

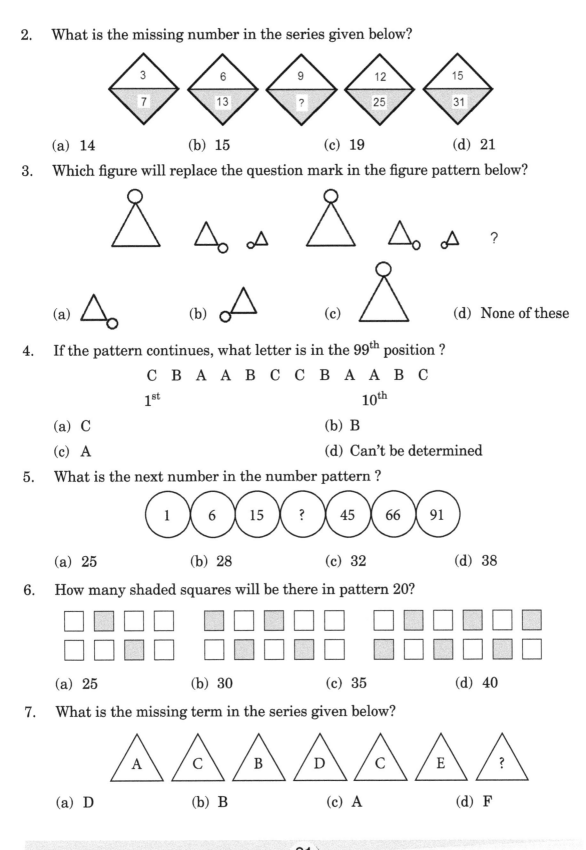

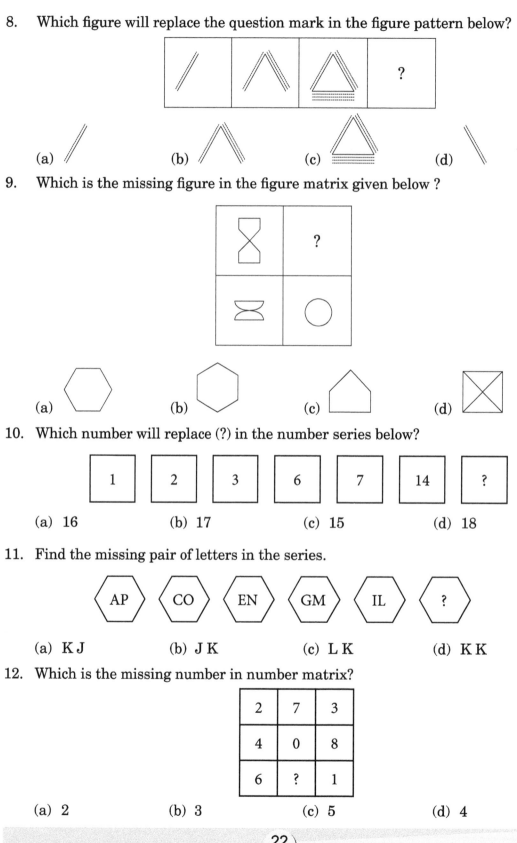

13. Which of the following figures will complete the fig. (X)?

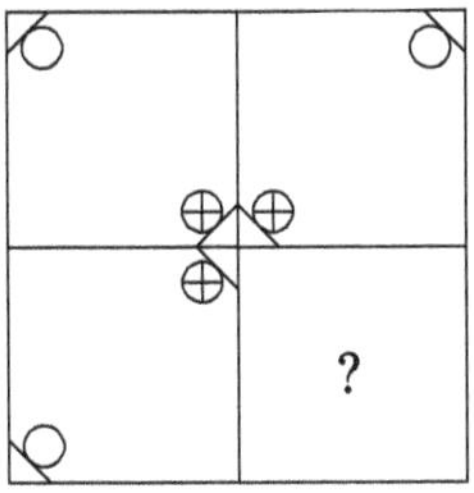

Fig. (X)

(a) 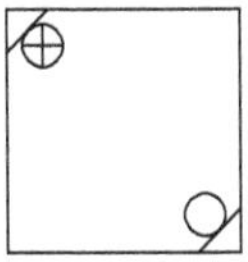   (b) 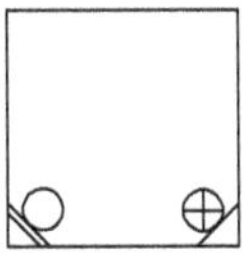   (c) 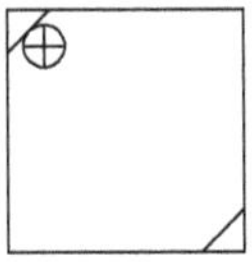   (d)

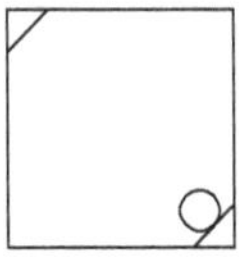

14. What is the sum of the numbers in pattern 4?

Pattern 1 — 2
Pattern 2 — 4, 6
Pattern 3 — 8, 10, 12

(a) 68   (b) 58   (c) 62   (d) 64

15. Find the missing pair of letters in the series.

CA, GD, ?, OJ, SM

(a) I F   (b) H E   (c) K G   (d) J G

16. Write the number that continues each sequence in the most sensible way.

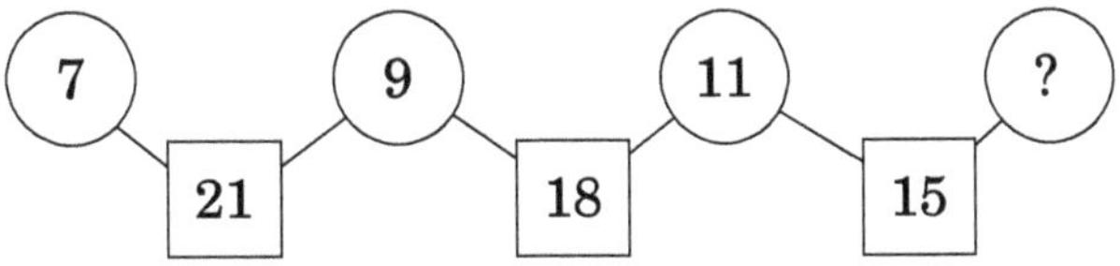

7, 21, 9, 18, 11, 15, ?

(a) 14   (b) 16   (c) 17   (d) 13

17. Which is the missing figure?

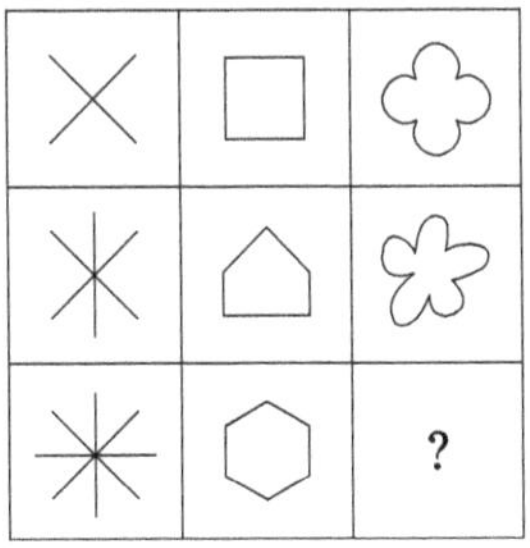

(a)    (b)    (c) 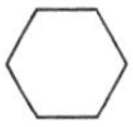   (d)

23

18. What is the missing number in the given number pattern?

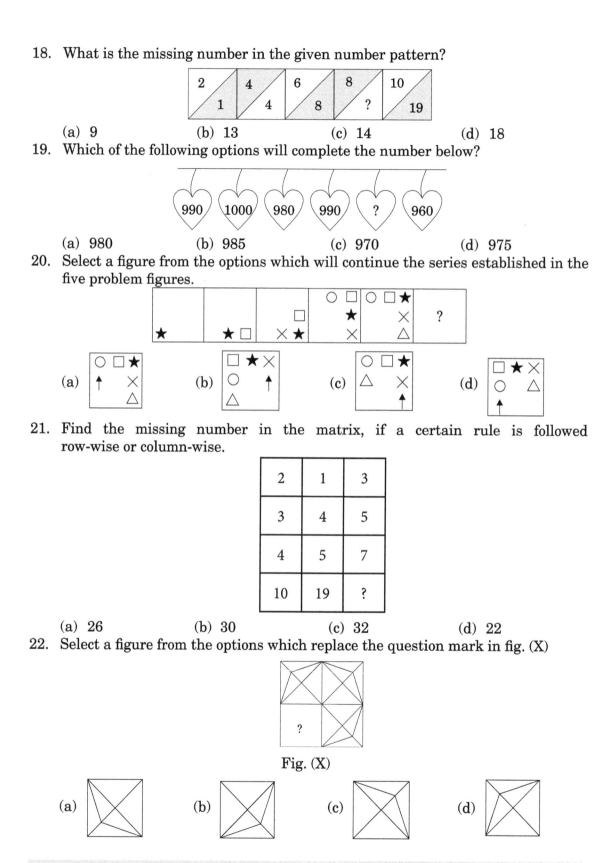

   (a) 9   (b) 13   (c) 14   (d) 18

19. Which of the following options will complete the number below?

   (a) 980   (b) 985   (c) 970   (d) 975

20. Select a figure from the options which will continue the series established in the five problem figures.

21. Find the missing number in the matrix, if a certain rule is followed row-wise or column-wise.

   (a) 26   (b) 30   (c) 32   (d) 22

22. Select a figure from the options which replace the question mark in fig. (X)

Fig. (X)

23. .... will replace the (?) to continue the given pattern

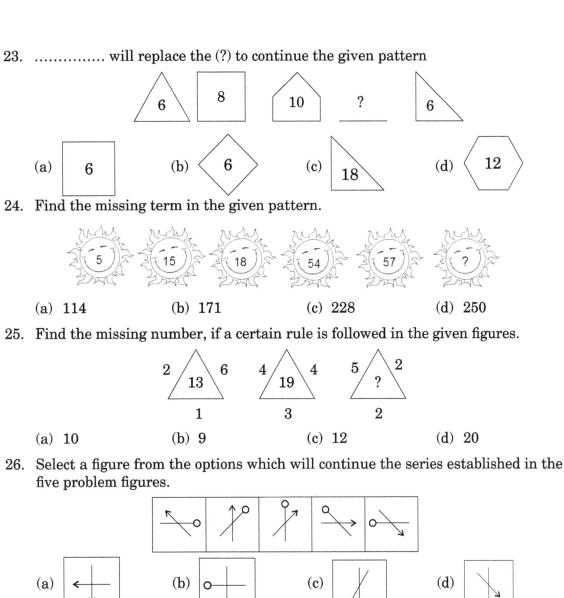

24. Find the missing term in the given pattern.

(a) 114 (b) 171 (c) 228 (d) 250

25. Find the missing number, if a certain rule is followed in the given figures.

(a) 10 (b) 9 (c) 12 (d) 20

26. Select a figure from the options which will continue the series established in the five problem figures.

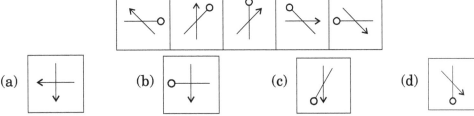

27. Which of the following options will complete the fig. (X)?

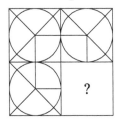

Fig. (X)

(a)   (b)   (c)   (d)

28. Which letter will replace the (?) in the given series?

R O L I ? C

(a) D (b) F (c) E (d) G

29. Which number will replace the question mark in number series below?

2, 6, 18, 54, ?, 486

(a) 162 (b) 108 (c) 100 (d) 216

30. Find the missing numbers A and B respectively.

2	4		6	11		7	B		A	5
1	3		2	7		6	8		3	3

(a) 5 and 6 (b) 9 and 7 (c) 4 and 3 (d) 5 and 9

31. Find the missing number. **(2018)**

6	6	18	12	30
3	12	9	24	?

(a) 15 (b) 60 (c) 10 (d) 20

32. Which of the following options will continue the given series? **(2019)**

23Z, 28X, 35V, 44T, 55R, ?

(a) 27U (b) 68P (c) 65U (d) 47U

33. Select the odd one out. **(2020)**
(a) GHJ (b) KLN (c) TVW (d) MNP

34. Study the given pattern carefully and tell the number of apples in Pattern 25 **(2020)**

Pattern 1   Pattern 2   Pattern 3

(a) 60 (b) 75 (c) 72 (d) 90

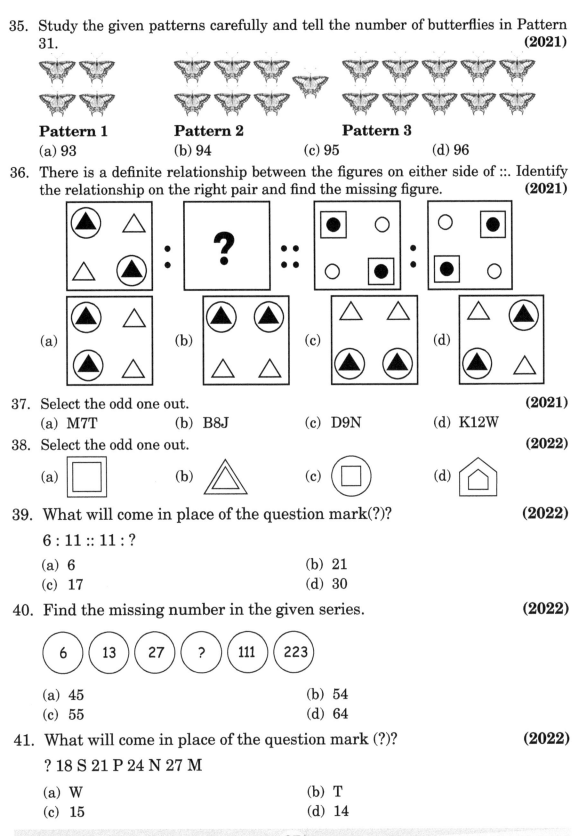

LEVEL-2

1. Find the missing letter in the given series.

   (a) N O   (b) L N   (c) O Q   (d) M O

2. Find the missing number in the given number series.

   (a) 110   (b) 120   (c) 100   (d) 150

3. Which figure will replace the question mark in figure pattern below?

   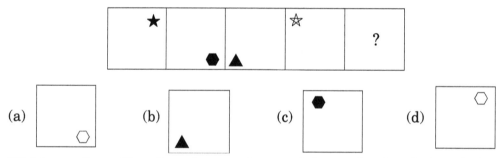

4. Which number will replace the question mark in number bond given below?

   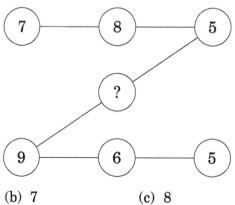

   (a) 6   (b) 7   (c) 8   (d) 4

5. What is the missing number in pattern below?

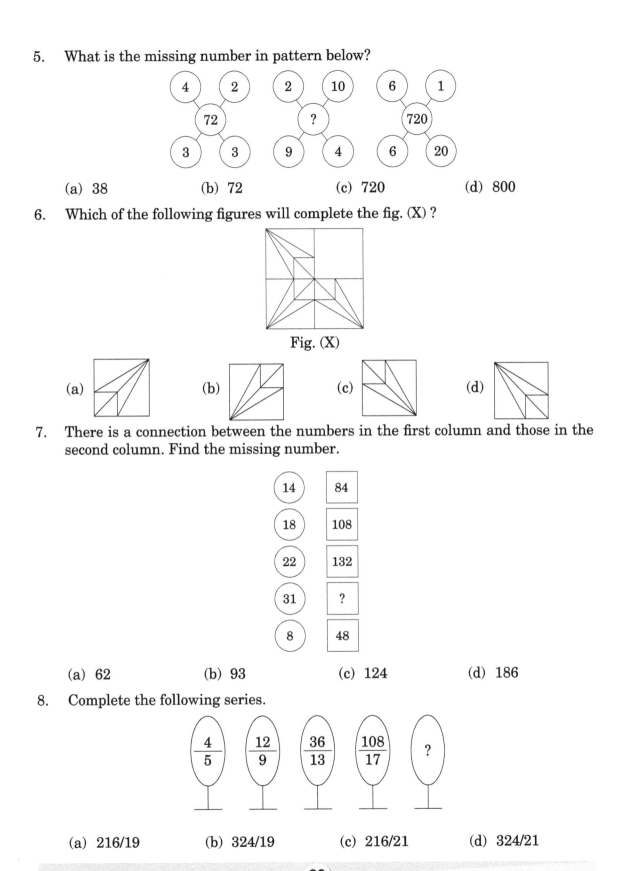

(a) 38   (b) 72   (c) 720   (d) 800

6. Which of the following figures will complete the fig. (X) ?

Fig. (X)

(a)   (b)   (c)   (d)

7. There is a connection between the numbers in the first column and those in the second column. Find the missing number.

(a) 62   (b) 93   (c) 124   (d) 186

8. Complete the following series.

(a) 216/19   (b) 324/19   (c) 216/21   (d) 324/21

9. Find the missing figure which completes the given figure pattern.

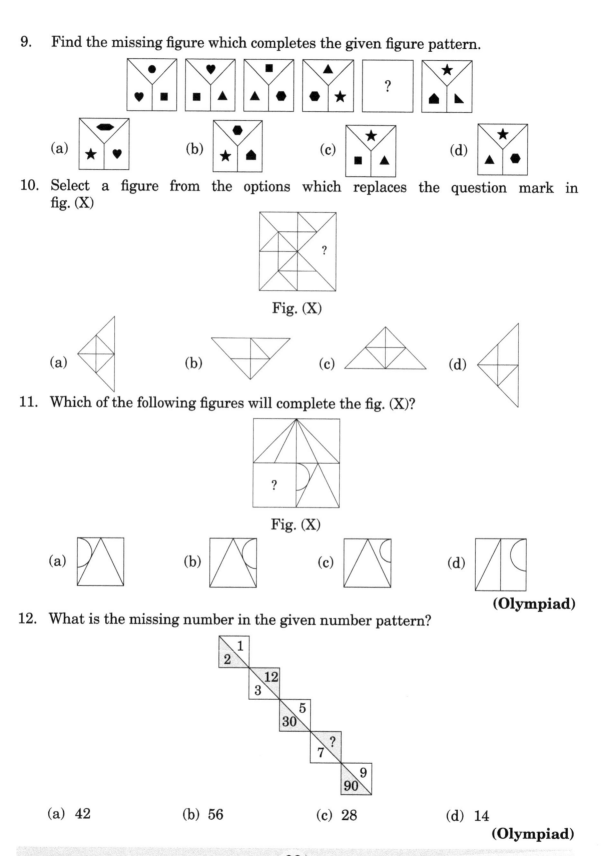

10. Select a figure from the options which replaces the question mark in fig. (X)

Fig. (X)

11. Which of the following figures will complete the fig. (X)?

Fig. (X)

(Olympiad)

12. What is the missing number in the given number pattern?

(a) 42 (b) 56 (c) 28 (d) 14

(Olympiad)

13. How many matchsticks are needed to make Pattern 5?

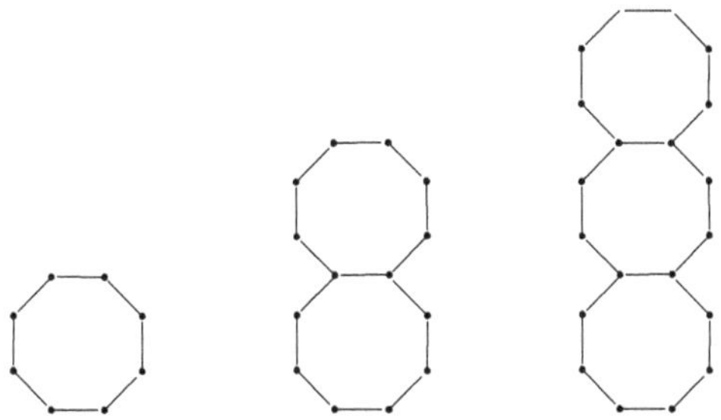

    Pattern 1   Pattern 2   Pattern 3

    (a) 54   (b) 36   (c) 43   (d) 35

    (Olympiad)

14. Fill the missing number in the pattern given below.

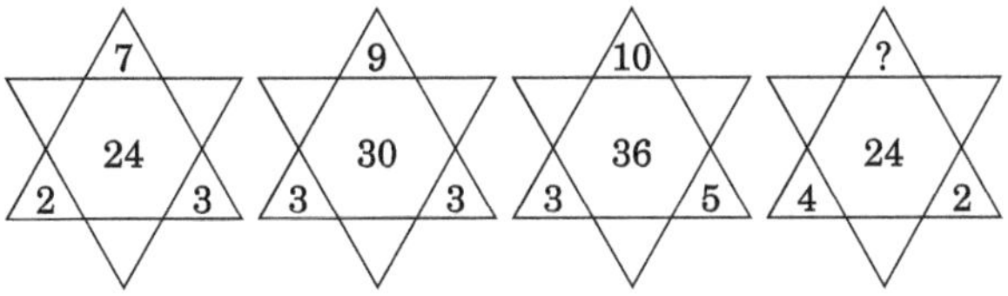

    (a) 6   (b) 8   (c) 4   (d) 5

    (Olympiad)

15. Which of the following figure will compete the given series below?

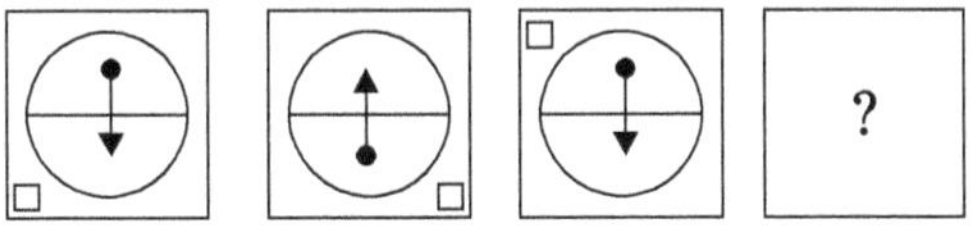

    (a) 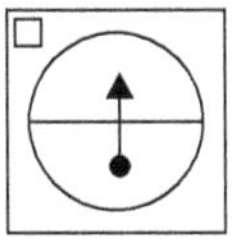   (b) 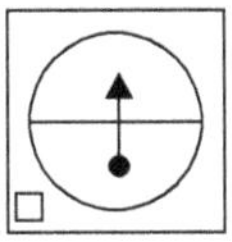   (c) 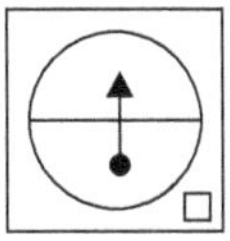   (d)

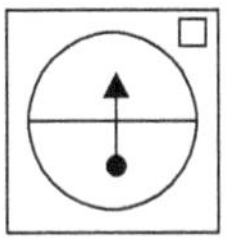

    (Olympiad)

16. Which of the following options will complete the Fig. (X)?

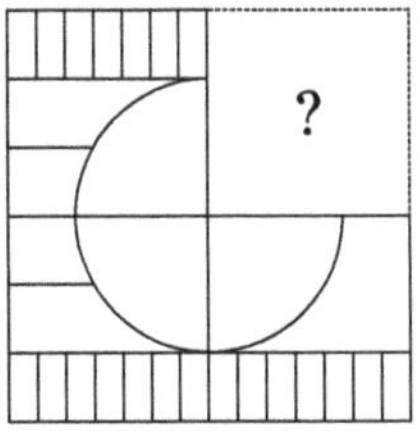

    Fig. (X)

    (a) 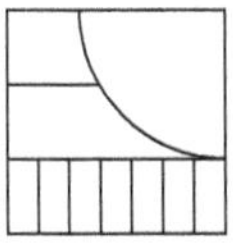   (b) 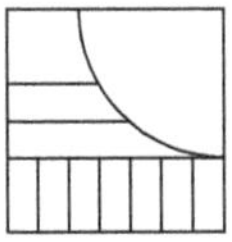   (c) 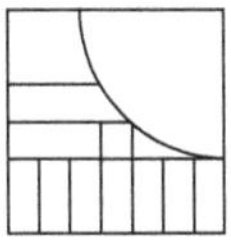   (d)

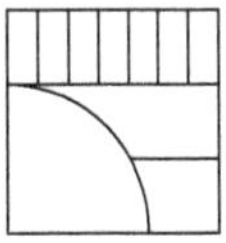

    (Olympiad)

17. Which of the following options will complete the number pattern below?

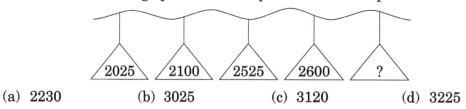

(a) 2230 (b) 3025 (c) 3120 (d) 3225

(Olympiad)

18. There is a matrix that follows a certain rule row-wise or column-wise. Find the missing number.

7	9	11
81	169	?
2	4	6

(Olympiad)

(a) 212 (b) 241 (c) 144 (d) 289

19. Select a figure from the options which will continue the series established in the five problem figures.

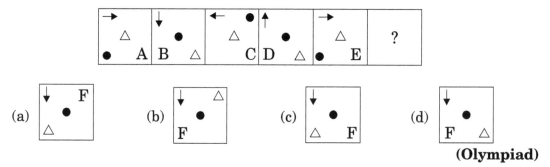

(Olympiad)

20. Find the missing number in the matrix, if a certain rule is followed row-wise or column-wise.

1	2	3
4	5	6
7	8	9
27	38	?

(a) 48 (b) 50 (c) 51 (d) 52

(Olympiad)

21. In the given number matrix, a certain rule is followed row-wise or column wise. Which number will replace the question mark?

4	6	3	8
2	8	4	4
6	5	?	10

(a) 3 (b) 6 (c) 2 (d) 7

(Olympiad)

22. Select a figure from the options which replace the question mark in fig. (X).

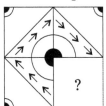

Fig. (X)

(a)   (b)   (c) (d)

(Olympiad)

23. How many circles will be there in Pattern 10?

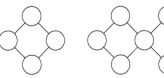

Pattern 1   Pattern 2   Pattern 3

(a) 24 (b) 33 (c) 27 (d) 31

(Olympiad)

24. Find the value of P and Q respectively, if each number is the sum of the two numbers directly below it.

(a) 8, 6
(b) 3, 6
(c) 5, 6
(d) 9, 10

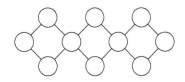

(Olympiad)

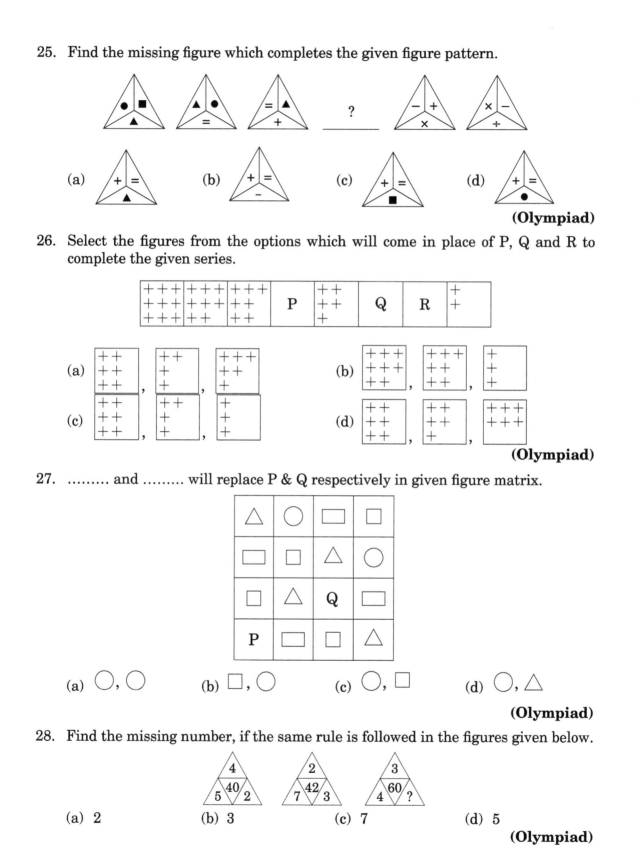

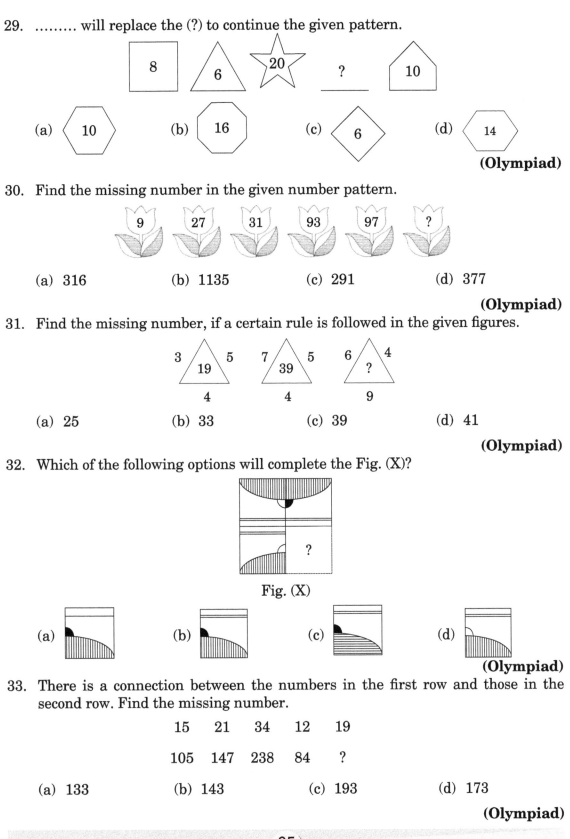

34. Which of the following options will complete the pattern in fig. (X)?

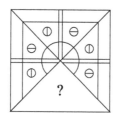

Fig. (X)

(a) 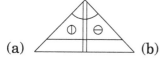 (b) 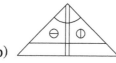 (c) 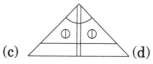 (d)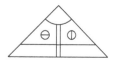

(Olympiad)

35. Find the missing number, if the wheel is rotated in the given direction.

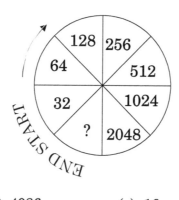

(a) 8 (b) 4086 (c) 16 (d) 4096

(Olympiad)

36. There is a certain relationship between the pair of letters on the either side of :: Establish the relationship of the left pair and find the missing term. **(2022)**

$$\boxed{\text{MTR : PRT :: ? : XIJ}}$$

(a) ULI (b) VKH (c) VKG (d) UKH

37. Find the missing number.

| 8 | 27 | 84 | 255 | ? | 2307 |

(a) 712 (b) 765 (c) 768 (d) 718

Answers and Explanation

Level-1

1. **(d)** The pattern is as follows:

    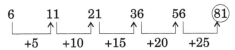

2. **(c)** The pattern is as follows:

    $B = A \times 2 + 1$

    Hence, number in lower part of third pattern is: $9 \times 2 + 1 = 19$

3. **(c)** The circle is moving from one corner to other in clockwise direction. And, the triangle reduces its size from figure to figure. So, option figure (c) will come next.

4. **(c)** The pattern repeats after 6 letters

    So, now position of

C	B	A
97th	98th	99th

5. **(b)** The pattern is as follows:

    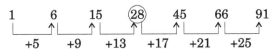

6. **(d)** Number of shaded squares in pattern 1 = 2

    Number of shaded squares in pattern 2 = 4

    Number of shaded squares in pattern 3 = 6

    So, Pattern followed is

    $(1 \times 2), (2 \times 2), (3 \times 2), \ldots$ i.e., 2, 4, 6, ...

    Hence, Number of shaded squares in pattern 20 =

    $20 \times 2 = 40$.

7. **(a)** The pattern is as follows:

    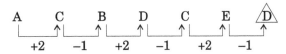

8. **(a)** Each figure repeats itself after 2 figure.

9. **(b)** The second figure in each row is obtained by joining the lower part of first figure with its upper part. The common side is then removed to form the second figure.

10. **(c)** The pattern is as follows:

    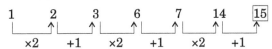

11. **(d)** Pattern followed is

    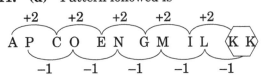

12. **(c)** Rule followed column wise = Sum of the numbers in each column is = 12.

13. **(a)**

14. **(a)** Numbers in pattern 4 = 14, 16, 18, 20

    So, the total sum = 14 + 16 + 18 + 20 = 68

15. (c) The pattern is as follows:

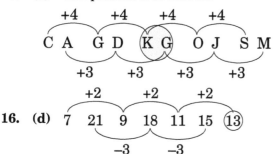

16. (d)

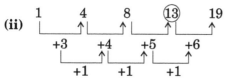

17. (d) Increasing pattern is followed.

18. (b) The pattern is as follows:

(i) $2 \xrightarrow{+2} 4 \xrightarrow{+2} 6 \xrightarrow{+2} 8 \xrightarrow{+2} 10$

(ii)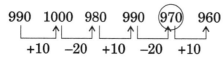

19. (c) Pattern followed is

990 1000 980 990 (970) 960
   +10   −20 +10 −20   +10

20. (d) The elements move half step anti-clockwise in each step. One element is added in each step, first to the right and then to the left of the main element.

21. (c) As, In 1st Column
= 3 × 4 − 2 = 10
In 2nd Column
= 4 × 5 − 1 = 19
Similarly, In 3rd Column
= 5 × 7 − 3 = 32

22. (a)

23. (d) The pattern followed is sides × 2 ie,

△ = 3 × 2 = 6

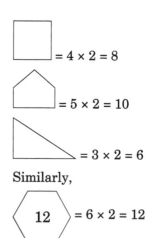

Similarly,

⬡ 12 = 6 × 2 = 12

24. (b) The pattern is as follows:

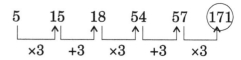

25. (c) As, In 1st figure :
2 × 6 + 1 = 13
In 2nd figure :
4 × 4 + 3 = 19
Similarly, In 3rd figure :
5 × 2 + 2 = 12

26. (c) On close observation, we find that arrow rotates 45° clockwise and the other like rotates 45° anti-clockwise in each successive figure.

27. (a)

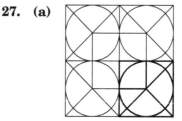

28. (b) The pattern is as follows:

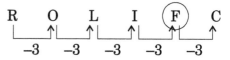

29. (a) The pattern followed is

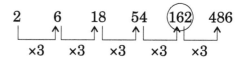

30. **(d)** Rule followed in each

A	B
C	D

$B = (A + D) - C$

So, $B = (7 + 8) - 6$

$B = 15 - 6$

$B = 9$

And $5 = (A + 3) - 3$

$5 = A + 3 - 3$

$A = 5$

31. **(a)** 15

32. **(b)** 68P

$23 + 5 = 28;\ Z - 2 = X$

$28 + 7 = 35;\ X - 2 = V$

$35 + 9 = 44;\ V - 2 = T$

$44 + 11 = 55;\ T - 2 = R$

$55 + 13 = 68;\ R - 2 = P$

33. **(c)** TVW

34. **(b)** Number of apples in given pattern = Pattern number × 3

Number of apples in pattern 25 = $25 \times 3 = 75$

35. **(b)** Number of butterflies in pattern 31 = (3 × Number of pattern) + 1 = (3 × 31) + 1 = 94

36. **(d)** The given figures on right pair are mirror images of each other.

37. **(c)**

$M \xrightarrow{+7} T$

$B \xrightarrow{+8} J$

$D \xrightarrow{+10} N$

$K \xrightarrow{+12} W$

38. **(c)**
39. **(b)**
40. **(c)**
41. **(a)**

Level-2

1. **(c)** The pattern followed is

$C \xrightarrow{+4} G \xrightarrow{+4} K \xrightarrow{+4} \boxed{O} \xrightarrow{+4} S$

$E \xrightarrow{+4} I \xrightarrow{+4} M \xrightarrow{+4} \boxed{Q} \xrightarrow{+4} U$

2. **(b)** The pattern followed is

$1 \xrightarrow{\times 2} 2 \xrightarrow{\times 3} 6 \xrightarrow{\times 4} 24 \xrightarrow{\times 5} \boxed{120} \xrightarrow{\times 6} 720$

3. **(d)** Inner element is repeating after third step after being unshaded. It is rotating 90° clockwise.

4. **(a)** Rule followed chain – wise is

Sum of the numbers in each chain is 20. ie

$7 + 8 + 5 = 20,\ 9 + 6 + 5 = 20$

Similarly, $9 + 6 + 5 = 20$

5. **(c)** The pattern followed is

As, $4 \times 2 \times 3 \times 3 = 72$

and, $6 \times 1 \times 6 \times 20 = 720$

Similarly, $2 \times 10 \times 9 \times 4 = 720$

6. **(a)**

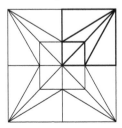

7. (d) The pattern is as follows:
14 × 6 = 84
18 × 6 = 108
22 × 6 = 132
31 × 6 = (186)
8 × 6 = 48

8. (d) The pattern followed is:

4 →(×3) 12 →(×3) 36 →(×3) 108 →(×3) (324)

5 →(+4) 9 →(+4) 13 →(+4) 17 →(+4) (21)

9. (b) The missing figure which completes the given figure pattern is

10. (d)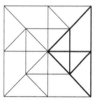

11. (b)

12. (b) The pattern followed is

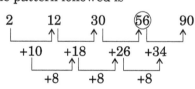

13. (b) The pattern followed is

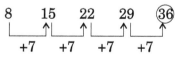

+7   +7   +7   +7

14. (a) As, (7 + 2 + 3) × 2 = 24
(9 + 3 + 3) × 2 = 30
and, (10 + 3 + 5) × 2 = 36
Similarly,
((6) + 4 + 2) × 2 = 24.

15. (d) Arrow moves up and down alternately and square moves anticlockwise direction with the gap of 1, 2, 3.

16. (d)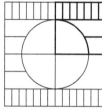

17. (b) The pattern followed is

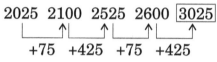

+75 +425 +75 +425

18. (d) As, 7 + 2 = $(9)^2$ = 81
and 9 + 4 = $(13)^2$ = 169
Similarly, 11 + 6 = $(17)^2$ = 289

19. (d) • Arrow and black dot are repeating their patterns at every fourth step.
• Triangle is repeating its pattern at every second step.
• Letter is moving 90° clockwise and anti clockwise alternatively after following this rule:

A →(+1) B →(+1) C →(+1) D →(+1) E

20. (c) In row 1 : (4 × 7) – 1 = 27
In row 2 : (5 × 8) – 2 = 38
Similarly,
In row 3 : (6 × 9) – 3 = 51

21. (a) The pattern followed is:
4 × 6 ⇒ 24 ⇒ 3 × 8
2 × 8 ⇒ 16 ⇐ 4 × 4
6 × 5 ⇒ 30 ⇔ × 10

22. (c)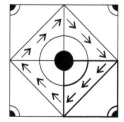

23. (d) The pattern followed is:

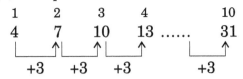

24. (c) The value of P and Q is 5 and 6 respectively.

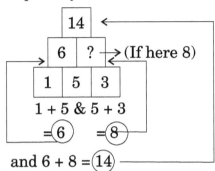

25. (b) Each step, element moves in clockwise direction and one new element is added to the below, i.e.

26. (c) The pattern is as follows :

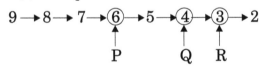

27. (a) Each row is the combination of figures △, ▭, ▢, ○, so, ○ and ○ will replace P & Q respectively in given figure matrix.

28. (d) As, In 1st figure :
$4 \times 5 \times 2 = 40$
and In 2nd figure :
$7 \times 2 \times 3 = 42$
Similarly, In 3rd figure :
$3 \times 4 \times 5 = 60$

29. (b) The pattern followed is : Number of Sides × 2
So, ⬣ no of sides = 8
and = 8 × 2 = 16

30. (c) The pattern is as follows :

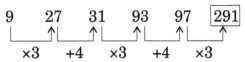

31. (b) As, In 1st figure :
$(3 \times 5) + 4 = 19$ and,
In 2nd figure : $(7 \times 5) + 4 = 39$
Similarly,
In 3rd figure : $(6 \times 4) + 9 = 33$

32. (b)

33. (a) The pattern followed is :
$15 \times 7 = 105$, $21 \times 7 = 147$,
$34 \times 7 = 238$, $12 \times 7 = 84$,
$19 \times 7 = 133$

34. (b)

35. (d) The pattern followed is: × 2 i.e.
$2048 \times 2 = 4096$

36. (d)

M T R   U K H
+3↓ −2↓ +2↓   +3↓ −2↓ +2↓
P R T   X I J

37. (c) $(8 \times 3) + 3 = 24 + 3 = 27$

$(27 \times 3) + 3 = 81 + 3 = 84$

$(84 \times 3) + 3 = 252 + 3 = 255$

$(255 \times 3) + 3 = 765 + 3 = 768$

$(768 \times 3) + 3 = 2304 + 3 = 2307$

CHAPTER 3

Alphabet Test

OBJECTIVES

- Students will learn how to arrange a single series of alphabets.
- They will learn to decode the logic involved in the alphabetical sequence.

INTRODUCTION

Alphabet is a group of English letters. Alphabet test is a test to solve the problems based on letters of English alphabet.

Some basic facts related to Alphabet Test are given below:

I. The Alphabet Series:

The English alphabet contain 26 letters as shown below:

A	B	C	D	E	F
G	H	I	J	K	L
M	N	O	P	Q	R
S	T	U	V	W	X
		Y	Z		

II. Letters positions in forward alphabetical order:

A	B	C	D	E	F	G	H
1	2	3	4	5	6	7	8
I	J	K	L	M	N	O	P
9	10	11	12	13	14	15	16
Q	R	S	T	U	V	W	X
17	18	19	20	21	22	23	24
Y	Z						
25	26						

III. Letters positions in backward or reverse alphabetical order:

Z	Y	X	W	V	U	T	S
1	2	3	4	5	6	7	8
R	Q	P	O	N	M	L	K
9	10	11	12	13	14	15	16
J	I	H	G	F	E	D	C
17	18	19	20	21	22	23	24
B	A						
25	26						

- Remember the word E J O T Y

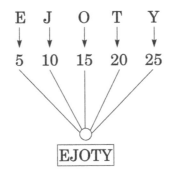

IV. A, E, I, O, U are vowels and remaining letters are consonants of English alphabet.

V. A-M (1-13) letters are the first half of English alphabet.

VI. N-Z (14-26) letters are the second half of English alphabet.

Types of Questions

Type 1: Alphabetical Order of Words

Arranging words in alphabetical order implies 'to arrange them in the order as they appear in a dictionary'. First consider the first letter of each word. Arrange the words in the order in which these letters appear in the English alphabet.

Example 1:

Arrange the following words as per order in the dictionary.

    A. Parrot   B. Sparrow   C. Peacock   D. Skylark

    (a) CADB   (b) ACDB   (c) BDCA   (d) ABCD

Ans. (b)

Explanation: The correct order is as follows :

    Parrot → Peacock → Skylark → Sparrow
      A   C   D   B

Example 2:

Arrange the following words as given in dictionary.

    1. Across   2. Admit   3. Advise   4. Alone

    (a) 1, 2, 3, 4   (b) 1, 2, 4, 3   (c) 1, 3, 2, 4   (d) 4, 3, 2, 1

Ans. (a)

Explanation: Here, first letter of all words is 'A'. For the second letter, two of the words have 'd'. We now move on to the third letter in each of these two words and then arranging the words accordingly, we get

    Across → Admit → Advise → Alone.

    So, 1, 2, 3, 4 is the correct order of the words.

    Hence, option (a) is correct.

Note: In some cases, two or more words begin with the same letter. Such words should be arranged in the order of second or third letters in the alphabet.

Example 3:

Which of the following words will come fourth in the English dictionary?

    (a) False   (b) Follow   (c) Faithfully   (d) Fool

Ans. (d)

Explanation: The given words can be arranged in the alphabetical order as:

            1   2   3   4
    Faithfully → False → Follow → Fool

Now, Clearly, 'Fool' comes fourth. So, the correct answer is (d).

Type 2: Letter-Gap Problems

In letter-gap problems, one has to find out as many letters in the same sequence between them in the given word as in the English alphabet.

4. How many letters are there in the word '**CHANNEL**' which have as many letters between them in the word as in the English alphabet?

   (a) One (b) Two (c) Three (d) Four

Ans. (b)

Explanation: According to the question:

So, such number of pairs are AC and LN.

Type 3: Rule Detection

In rule detection, four options are given as the group of letters and out of these four groups of letters, students are asked to choose the correct alternative that follows a certain rule in a particular manner.

5. Find out which letter groups contains more than two vowels?

   (a) B D E J O L   (B) J K A P I X   (c) P R A Q E O   (d) Z I L E R S

Ans. (c)

Explanation: P R A Q E O has more than two vowels – A, E and O

Type 4: Alphabetical Quibble

In these types of questions, generally a letter-series of English alphabets from A to Z or a randomised sequence of letters is given. The students are required to find out how many times a letter fulfills the certain condition.

6. The given question is based on the following alphabet series:

   A B C D E F G H I J K L M N O P Q R S T U V W X Y Z

In the English alphabet, which letter will be the seventh from the right end?

   (a) S (b) T (c) Q (d) P

Ans. (b)

Explanation: Counting from the right end of the given alphabet series, i.e. from Z, the seventh letter will be T.

   A B C D E F G H I J K L M N O P Q R S T U V W X Y Z
                                        ↑
                                        7th From the right end

So, option (b) is correct.

Type 5: Word Formation By Unscrambling Letters

In these types of questions, a set of English letters is given in a jumbled order. The student is required to arrange these letters to form a meaningful word.

7. Select the combination of numbers so that the letters arranged accordingly will form a meaningful word.

T	R	I	F	U
1	2	3	4	5

   (a) 4, 2, 5, 3, 1   (b) 3, 1, 2, 4, 5   (c) 4, 3, 2, 1, 5   (d) 5, 3, 2, 1, 4

   Ans. (a)

   Explanation: From the given letters, when arranged in the order 4, 2, 5, 3, 1 form the word 'FRUIT'. Hence, option (a) is correct.

Type 6: Word Formation Using Letters of a Given Word

In these types of questions, students have to form words using letters of a given word.

8. In the following question, choose one word which can not be formed from the letters of the given word.

   C O M M U N I C A T I O N

   (a) ACTION   (b) UNION   (c) NATION   (d) UNISON

   Ans. (d)

   Explanation: The word 'UNISON' cannot be formed because letter 'S' is not present in the given word.

LEVEL-1

1. Arrange the given words as they are arranged in the dictionary.
   1. Land   2. Lamp   3. Landscape   4. Lantern
   (a) 2,1,4,3   (b) 2,1,3,4   (c) 1,2,3,4   (d) 1,3,4,2

2. In the following question, a group of letters is given which are numbered 1, 2, 3, 4 and 5. Given below are four alternatives containing combinations of these numbers. Select the combination of numbers so that letters arranged accordingly, form a meaningful word.

   R U S G A
   1 2 3 4 5

   (a) 1, 5, 4, 2, 3   (b) 5, 3, 4, 1, 2   (c) 3, 2, 4, 5, 1   (d) 4, 5, 3, 2, 1

3. Arrange the following words in a meaningful/logical order.
   1. Work   2. Day   3. Night   4. Sleep
   (a) 4,3,1,2   (b) 2,1,4,3   (c) 2,1,3,4   (d) 1,2,3,4
4. Which word **cannot** be made from the letters of the given word?
   TEACHER
   (a) Tractor   (b) Reach   (c) Eater   (d) Earth
5. Which word **can** be formed from the letters of the given word?
   DICTIONARY
   (a) Nation   (b) Addition   (c) Binary   (d) Dairy
6. Arrange the given words as they are arranged in the dictionary.
   1. Floor   2. Flask   3. Flower   4. Flock
   (a) 2,3,4,1   (b) 2,4,1,3   (c) 1,4,3,2   (d) 4,3,1,2
7. Arrange the following words in a meaningful/logical order.
   1. Shoulder   2. Palm   3. Elbow   4. Wrist
   5. Finger
   (a) 5,2,4,3,1   (b) 5,4,2,3,1   (c) 3,4,5,2,1   (d) 3,1,4,2,5

DIRECTIONS (Qs. 8 & 9) In the following question, a group of letters is given which are numbered 1, 2, 3, 4 and 5. Given below are four alternatives containing combinations of these numbers. Select the combination of numbers so that letters arranged accordingly, form a meaningful word.

8.　　　　　　　E　I　N　K　F
　　　　　　　　1　2　3　4　5
   (a) 1,5,2,3,4   (b) 3,2,1,4,5   (c) 4,3,2,5,1   (d) 4,1,2,3,5
9.　　　　　　　R　T　B　I　H
　　　　　　　　1　2　3　4　5
   (a) 5,4,1,2,3   (b) 3,4,1,2,5   (c) 2,1,3,5,4   (d) 1,4,2,3,5

DIRECTIONS (Qs. 10 & 11) : Which word **cannot** be made from the letters of the given word?

10.　　　　　　　　**GENERATE**
   (a) Rate   (b) Great   (c) Gate   (d) Never
11.　　　　　　　　**CONTENTION**
   (a) Note   (b) Notion   (c) Tonic   (d) Nation
12. Arrange the given words as they are arranged in the dictionary.
   1. Format   2. Forgive   3. Forget   4. Forgo
   (a) 1,2,3,4   (b) 4,3,2,1   (c) 3,2,1,4   (d) 3,2,4,1

13. Which word **can** be made from the letters of the given word?

REASONABLE

   (a) Rest   (b) Best   (c) Snow   (d) Noble

DIRECTIONS (Qs. 14-18): In the following questions, a group of letters is given which are numbered 1, 2, 3, 4 and 5. Given below are four alternatives containing combinations of these numbers. Select the combination of numbers so that letters arranged accordingly, form a meaningful word.

14. H A P S E
    1 2 3 4 5
   (a) 4,1,2,3,5   (b) 4,2,1,3,5   (c) 2,1,3,4,5   (d) 3,5,2,1,4

15. R A J M O
    1 2 3 4 5
   (a) 3,5,1,2,4   (b) 1,2,3,4,5   (c) 4,2,3,5,1   (d) 5,4,1,2,3

16. M T H O U
    1 2 3 4 5
   (a) 1,4,2,5,3   (b) 1,4,5,2,3   (c) 3,4,5,2,1   (d) 2,3,1,4,5

17. T N G I H
    1 2 3 4 5
   (a) 2,4,5,3,1   (b) 1,4,2,5,3   (c) 2,4,3,5,1   (d) 1,5,2,4,3

18. N C U E L
    1 2 3 4 5
   (a) 3,1,4,5,2   (b) 1,5,4,3,2   (c) 3,2,1,5,4   (d) 3,1,2,5,4

DIRECTIONS (Qs. 19-20): Which word **cannot** be made from the letters of the given word?

19. THOUSAND
   (a) Sand   (b) Hand   (c) House   (d) Aunt

20. INTELLIGENT
   (a) Gentle   (b) Hilt   (c) Intel   (d) Elite

21. Two letters in the word 'LEMON' have as many letters between them in the word as in the alphabet. Which one of the two letters comes earlier in the alphabet?
   (a) E   (b) L   (c) M   (d) N

22. A meaningful word starting with A is made from the first, the second, the fourth, the fifth and the sixth letters of the word 'CONTRACT'. Which of the following is the middle letter of the word?
   (a) C   (b) O   (c) R   (d) T

DIRECTIONS (Qs. 23-25): Which word **can** be made from the letters of the given word?

23. FORECAST
   (a) Cash   (b) Fire   (c) Earn   (d) Rest

24. CHARACTER
   (a) Charge   (b) Chart   (c) Hurt   (d) Term

25. STRENGTH
    (a) Rent (b) Turn (c) Sight (d) Hanger

DIRECTIONS (Qs. 26-28) : Arrange the given words as they are arranged in the dictionary.

26. 1. Range 2. Rain 3. Rein 4. Ranger
    (a) 2,3,4,1 (b) 2,4,3,1 (c) 2,1,4,3 (d) 2,4,1,3

27. 1. Bound 2. Bonus 3. Bunch 4. Board
    (a) 4,2,1,3 (b) 4,3,2,1 (c) 1,4,2,3 (d) 2,4,3,1

28. 1. Clutch 2. Club 3. Cloth 4. Clone
    (a) 4,3,2,1 (b) 3,2,4,1 (c) 2,4,1,3 (d) 2,1,3,4

29. How many independent words can 'HEARTLESS' be divided into without changing the order of the letters and using each letter only once ?
    (a) 2 (b) 3 (c) 4 (d) 5

30. From the word 'BEHIND', how many independent words can be made without changing the order of the letters and using each letter only once ?
    (a) 1 (b) 2 (c) 3 (d) 4

31. Some letters are numbered 1, 2, 3, 4, 5 and 6 as given. Arrange the letters to form a meaningful English word and select the correct option. **(2020)**

E	A	M	G	D	A
1	2	3	4	5	6

(a) 5, 2, 3, 4, 1, 6 (b) 5, 6, 3, 2, 4, 1 (c) 6, 1, 3, 4, 2, 5 (d) 2, 1, 3, 5, 6, 4

32. Some alphabets are coded in a certain code as given below. **(2021)**

Letters	A	E	F	M	R
Codes	#	*	?	▯	▯

What will be the code for FARMER?

(a) # ? ↑ ↓ * ↓ (b) ? ↓ # ↑ ↓ * (c) # ? ↓ ↑ ↓ * (d) ? # ↓ ↑ * ↓

33. Arrange the given words as they occur in a dictionary and select the correct option. **(2021)**

    1. Machine   2. Muscle
    3. Mackle   4. Magnet
    5. Mythic

    (a) 1, 3, 4, 2, 5 (b) 1, 4, 3, 2, 5 (c) 2, 3, 1, 4, 5 (d) 3, 1, 2, 5, 4

34. Arrange the given words as they occur in a dictionary. **(2022)**
    1. Sacrifice 2. Scratch
    3. Safety 4. Scare
    5. Sample
    (a) 3, 5, 1, 4, 2 (b) 1, 3, 5, 4, 2 (c) 2, 3, 1, 5, 4 (d) 1, 5, 3, 2, 4

35. Which of the following words CANNOT be formed from the letters of the given word? **(2022)**

    POTASSIUM

    (a) STAMP (b) UPMOST (c) MOIST (d) ADOPT

36. Find the odd one out. **(2022)**
    (a) BF (b) CG (c) JP (d) GK

37. What will come in place of the question mark(?)? **(2022)**
    E : 10 : : G : ?
    (a) 15 (b) 14 (c) 18 (d) 20

38. If 'SHOW' is coded as 'TGPV', then how will 'MIND' be coded? **(2022)**
    (a) LJMF (b) NJMC (c) NHOF (d) NHOC

39. If H = 8, HE = 13 and HEN = 27, then HENDL = ? **(2022)**
    (a) 47 (b) 38 (c) 46 (d) 43

LEVEL-2

1. Some letters are given which are numbered 1,2,3,4,5 and 6. Find the combination of numbers so that the letters are arranged accordingly to form a meaningful word.

    L F R E O W
    1 2 3 4 5 6

    (a) 2,1,5,6,4,3 (b) 2,1,6,5,4,3 (c) 1,5,6,4,3,2 (d) 3,1,4,6,5,2

DIRECTIONS (Qs. 2-3): Which word **cannot** be made from the letters of the given word?

2. MISFORTUNE
    (a) Fort (b) Turn (c) Soft (d) Roam

3. SIGNATURE

   (a) Sight   (b) Gain   (c) Nature   (d) Gate

4. If it is possible to form a word with the first, fourth, seventh and eleventh letters in the word 'SUPERFLUOUS', write the first letter of that word. Otherwise, X is the answer.

   (a) S   (b) L   (c) X   (d) E

5. If you pick up from the following alphabet, the sixth and the fourteenth letters from your right and then pick up the fifth and twentieth letters from your left and form a meaningful word, what is the first letter of that word?

   A B C D E F G H I J K L M
   N O P Q R S T U V W X Y Z

   (a) M
   (b) E
   (c) No word can be formed
   (d) More than one word can be formed

DIRECTIONS (Qs. 6-7): Arrange the given words as they are arranged in dictionary.

6. 1. Chemistry 2. Chamber 3. Cheap 4. Cheerful

   (a) 2,1,3,4   (b) 3,4,2,1   (c) 2,4,3,1   (d) 2,3,4,1

7. 1. Genuine 2. Gender 3. Gentle 4. General

   (a) 2,1,3,4   (b) 2,4,3,1   (c) 1,3,4,2   (d) 3,4,2,1

8. How many meaningful English words can be formed from the letters **IFEN** using each letter only once in each word?

   (a) One   (b) Two   (c) Three   (d) None of these

9. How many meaningful English words can be formed from the letters **ROWK** using each letter only once in each word?

   (a) Two   (b) One   (c) Three   (d) None

10. How many meaningful English words can be formed from the letters **MELA** using each letter only once in each word?

    (a) One   (b) Two   (c) Three   (d) Four

DIRECTIONS (Qs.11-13): Arrange the words in a meaningful and logical order and then select the appropriate sequence from the options provided below each of the groups of words.

11. 1. District   2. Village   3. State   4. Block
    (a) 2,1,4,3   (b) 2,3,4,1   (c) 2,4,1,3   (d) 3,2,1,4
12. 1. Honey   2. Flower   3. Honey Bee   4. Wax
    (a) 1,3,4,2   (b) 2,1,4,3   (c) 2,3,1,4   (d) 4,3,2,1
13. 1. Farmer   2. Seed   3. Food   4. Cultivation
    (a) 1,2,4,3   (b) 2,1,3,4   (c) 4,2,3,1   (d) 3,2,4,2
14. If the words in the sentence, "She showed several sample snaps" are rearranged in the alphabetical order, which will be the middle word?
    (a) snaps   (b) sample   (c) several   (d) she
15. Number of the letters skipped in between adjacent letters in the series is two. Which of the following alternatives observe this rule?
    (a) SPMLI   (b) TSPNKH   (c) UROLIF   (d) WTQNKJ
16. In the following letter sequence, how many n's are followed by m but not preceded by h?
    a g r h t n m b c n m l b u v n m h e r h
    n m g f e h n m e c n m w q a n m h l b
    (a) 4   (b) 5   (c) 6   (d) 7

DIRECTIONS (Qs. 17-18): Some letters are given which are numbered 1,2,3,4, 5 and 6. Find the combination of numbers so that the letters are arranged accordingly to form a meaningful word.

17. T E M R H O
    1 2 3 4 5 6
    (a) 3,2,4,6,1,5   (b) 3,6,1,5,2,4   (c) 2,1,3,6,5,4   (d) 1,4,2,6,3,5
18. A K T E R M
    1 2 3 4 5 6
    (a) 6,1,5,2,4,3   (b) 2,1,3,4,5,6   (c) 1,2,6,5,4,3   (d) 6,2,1,5,4,3
19. Which of the following CANNOT be formed from the letters of the given word?
    ATTRIBUTABLE
    (a) BATTER   (b) TRIAL   (c) EAT   (d) ATTITUDE

    (Olympiad)

20. Arrange the given words as they are arranged in dictionary.
    1. Asia   2. Australia   3. America   4. Afghanistan
    5. Africa
    (a) 2, 3, 4, 5, 1   (b) 4, 5, 3, 2, 1   (c) 4, 3, 2, 1, 5   (d) 4, 5, 3, 1, 2

    (Olympiad)

21. If a meaningful word be formed using the five letters RCONW each only once, then the fourth letter of that word is your answer. If more than one such word can be formed your answer would be 'X' and if no such word can be formed, your answer is 'M'.
    (a) M   (b) W   (c) X   (d) N
    (Olympiad)

22. If it is possible to make a meaningful word with the 1st, 4th, 7th and 11th letters of the word INTERPRETATION', which of the following will be the third letter of that word? If more than one such word can be made, give 'M' as the answer and if no such word can be formed, give 'X' as the answer.
    (a) M   (b) I   (c) E   (d) X
    (Olympiad)

23. If a meaningful word can be formed with 2nd, 3rd, 6th and 7th letters of the alphabetical order of the letters of the word 'INDIRECT', then 2nd letter of the word is your answer. If more than one such word can be formed, then 'X' is your answer, and if no such word can be formed then, 'M' is your answer.
    (a) D   (b) N   (c) M   (d) X
    (Olympiad)

24. Arrange the given words in alphabetical order and choose which word comes in Middle.
    Jealous, Jargon, Judiciary, Jockey, Javelin
    (a) Jargon   (b) Javelin   (c) Jockey   (d) Jealous
    (Olympiad)

25. Find the combination of numbers from the options so that letters arranged accordingly forms a meaningful word.
    E R B K N O
    1 2 3 4 5 6
    (a) 3,2,6,1,4,5   (b) 3,2,6,4,1,5   (c) 3,6,2,1,4,5   (d) 3,2,1,6,5,4
    (Olympiad)

26. Arrange the following words in a logical sequence.
    1. Evening   2. Morning   3. Night   4. Afternoon
    (a) 1,2,3,4   (b) 2,4,1,3   (c) 2,3,1,4   (d) 2,4,3,1
    (Olympiad)

27. Which of the following words can't be formed from given logo

(a) VOTE (b) STOP (c) NEWS (d) TUBE

(Olympiad)

28. Some letters are given which are numbered 1, 2, 3, 4, 5 and 6 and followed by four options containing combinations of these numbers. Find the combination of numbers so that letters are arranged accordingly to form a meaningful word.

    E H N T O R
    1 2 3 4 5 6

    (a) 2,5,3,4,1,6   (b) 5,6,2,3,1,4   (c) 4,2,6,5,1,3   (d) 4,2,6,5,3,1

(Olympiad)

29. How many meaningful English words can be formed from the letters ADRW using each letter only once in each word?

    (a) One   (b) Two   (c) Three   (d) None of these

(Olympiad)

30. Some letters given are numbered 1, 2, 3, 4 and 5 followed by four options containing combination of these numbers. Find the combination of number so that letters are arranged accordingly to from a meaningful word.

    U J C I E
    1 2 3 4 5

    (a) 1,2,3,4,5   (b) 2,4,1,5,3   (c) 2,1,4,3,5   (d) 3,1,2,4,5

(Olympiad)

31. Which of the following words can be formed from the letters of the given word? **(2018)**

    SUPERSTITIOUS

    (a) TUTION   (b) PURSUIT   (c) RESIDENT   (d) SUSPECT

32. Some letters are given which are numbered as 1, 2, 3, 4, 5 and 6. Find the combination of numbers so that letters are arranged accordingly to form a meaningful word. **(2019)**

    O E T S N F
    1 2 3 4 5 6

    (a) 4, 1, 3, 5, 2, 6
    (b) 4, 1, 6, 3, 2, 5
    (c) 5, 2, 3, 1, 6, 4
    (d) 5, 6, 4, 1, 3, 2

Answers and Explanation

Level-1

1. **(b)** The given words can be arranged as:
   Lamp → Land → Landscape → Lantern
   2 → 1 → 3 → 4
2. **(c)** 3, 2, 4, 5, 1 = S U G A R
3. **(c)** The meaningful/logical order of the words is as following:
   Day → Work → Night → Sleep
   2 → 1 → 3 → 4
4. **(a)**
   - TRACTOR can not be formed from the given word as there is only 'T' and 'R' in the given word.
   - There is no 'O' in the given word.
5. **(d)** DAIRY is the word which can be formed form the given word.
6. **(b)** The given words can be arranged as:
   Flask → Flock → Floor → Flower
   2 → 4 → 1 → 3
7. **(a)** The meaningful/logical order of the words is as following:
   Finger → Palm → Wrist → Elbow → Shoulder
   5 → 2 → 4 → 3 → 1
8. **(c)** 4,3,2,5,1 = K N I F E
9. **(b)** 3,4,1,2,5 = B I R T H
10. **(d)** NEVER cannot be made as there is no 'V' in the given word.
11. **(d)** NATION cannot be made as there is no 'A' in the given word.
12. **(d)** The given words can be arranged as:
    Forget → Forgive → Forgo → Format
    3 → 2 → 4 → 1
13. **(d)** NOBLE can be formed form the given word.
14. **(a)** 4,1,2,3,5 = S H A P E
15. **(c)** 4,2,3,5,1 = M A J O R
16. **(b)** 1,4,5,2,3 = M O U T H
17. **(c)** 2,4,3,5,1 = N I G H T
18. **(d)** 3,1,2,5,4 = U N C L E
19. **(c)** E of the word HOUSE is not in the given word.
20. **(b)** H of the word HILT is not in the given word.
21. **(b)**

Letters in the word	Letters in the alphabet
L E M O	L M N O

22. **(d)** The first, second, fourth and sixth letters of the word 'CONTRACT' are C, O, T, R, A respectively. The word formed is ACTOR, in which the middle letter is T.
23. **(d)** REST can be formed from the given word.
24. **(b)** CHART can be formed from the given word.
25. **(a)** RENT can be formed from the given word.
26. **(c)** 2,1,4,3 = Rain, Range, Ranger, Rein
27. **(a)** 4,2,1,3 = Board, Bonus, Bound, Bunch
28. **(a)** 4,3,2,1 = Clone, Cloth, Club, Clutch
29. **(b)** The words are HE, ART and LESS.
30. **(b)** The words are BE and HIND.
31. **(b)** 5,6,3,2,4,1 = DAMAGE
32. **(d)** FARMER : ?#↓↑*↓
33. **(a)** 1, 3, 4, 2, 5; Machine, Mackle, Magnet, Muscle, Mythic.
34. **(b)** 1, 3, 5, 4, 2; Sacrifice, Safety, Sample, Scare, Scratch
35. **(d)** Letter D is not present in the given word.
36. **(c)** 37. **(b)** 38. **(d)** 39. **(d)**

Level-2

1. (a) 2,1,5,6,4,3 = F L O W E R
2. (d) A of the word ROAM is not in the given word.
3. (a) H of the word SIGHT is not in the given word.
4. (b) The first, fourth, seventh and eleventh letters of the word SUPERFLUOUS are S, E, L and S respectively. The word formed is LESS. The first letter is L.
5. (a) The sixth and fourteenth letters from the right are U and M respectively. The fifth and twentieth letters from the left are E and T respectively. Clearly, the word formed is MUTE. So, the first letter is M.
6. (d) 2,3,4,1 = Chamber Cheap Cheerful Chemistry
7. (b) 2,4,3,1 = Gender General Gentle Genuine
8. (a) 'FINE' can be formed from the given letters.
9. (b) 'WORK' can be formed from the given letters.
10. (c) MALE, LAME and MEAL can be formed from the given letters.
11. (c) 2,4,1,3 = Village → Block → District → State
12. (c) 2,3,1,4 = Flower → Honey Bee → Honey → Wax
13. (a) 1,2,4,3 = Farmer → Seed → Cultivation → Food
14. (d) The alphabetical order is : sample, several, she, showed, snaps. so, "she" is the middle word.
15. (c)

<u>U</u>	T S	<u>R</u>	Q P	<u>O</u>	N M	<u>L</u>	K J	<u>I</u>	H G	<u>F</u>
	2		2		2		2		2	

16. (b) a g r h t **n** m b c **n** m l b u v **n** m h e r h n m g f e h n m e c **n** m w q a **n** m h l b
17. (b) 3,6,1,5,2,4 = M O T H E R
18. (a) 6,1,5,2,4,3 = M A R K E T
19. (d) D of the word ATTITUDE is not in the given word.
20. (d) 4, 5, 3, 1, 2 = Afghanistan → Africa → America → Asia → Australia
21. (b) Only one word can be formed, i.e. CROWN
22. (a) The meaningful word with the 1st, 4th, 7th and 11th letters of the word is TIRE, RITE and TIER.
23. (d) Alphabetical order
    1 2 3 4 5 6 7 8
    Ⓒ Ⓓ Ⓔ I I Ⓝ Ⓡ T
    REND, NERD words can be formed.
24. (d) The words in alphabetical order as: Jargon, Javelin, <u>Jealous</u>, Jockey, Judiciary
    So, Jealous in middle.
25. (b) 3,2,6,4,1,5 = BROKEN
26. (b) 2,4,1,3 = Morning → Afternoon → Evening → Night
27. (d) 'TUBE' word can't be formed from given logo.
28. (d) 4,2,6,5,3,1 = THRONE
29. (b) DRAW, WARD can be formed from the given letters.
30. (c) 2,1,4,3,5 = JUICE
31. (b) PURSUIT can be formed from the letters of SUPERSTITIOUS.
32. (b) 4, 1, 6, 3, 2, 5; SOFTEN

CHAPTER 4

Coding-Decoding

OBJECTIVE
- Students will develop the ability to understand the logic that codes a particular message to read the message.

INTRODUCTION
A code means arrangement of letters. Therefore, coding is a method of transforming any instruction from the given form to the required form.

CODING
A particular code pattern is used to express a word in English language to express it as a different word. The coded word itself does not make any sense unless we know the code, i.e. unless we know the pattern or code that has been followed.

DECODING
Decoding helps in tracing out the actual meaning of a coded letter/word/sentence.

TYPES OF CODING
1. Letter Coding
2. Number Coding
3. Substitution Coding
4. Sentence Coding
5. Symbols Coding

1. LETTER CODING
In these questions, code values are given to a word in terms of letters. A particular letter stands for another letter in letter coding.

Example 1:

In a certain code language, TEACHER is written as VGCEJGT, then how will CHILDREN be written in that code language?

(a) ENAGITEV
(b) PGTFNKJE
(c) EJKNFTGP
(d) MGAETVIE

Ans. (c)

Explanation:

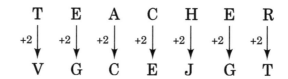

Similarly,

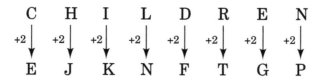

Hence, answer is (c).

2. NUMBER CODING

In these questions, either numerical code values are assigned to a word or alphabetical code values are assigned to numbers.

Example 2:

If in a certain code TERM is coded as 2345, SHAPE is coded as 67893, then what will be code for PASTE?

(a) 98632 (b) 98623 (c) 32689 (d) 23689

Ans. (b)

Explanation : The alphabets are coded as follows :

T	E	R	M	S	H	A	P
2	3	4	5	6	7	8	9

So, PASTE is coded as 98623.

3. SUBSTITUTION CODING

In these types of questions, a particular word is assigned to a certain substituted name and a question is asked to be answered in that substituted name.

Example 3:

If Parrot is known as Peacock, Peacock is known as Swallow, Swallow is known as Pigeon and Pigeon is known as Sparrow, then what would be the name of National Bird of India?

(a) Parrot (b) Peacock (c) Pigeon (d) Swallow

Ans. (d)

Explanation : We know that Peacock is the National Bird but here Peacock is known as Swallow. So, option (d) is correct.

4. SENTENCE CODING

In these types of questions, a group of words will be coded.

Example 4:

If 'drink fruit juice' is written as 'tee see pee', 'juice is sweet' is written as 'see kee lee' and 'he is intelligent' is written as 'lee ree mee'. What will be the code for 'sweet' in that code language?

    (a) see   (b) kee   (c) pee   (d) lee

Ans. (b)

Explanation:

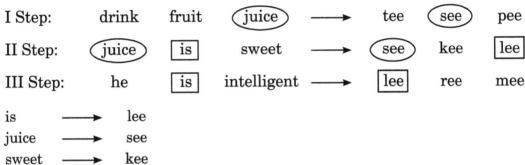

In first and second step we get the code of 'juice' which is 'see'. In the same manner, from second and third step we get the code of 'is' which is 'lee'. In the second step, the remaining word is "sweet' and the remaining code is "kee".

Hence, answer is (b).

5. SYMBOLS CODING

In these types of questions, either alphabetical code values are assigned to symbols or symbols are assigned to alphabets.

Example 5:

In a certain code 'TOME' is written as '@ $ * ?' and ARE is written as '• £?'. How can 'REMOTE' be written in that code.

    (a) £ ? • $ @ ?   (b) @ ? * $ @ ?

    (c) £ ? * $ @ ?   (d) None of these

Ans. (c)

Explanation:

From the data we have

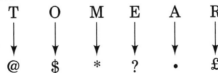

Hence, REMOTE is coded as £ ? * $ @ ?

So, (c) is the answer.

LEVEL-1

1. If HOSPITAL is written as 32574618 in a certain code, how would POSTAL be written in that code?

   (a) 752618   (b) 725618   (c) 725168   (d) 725681

2. If SPARK is coded as TQBSL, what will be the code for FLAME?

   (a) GMBNF   (b) GNBNF   (c) GMCND   (d) GMBMF

3. In a certain code SOBER is written as RNADQ. How LOTUS can be written in that code?

   (a) KMSTR   (b) MPUWT   (c) KNSTR   (d) LMRST

4. If WATER is written as YCVGT then what is written as FIRE?

   (a) IRFE   (b) HKTG   (c) REFI   (d) ERIF

5. If PALE is coded as 2134, EARTH is coded as 41590, then how is PEARL coded as?

   (a) 29530   (b) 25430   (c) 25413   (d) 24153

6. If orange is called butter; butter is called soap, soap is called ink, ink is called honey and honey is called orange, which of the following is used for washing clothes?

   (a) Honey   (b) Butter   (c) Ink   (d) Soap

7. If the animals which can walk are called swimmers, animals who crawl are called flying, those living in water are called snakes and those which fly in the sky are called hunters, then what will a lizard be called?

   (a) Hunters   (b) Snakes   (c) Swimmers   (d) Flying

8. If DELHI is coded as 73541 and CALCUTTA as 82589662, how can CALICUT be coded?

   (a) 5279431   (b) 5978213   (c) 8251896   (d) 8543691

9. If PIGEON is coded as 7 and BELIEVED is coded as 9, then what is the code number for CONTINUOUS?

   (a) 10   (b) 11   (c) 12   (d) 13

10. In a certain code, SISTER is written as SKUVGT. How is UNCLE written in that code?

    (a) TMBKD   (b) WPENG   (c) UMBKD   (d) UPENG

11. If in a certain code, HYDROGEN is written as YHRDGONE, then how can RAMAYANA be written in that code?

    (a) ARAMAYAN   (b) ANAYAMAR   (c) SBNBZBOB   (d) RMYNAAAA

12. If air is called green, green is called blue, blue is called sky, sky is called yellow, yellow is called water and water is called pink, then what is the color of clear sky?
    (a) Yellow   (b) Green   (c) Sky   (d) Blue
13. If PEAR is written as GFDN, then how is REAP written in that code?
    (a) FDNG   (b) NFDG   (c) DNGF   (d) NDFG
14. If LUXOR is coded as ORXLU, then CAMEL will be coded as?
    (a) LEMAC   (b) ACMLE   (c) ELMCA   (d) DBMFM
15. If FLATTER is coded as 7238859 and MOTHER is coded as 468159, then how is MAMMOTH coded?
    (a) 4344651   (b) 4344681   (c) 4146481   (d) 4346481
16. If sky is called sea, sea is called water, water is called air, air is called cloud and cloud is called river, then what do we drink when thirsty?
    (a) Sky   (b) Water   (c) Cloud   (d) Air
17. If SEASONAL is written as ESASONLA, then how can SEPARATE be written in that code?
    (a) ETARAPES   (b) ESAPARET   (c) ESPARAET   (d) SEAPARATE
18. In a certain code, RAGHAVAN is written as RBGIAWAO, then how can MATHAVAN be written in that code?
    (a) OAWAITBM   (b) MBTIAWAO   (c) NAVAHTAM   (d) NBUIBWBO
19. If ABC = 6, then DEF = ?
    (a) 3   (b) 7   (c) 10   (d) 15
20. If lead is called stick, stick is called nib, nib is called needle, needle is called rope and rope is called thread, what will be fitted in a pen to write with it?
    (a) Needle   (b) Stick   (c) Nib   (d) Rope
21. In a certain code language, GRAPE is written as 27354 and FOUR is written as 1687. How is GROUP written in that code?
    (a) 27384   (b) 27684   (c) 27685   (d) 27658
22. If FRIEND is coded as DPGCLB, then how will you code ENEMY?
    (a) FOFNZ   (b) CLCKW   (c) YMENE   (d) ZNFOF
23. If EQUATION is coded as FSVCUKPP, then how DONKEY can be coded?
    (a) EQOMFA   (b) EPOLFZ   (c) YEKNOD   (d) FQPMGA
24. If MALE is coded as OCJC, then how HOME can be coded?
    (a) IPNF   (b) HPMF   (c) OHEM   (d) JQKC
25. If rose is called popy, popy is called lily, lily is called lotus and lotus is called glandiola, which is the king of flowers?
    (a) Rose   (b) Popy   (c) Glandiola   (d) Lotus

DIRECTIONS (Qs. 26-30): In each of the questions given below, a group of digits followed by four combinations of letter codes labelled (a), (b), (c) and (d) are given. You have to find out which of the combinations is correct coded from of the group of digits as per the following codes and conditions.

Digit code	9	3	2	8	1	5	7	0	4
Letter code	M	E	B	N	K	R	H	T	D

Conditions :

(i) If the first digit is an odd number, then it is to be coded as 'X'.

(ii) If the last digit is an even number, then it is to be coded as 'Y'.

26. 32140
    (a) EBKDT (b) XBKDT (c) EBKDY (d) XBKDY

27. 01574
    (a) TKRHD (b) BTRHX (c) TKRHY (d) XTRHY

28. 91573
    (a) MKRHY (b) XKRHX (c) MKRHX (d) XKRHE

29. 42082
    (a) DBTNY (b) YBTNB (c) DBTNX (d) XBTNB

30. 01230
    (a) XKBEX (b) TKBEY (c) YKBEY (d) YKBEX

31. If 'triangle' is coded as 9, 'square' is coded as 16, then 'circle' is coded as _____ .
    (2018)
    (a) 0 (b) 16 (c) 100 (d) 25

32. In a certain code language, if SMART is coded as MSATR, then how will HORSE be coded in the same code language? **(2020)**
    (a) RHOES (b) ROHES (c) OHSRE (d) OHRES

33. If 'School' is called 'Home'. 'Home is called 'office'. 'Office' is called 'Market' and 'Market' is called 'Bus stop', then we buy vegetables from. **(2020)**
    (a) Office (b) Market (c) Bus stop (d) Home

34. If 'pen' is called 'bag', 'bag' is called 'table', 'table' is called 'book' and 'book' is called 'blackboard', then we can put our books in _____. **(2022)**
    (a) table (b) bag (c) blackboard (d) pen

LEVEL-2

1. If PAINT is coded as 74128 and EXCEL is coded as 93596, then how is ACCEPT coded?
   (a) 459578 (b) 455978 (c) 457958 (d) 459758

2. If MOBILE is written as NOCIME, then how DIVINE can be written in that code?
   (a) EIWIOE (b) EJWJOF (c) IDIVEN (d) ENIVID

3. If room is called bed, bed is called window, window is called flower and flower is called cooler, on what would a man sleep?
   (a) Bed (b) Cooler (c) Window (d) Flower

4. In a certain code, BASKET is written as 5$3%#1 and TRIED is written as 14*#2. How is SKIRT written in that code?
   (a) 3%*41 (b) 3*%41 (c) 3%#41 (d) 3#4%1

5. In a certain code language, 123 means 'bright little boy' and 145 means 'beautiful is boy'. Which digit in that language means 'boy'?
   (a) 2 (b) 3 (c) 4 (d) 1

6. In a certain code, the following numbers are coded by assigning signs

1	2	3	4	5	6	7	8	9
<	+	=	@	!	$	>	#	&

   Which number can be decoded from the given symbols?

   @ > ! & +

   (a) 29574 (b) 47295 (c) 47592 (d) 21638

DIRECTIONS (Qs.7-11): Study the following information carefully and answer the questions given below it.

Alphabets in the letters are to be coded as follows:

C	A	R	W	U	B	N	Q	E
2	4	3	7	9	6	1	5	8

Conditions:
(i) If the first as well as last letters are vowels, both are to be coded as @.
(ii) If the first as well as last letters are consonants, both are to be coded as %.

7. AWBUQ
   (a) @769@ (b) 47695 (c) @7695 (d) 4769@

8. RNABE
    (a) 31468 (b) %1468 (c) 3146% (d) %146%
9. ECRBU
    (a) 82369 (b) @2369 (c) @236@ (d) 8236@
10. NQEAR
    (a) 15843 (b) %5843 (c) 1584% (d) %584%
11. WUABE
    (a) 79468 (b) %9468 (c) 7946@ (d) %946%

DIRECTIONS (Qs. 12-15): Study the following information carefully and answer the following questions.

(i) 'She is brave' means 'L M N'.

(ii) 'He has great smile' means 'A C D B'.

(iii) 'She always smile' means 'R C N'.

12. What is the code for 'She'?
    (a) L (b) M (c) N (d) C
13. What is the code for 'Smile'?
    (a) A (b) C (c) D (d) N
14. What is the code for 'always'?
    (a) R (b) L (c) B (d) A
15. What is the code for 'she smile'?
    (a) RN (b) LC (d) AB (d) NC
16. If in a code language, PARENT is coded as SAUEQT, then how CHILDREN can be coded in that same code?
    (a) FHLLGRHN (b) DIJMESFO (c) NERDLIHC (d) DHJLERFN
17. If bangle is called cassette, cassette is called table, table is called game and game is called cupboard, then which is played in the tape recorder?
    (a) Bangle (b) Cassette (c) Table (d) Cupboard
18. If in a certain code language DASHE is written as 21845, then how would SHADE be written in that same code language?
    (a) 84215 (b) 84152 (c) 84125 (d) 84124
19. In a certain code language FLOWERS is written as OLFXSRE, then how SUPREME can be written in that same code?
    (a) PUSREME (b) PVSSFNF (c) EMERPUS (d) PUSSEME
20. If A = 1, BE = 7, then ADD = ?
    (a) 3 (b) 6 (c) 9 (d) 12

21. Hitesh asked Piya, "If SAFER is coded as 5@3#2 and RIDE is coded as 2&%#, then how would FEDS be written in same code?"

    (a) 3#%5   (b) 3#&5   (c) 3@%5   (d) 3#%2

22. If 'GREEN' is coded as '35664' and 'PARROT' is coded '715592', then how will 'REPEAT' be coded? **(Olympiad)**

    (a) 569612   (b) 567612   (c) 597613   (d) 567611

23. If 'Book' means 'Watch'; 'Watch' means 'Bag'; 'Bag' means 'Pen'; and 'Pen' means 'Pencil', then which is used to read time? **(Olympiad)**

    (a) Book   (b) Watch   (c) Bag   (d) Pen

24. In a certain code language, 'MAN' is coded as 28 and 'GIRL' is coded as 46, then 'WOMEN' will coded be as **(Olympiad)**

    (a) 69   (b) 70   (c) 80   (d) 83

25. If 'Rain' is called 'Road'; Road is called 'Water'; 'Water' is called 'Cloud'; 'Cloud' is called 'Sky'; 'Sky' is called' Sea'; 'Sea' is called 'Path', where do aeroplanes fly? **(Olympiad)**

    (a) Road   (b) Sky   (c) Sea   (D) Water

26. In a certain code, GIGANTIC is written as GIGTANCI. How is MIRACLES written in that code? **(Olympiad)**

    (a) MIRLCAES   (b) MIRLACSE   (c) RIMCALSE   (d) RIMLCAES

27. In a certain code, INSTITUTION is written as NOITUTITSNI. How is PERFECTION written in that code? **(Olympiad)**

    (a) NOICTEFREP
    (b) NOITCEFERP
    (c) NOITCEFRPE
    (d) NOITCEFREP

28. If 'PAPER' is written as QBQFS and 'SCHOOL' is written as TDIPPM, then 'BOUQUET' will be written as .... **(Olympiad)**

    (a) CPVRVFV   (b) CPVRVFU   (c) CPRVFVU   (d) CPVRVGW

29. If 'Train' is called 'Bus'; 'Bus' is called 'Tractor'; 'Tractor' is called 'Car'; 'Car' is called 'Scooter'; 'Scooter' is called' Bicycle'; 'Bicycle' is called 'Rickshaw', then which is used to plough a field? **(Olympiad)**

    (a) Train   (b) Bus   (c) Tractor   (d) Car

30. If 'White' is called 'Blue'; 'Blue' is called 'Red'; 'Red' is called 'Yellow'; 'Yellow' is called 'Green'; 'Green' is called' Black'; 'Black' is called 'Violet', and 'Violet' is called 'Orange', then what would be the colour of human blood? **(Olympiad)**

    (a) Red   (b) Yellow   (c) Green   (d) Violet

31. In a certain code language, if 'ANIMAL', is coded as '123415' and 'CAMEL' is coded as '61475', then how will 'CINEMA' be coded in that language? **(2022)**

    (a) 637421
    (b) 632147
    (c) 632741
    (d) 647231

Answers and Explanation

Level-1

1. **(b)** As,

   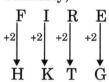

   Similarly,

   P O S T A L
   ↓ ↓ ↓ ↓ ↓ ↓
   7 2 5 6 1 8

2. **(a)** As,

   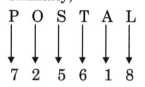

   Similarly,

   F L A M E
   +1↓ +1↓ +1↓ +1↓ +1↓
   G M B N F

3. **(c)** As,

   S O B E R
   -1↓ -1↓ -1↓ -1↓ -1↓
   R N A D Q

   Similarly,

   L O T U S
   -1↓ -1↓ -1↓ -1↓ -1↓
   K N S T R

4. **(b)** As,

   W A T E R
   +2↓ +2↓ +2↓ +2↓ +2↓
   Y C V G T

   Similarly,

   F I R E
   +2↓ +2↓ +2↓ +2↓
   H K T G

5. **(d)** As,

   P A L E
   ↓ ↓ ↓ ↓
   2 1 3 4

   and

   E A R T H
   ↓ ↓ ↓ ↓ ↓
   4 1 5 9 0

   So,

   P E A R L
   ↓ ↓ ↓ ↓ ↓
   2 4 1 5 3

6. **(c)** Clearly, soap is used for washing clothes. But soap is called ink. So, Ink is used for washing clothes.

7. **(d)** Clearly, a lizard crawls and the animals that crawl are called flying. So, lizard is called flying.

8. **(c)** As,

   D E L H I
   ↓ ↓ ↓ ↓ ↓
   7 3 5 4 1

   and

   C A L C U T T A
   ↓ ↓ ↓ ↓ ↓ ↓ ↓ ↓
   8 2 5 8 9 6 6 2

So,

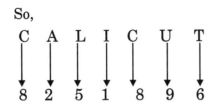

9. **(b)** Here, the pattern is: Numbers of letters + 1.

So, number of letters in CONTINUOUS = 10

Therefore, required code number = number of letters + 1 = 10 + 1

= 11

10. **(d)** As,

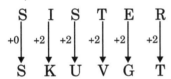

Similarly,

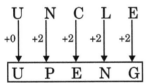

11. **(a)** As,

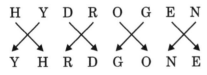

Similarly,

12. **(c)** The colour of clear sky is blue and as given blue is called sky. So, the colour of clear sky is sky.

13. **(b)** As,

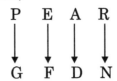

Similarly,

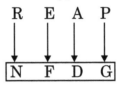

14. **(c)** As,

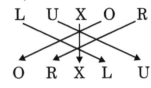

Similarly,

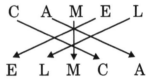

15. **(b)** As,

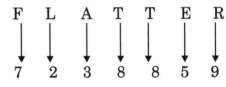

and,

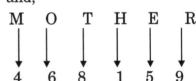

So,

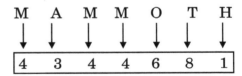

16. **(d)** As, we know that, one drinks water when thirsty and as given water is called air.

17. (c) As,

Similarly,

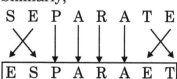

18. (b) As,

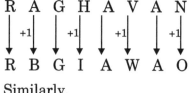

Similarly,

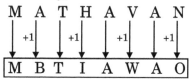

19. (d) As,
A B C (Positional Value)
1 + 2 + 3 = 6

Similarly,
D E F (Positional Value)
4 + 5 + 6 = 15

20. (a) As, nib is fitted in the pen to write with it. But, as given nib is called needle.

21. (c) As,

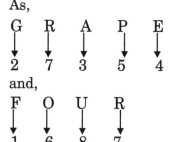

So,

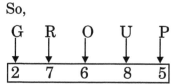

22 (b) As,

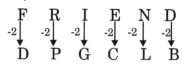

Similarly,

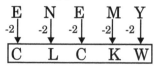

23. (a) As,

E Q U A T I O N
+1 +2 +1 +2 +1 +2 +1 +2
F S V C U K P P

Similarly,

D O N K E Y
+1 +2 +1 +2 +1 +2
E Q O M F A

24. (d) As,

M A L E
+2 +2 -2 -2
O C J C

Similarly,

H O M E
+2 +2 -2 -2
J Q K C

25. (c) As, we know that, the king of flowers is the lotus. But, here lotus is called glandiola.

26-30:

26. (b) Condition (i) is applied:
So, 32140 = XBKDT

27. (c) Condition (ii) is applied:
So, 01574 = TKRHY

28. (d) Condition (i) is applied:
So, 91573 = XKRHE

29. (a) Condition (ii) is applied:
So, 42082 = DBTNY

30. (b) Condition (ii) is applied:
So, 01230 = TKBEY

31. (a) A triangle has 3 sides and a circle has no sides
Coding digit for triangle
= (number of sides)^2 = $(3)^2$ = 9
Coding digit for circle
= (number of sides)^2 = $(0)^2$ = 0

32. (d) In the given code language, alphabet at 1st position is interchanged with 2nd position and and alphabet at 4th position is interchanged with 5th position. Following the same rule in HORSE, it can be coded as OHRES

33. (c) We buy vegetables from Market and Market is called Bus Stop.

34. (a) We can put our books in bag and bag is called table.

Level-2

1. (b) As,

P A I N T
↓ ↓ ↓ ↓ ↓
7 4 1 2 8

and

E X C E L
↓ ↓ ↓ ↓ ↓
9 3 5 9 6

So,

A C C E P T
↓ ↓ ↓ ↓ ↓ ↓
| 4 5 5 9 7 8 |

2. (a) As,

M O B I L E
+1↓ ↓ +1↓ ↓ +1↓ ↓
N O C I M E

Similarly,

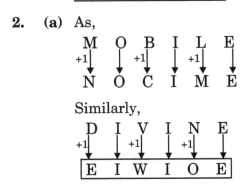

3. (c) As we know that, a man sleeps on a bed but in the question, bed is called window.

4. (a) As,

B A S K E T
↓ ↓ ↓ ↓ ↓ ↓
5 $ 3 % # 1

and,

T R I E D
↓ ↓ ↓ ↓ ↓
1 4 * # 2

So,

S K I R T
↓ ↓ ↓ ↓ ↓
| 3 % * 4 1 |

5. (d) According to the given information,

① 2   3 → bright light (boy) .... (i)

① 4   5 → beautiful is (boy) .... (ii)

From eq. (i) and (ii)

① → (boy)

So, boy means 1.

6. (c)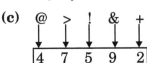

7-11:

7. **(b)** AWBUQ = 47695, no condition is applied.
8. **(a)** RNABE = 31468, no condition is applied.
9. **(c)** Condition (i) is applied, so ECRBU = @236@
10. **(d)** NQEAR = %584% as condition (ii) is applied.
11. **(a)** WUABE = 79468

12-15:

She is brave → L M N ...(i)

He has great ⟨smile⟩ → A Ⓒ D B ...(ii)

She |always| ⟨smile⟩ → |R| Ⓒ N ...(iii)

12. **(c)** From equations (i) and (iii), we get the code for 'she' is 'N'.
13. **(b)** From equations (ii) and (iii), we get the code for 'smile' is 'C'.
14. **(a)** From equation (iii) we get the code for 'always' is 'R'.
15. **(d)** From equation (i), (ii) and (iii) we get the code for 'she smile' is 'NC'.
16. **(a)** As,

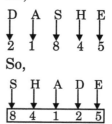

Similarly,

C H I L D R E N
+3 ↓ +3 ↓ +3 ↓ +3 ↓
| F H L L G R H N |

17. **(c)** As we know that, cassette is played in the tape recorder. But a cassette is called table. So, a table will be played in the tape recorder.

18. **(c)** As,

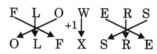

So,

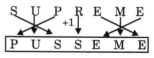

19. **(d)** as,

F L O W E R S
       +1↓
O L F X S R E

Similarly,

S U P R E M E
       +1↓
| P U S S E M E |

20. **(c)** As,
A = 1 (1 is A's positional value)
B = 2 (2 is B's positional value)
E = 5 (5 is E's positional value)
B + E = 2 + 5 = 7
Similarly, A + D + D
= 1 + 4 + 4 = 9

21. **(a)** As,

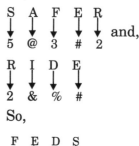 and,

So,

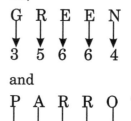

22. **(b)** As,

G R E E N
↓ ↓ ↓ ↓ ↓
3 5 6 6 4

and

P A R R O T
↓ ↓ ↓ ↓ ↓ ↓
7 1 5 5 9 2

So,

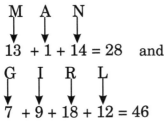

23. **(a)** As we know that, we used to read time by watch. But, as given, book means watch. So, the time is read by book.

24. **(b)** As,

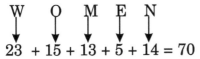

   $13 + 1 + 14 = 28$ and

   G I R L

   $7 + 9 + 18 + 12 = 46$

   Similarly,

   W O M E N

   $23 + 15 + 13 + 5 + 14 = 70$

25. **(c)** Aeroplanes fly in the sky. But, as given sky is called sea.

26. **(b)** As,

   Similarly,

27. **(d)** As,

   INSTITUTION $\xrightarrow{\text{Reversed}}$

   NOITUTITSNI

   Similarly,

   PERFECTION $\xrightarrow{\text{Reversed}}$

   NOITCEFREP

28. **(b)** As,

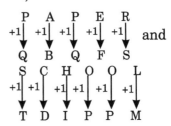

   Similarly,

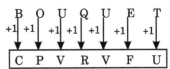

29. **(d)** A field is ploughed by tractor. But, as given, tractor is called car. So, car is used to plough a field.

30. **(b)** The colour of human blood is red. But as given, Red is called Yellow.

31. **(c)**

CHAPTER 5

Blood Relations

OBJECTIVES

- Students will be able to know the relation between two people by using the given information.
- They will learn to analyse the whole chain of relations and decipher the direct relationship between the people concerned.

INTRODUCTION

In blood relations, certain information is given about the members of the family in the question. Based on that information, students need to find out the relationship between particular members of the family. They should have the knowledge of blood relations, in order to solve these questions.

To remember easily, the relations may be divided into two sides as given below:

1. **Relations of Paternal side:**
    1. Father's father → Grandfather
    2. Father's mother → Grandmother
    3. Father's brother → Uncle
    4. Father's sister → Aunt
    5. Children of uncle → Cousin
    6. Wife of uncle → Aunt
    7. Children of aunt → Cousin
    8. Husband of aunt → Uncle

2. **Relations of Maternal side:**

   1. Mother's father → Maternal grandfather
   2. Mother's mother → Maternal grandmother
   3. Mother's brother → Maternal Uncle
   4. Mother's Sister → Aunt
   5. Children of maternal uncle → Cousin
   6. Wife of maternal uncle → Maternal aunt

Relations from one generation to next:

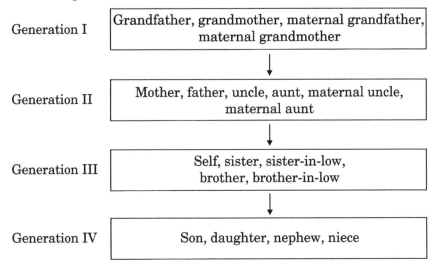

Example 1:

Rahul is the brother of Sonia. Sonia is the mother of Keshav. How is Keshav related to Rahul?

(a) Son (b) Nephew (c) Father (d) Brother

Sol. (b)

Explanation: Sonia is the sister of Rahul and Keshav is the son of Sonia. So, Keshav is the son of Rahul's sister. i.e., nephew.

The relation diagram can be represented as shown below:

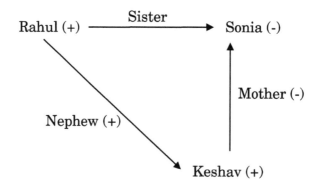

Example 2:

Pointing to a man, a lady said "His mother is the only daughter of my mother". How is the lady related to the man?

(a) Mother (b) Sister (c) Aunt (d) Daughter

Sol. (a)

Explanation: The only daughter of lady's mother is lady herself. So, she is the mother of the man.

The relation diagram can be represented as shown below:

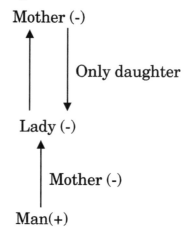

DIRECTIONS (Examples 3 & 4): Read the following information carefully and answer the questions, which follow.

(i) 'A × B' means 'A is the father of B'.

(ii) 'A + B' means ' A is the mother of B'.

(iii) 'A – B' means 'A is the sister of B'.

(iv) 'A ÷ B' means 'A is the brother of B'.

Example 3:

In the expression P × Q ÷ R, how is P related to R?

(a) Daughter (b) Mother (c) Father (d) Brother

Sol.(c)

Explanation: P × Q ÷ R,

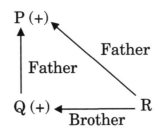

So, P is the father of R.

Example 4:

Which of the following represents 'N is the father of M'?

(a) L – N × M
(b) L + N – M
(c) L × N + M
(d) None of the above

Sol. (a)

Explanation: From option (a), L – N × M

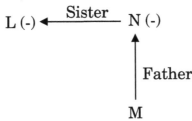

Example 5:

Puneet is the brother of Akshay. Kanak is the sister of Akshay. How is Puneet related to Kanak?

(a) Son (b) Father (c) Nephew (d) Brother

Sol.(d)

Explanation: According to the given question, the relation diagram can be represented as shown below:

Puneet (+) ←—Brother—— Akshay (+) ——Sister—→ Kanak (–)
　　　↑_____Brother_____↑

So, Puneet is the brother of Kanak.

LEVEL-1

1. Pointing to a woman, I said, "She is the mother of my father's sister". How is that woman related to me?

   (a) Mother   (b) Daughter   (c) Sister   (d) Grandmother

2. Looking at a photographer, a person said, "I have no brother or sister but that man's father is my father's son". At whose photographer was the person looking at?

   (a) His father's   (b) His son's   (c) His nephew's   (d) His own

3. If P $ Q means P is the brother of Q, P # Q means P is the mother of Q, P * Q means P is the daughter of Q, in A # B $ C, who is the brother?

   (a) A   (b) C   (c) B   (d) None of these

4. A party consists of grandmother, father, mother, two sons and their wives and two daughters of each of the sons. How many females are there in all?

   (a) 6   (b) 8   (c) 10   (d) 12

5. Megha and Risha are sisters. Nishant and Harsh are brothers. Megha is the mother of Nishant. How is Risha related to Harsh?

   (a) Aunt   (b) Mother   (c) Grandmother   (d) Sister

6. I am brother of Hemant and Neha is my sister, Mr. Jayant is my father's father. How is Neha related to Mr. Jayant?

   (a) Mother
   (b) Daughter
   (c) Granddaughter
   (d) Sister

7. If Anup is the brother of Bina; Bina is the sister of Chetan; and Chetan is the father of Dimple, how Dimple is related to Anup?

   (a) Brother
   (b) Sister
   (c) Nephew
   (d) Cannot be determined

8. Introducing a boy, a girl said, "He is the son of the daughter of the father of my uncle." How is the boy related to the girl?

   (a) Son-in-law   (b) Uncle   (c) Nephew   (d) Brother

DIRECTIONS (Qs. 9-10): Study the following information carefully and answer the questions.

   (i) A + B means A is the mother of B.

   (ii) A - B means A is the sister of B.

(iii) A * B means A is the father of B.

(iv) A × B means A is the brother of B.

9. Which of the following means Q is the grandfather of S?

   (a) Q + R * S   (b) Q * R + S   (c) S – Q + R   (d) None of these

10. Which of the following means I is the uncle of K?

    (a) I + J + K   (b) J * K – I   (c) I × J * K   (d) None of these

11. Pointing to a lady, Shohbit said, "Her granddaughter is the only daughter of my brother." How is the lady related to Shohbit?

    (a) Mother   (b) Sister   (c) Daughter   (d) Grandmother

12. Vikas said - "This girl is the wife of the grandson of my mother". How is Vikas related to the girl?

    (a) Husband   (b) Father   (c) Father-in-law   (d) Brother

13. When Nitin saw Varun, he recalled, "He is the son of the father of my daughter." Who is Varun?

    (a) Brother-in-law   (b) Uncle   (c) Brother   (d) None of these

14. Ashok is the brother of Bani, Bani is the daughter of Chandni and Deepak is the father of Ashok. Then, how is Chandni related to Deepak?

    (a) Husband   (b) Wife   (c) Granddaughter   (d) Grandfather

15. Pointing to Varman, Madhav said, "I am the only son of one of the sons of his father." How is Varman related to Madhav?

    (a) Uncle
    (b) Father or Uncle
    (c) Nephew
    (d) Father

DIRECTIONS (Qs. 16-20): Study the following information carefully and answer the questions.

Members of a family Ankit, Kajal, Chetan, Diya, Mohit, Shikha and Gajendra are sitting together. Ankit is the son of Gajendra who is brother of Shikha. Shikha is mother of Mohit and Kajal. Mohit is brother of Kajal and Kajal is sister of Chetan. Chetan is a male. Diya is a female and child of Chetan.

16. How is Kajal related to Ankit?

    (a) Aunt   (b) Sister-in-law   (c) Cousin   (d) Mother

17. Who is uncle of Chetan?

    (a) Gajendra   (b) Ankit   (c) Mohit   (d) None of these

18. How many male members are there in the family?

    (a) 2   (b) 4   (c) 3   (d) 5

19. Which of the following is the correct statement?
    (a) Gajendra is the father of Chetan
    (b) Diya is the Child of Ankit
    (c) Kajal is the cousin of Ankit
    (d) None of the above

20. Who is the child of Chetan?
    (a) Ankit (b) Kajal (c) Mohit (d) Diya

21. In a 4 members family, R is the wife of P while L is the son of P and R. D is the grandson of P. How is D related to L? **(2022)**
    (a) Father (b) Son (c) Brother (d) Uncle

LEVEL-2

1. If A + B means A is the brother of B; A % B means A is the father of B and A × B means A is the sister of B. Which of the following means M is the uncle of P?
    (a) M % N × P (b) N × P % M (c) M + S % R (d) M + K % T × P

2. Introducing a lady, Sahil said, "She is the mother of the only daughter of my son." How that lady is related to Sahil?
    (a) Daughter-in-law
    (b) Daughter
    (c) Sister
    (d) Sister-in-law

3. A man said to Vansh, "Your mother's husband is my brother-in-law". How is man related to Vansh?
    (a) Father
    (b) Uncle
    (c) Brother
    (d) Father-in-law

4. If A + B means B is the brother of A; A × B means B is the husband of A; A - B means A is the mother of B and A % B means A is the father of B, which of the following relations shows that Q is the grandmother of T?
    (a) P × Q % R – T
    (b) P × Q % R + T
    (c) Q - P + R % T
    (d) None of these

5. A, B and C are sisters. D is the brother of E and E is the daughter of B. how is A related to D?
    (a) Cousin (b) Aunt (c) Sister (d) Niece

6. Dipanshu has a brother Aniket. Dipanshu is the son of Prem. Nitesh is Prem's father. In terms of relationship, what is Aniket of Nitesh?
    (a) Brother (b) Son (c) Grandson (d) Grandfather

7. If P $ Q means P is the father of Q; P # Q means P is the mother of Q and P * Q means P is the sister of Q, then N # L $ P * Q shows which of the relation of Q to N?

   (a) Grand daughter (b) Nephew
   (c) Grandson (d) Data inadequate

DIRECTIONS (Qs. 8-10): Read the following information and answer the questions given below:

Priyansh is the son of Sumit. Kavya, Sumit's sister, has a son Rithvik and a daughter Nitanya. Rakesh is the maternal uncle of Rithvik.

8. How is Priyansh related to Rithvik?

   (a) Uncle (b) Brother (c) Cousin (d) Nephew

9. How is Nitanya related to Rakesh?

   (a) Niece (b) Wife (c) Daughter (d) Sister

10. How many nephews does Rakesh have?

    (a) Nil (b) One (c) Two (d) Three

11. Pointing to a photograph Anusha said, "He is the son of the only son of my grandfather." How is the man in the photograph related to Anusha?

    (a) Son (b) Brother
    (c) Uncle (d) Data inadequate

12. Pointing to a person, Praveen said, "His only brother is the father of my daughter's father". How is the person related to Praveen?

    (a) Father (b) Brother-in-law (c) Uncle (d) Grandfather

13. P is the mother of K; K is the sister of D; D is the father of J. How is P related to J?

    (a) Aunt (b) Mother (c) Sister (d) Grandmother

14. Pointing to Gopi, Nalni says, "I am the daughter of the only son of his grandfather." How Nalni is related to Gopi?

    (a) Daughter (b) Sister (c) Niece (d) Mother

15. If P + Q means P is the father of Q, P × Q means P is the brother of Q, P − Q means P is the mother of Q, then which of the following is definitely true about C − A + B?

    (a) B is the son of A (b) A is the son of C
    (c) B is the father of A (d) C is the mother of B

DIRECTIONS (Qs. 16-19): Read the following information carefully and answer the questions given below:

   (i) A + B means A is the son of B
   (ii) A − B means A is the wife of B

(iii) A × B means A is the brother of B

(iv) A ÷ B means A is the mother of B

(v) A = B means A is the sister of B

16. What does P + R − Q mean?
    (a) Q is the father of P
    (b) Q is the son of P
    (c) Q is the uncle of P
    (d) Q is the brother of P

17. What does P × R ÷ Q mean?
    (a) P is the brother of Q
    (b) P is the father of Q
    (c) P is the uncle of Q
    (d) P is the nephew of Q

18. What does P = R + Q mean?
    (a) P is the aunt of Q
    (b) P is the daughter of Q
    (c) P is the niece of Q
    (d) P is the sister of Q

19. What does P = R ÷ Q mean?
    (a) P is the aunt of Q
    (b) P is the sister of Q
    (c) Q is the niece of P
    (d) Q is the daughter of P

20. A's son B is married with C whose sister D is married to E, the brother of B. How D is related to A?
    (a) Cousin
    (b) Sister
    (c) Daughter's-in-law
    (d) Sister-in-law

DIRECTIONS (Qs. 21-25): Study the following information carefully and answer the questions given below it:

There are six persons A,B,C,D,E and F. C is the sister of F. B is the brother of E's husband. D is the father of A and grandfather of F. There are two fathers, three brothers and a mother in the group.

21. Who is the mother?
    (a) A
    (b) B
    (c) D
    (d) E

22. Who is E's husband?
    (a) B
    (b) C
    (c) A
    (d) F

23. How many male members are there in the group?
    (a) One
    (b) Two
    (c) Three
    (d) Four

24. How is F related to E?
    (a) Uncle
    (b) Husband
    (c) Son
    (d) Daughter

25. Which of the following is a group of brothers?
    (a) ABF   (b) ABD   (c) BFC   (d) BDF

26. A is the brother of B. A is the brother of C. To find what is the relation between B and C, what minimum information from the following is necessary?
    1. Sex of C   2. Sex of B
    (a) only 1   (b) only 2   (c) Either 1 or 2   (d) Both 1 and 2

27. How is L related to Z in the given family tree? **(2022)**

    Note:
    (i) '⇔' is used for husband and wife
    (ii) '|' is used for parents (Father and mother). Parents are put on the top while children are put at the bottom
    (iii) '−' or minus sign is used for female
    (iv) '+' or plus sign is used for male
    (v) '—' sign is used for sibling

    (a) Grandfather
    (b) Grandmother
    (c) Great maternal grandfather
    (d) Great paternal grandfather

28. How is P related to N in the given family tree? **(2022)**

    Note:
    (i) '⇔' is used for husband and wife
    (ii) '|' is used for parents (Father and mother). Parents are put on the top while children are put at the bottom
    (iii) '−' or minus sign is used for female
    (iv) '+' or plus sign is used for male
    (v) '—' sign is used for sibling

    (a) Father
    (b) Paternal Uncle
    (c) Maternal Uncle
    (d) Son

Answers and Explanation

Level-1

1. **(d)** My father's sister is my aunty and my aunty's mother is also my father's mother. So, she is my grandmother.
   The relation diagram can be represented as shown below:

   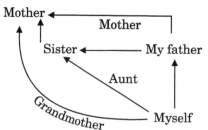

2. **(b)** According to the given question, the relation diagram can be represented as:

   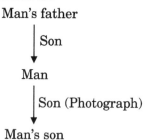

   It is clearly shown that the photo is of his son.

3. **(c)** A is the mother of B and B is the brother of C. So, B is the brother.

4. **(b)** Here, Grandmother = 1
   Mother = 1
   Wives = 2
   Daughters = 2+2 = 4
   So, in all there are = 1+1+2+4 = 8 females.

5. **(a)** The relation diagram can be represented as :

   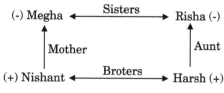

   So, Risha is aunt to Harsh.

6. **(c)** The relation diagram can be represented as shown below:

   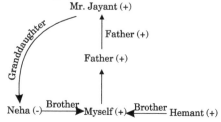

   So, Neha is granddaughter of Mr. Jayant.

7. **(d)** The relation diagram can be represented as shown below:

   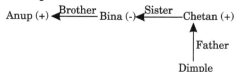

   The gender of dimple is not known. So, we cannot be determine the relation.

8. **(d)** The father of the boy's uncle → the grandfather of the boy and daughter of the grandfather → sister of father.

9. **(b)** Option (b) Q * R + S

   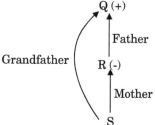

   So, Q is the grandfather of S.

10. (c) From option (c), I × J * K

I (+) ←—Brother— J (+)
                    ↑
                    | Father
                    K

11. (a) Daughter of Shohbit's brother → niece of Shohbit. Thus the granddaughter of the woman is Shohbit's niece.

Hence, the lady is the mother of Shohbit.

12 (c) The girl is the wife of grandson of Vikas's mother i.e., the girl is the wife of son of Vikas. Hence, Vikas is the father-in-law of the girl.

13. (a) Nitin's daughter's mother -- Nitin's wife;

Nitin's wife's father - Nitin's father-in-law;

Father-in-law's son - Nitin's brother-in-law.

So, Varun is Nitin's brother-in-law.

14. (b) The relation can be represented as

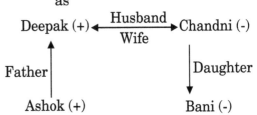

So, Chandni is wife of Deepak.

15. (b) Madhav is the only son of one of the sons of Varman's father → Either Varman is the father or uncle of Madhav.

16.-20: The relation diagram can be represented as shown below:

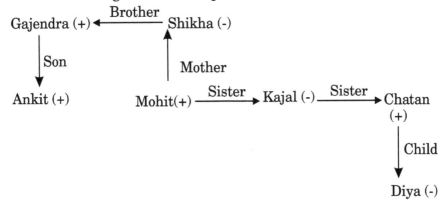

16. (c) According to the above diagram, Kajal is cousin to Ankit.

17. (a) According to the above diagram, Gajendra is the uncle of Chetan.

18. (b) There are 4 male members are there in the family.

19. (c) Kajal is the cousin of Ankit is the correct statement.

20. (d) According to the above diagram, Diya is the child of Chetan.

21. (b)

Level-2

1. **(d)** M + K → M is the brother of K
   K % T → K is the father of T
   T × P → T is the sister of P
   Therefore, K is the father of P and M is the uncle of P.

2. **(a)** The lady is the mother of Sahil's granddaughter. Hence, the lady is the daughter-in-law of Sahil.

3. **(b)** Vansh's mother's husband is father of Vansh. Brother-in-law of Vansh's father is Vansh's uncle.

4. **(c)** Q - P → Q is the mother of P
   P + R → R is the brother of P
   Hence, → Q is the mother of R
   R % T → R is the father of T.
   Hence, Q is the grandmother of T.

5. **(b)** E is the daughter of B and D is the brother of E. So, D is the son of B. Also, A is the sister of B. Thus, A is D's aunt.

6. **(c)** Aniket is the brother of Dipanshu and Dipanshu is the son of Prem. So, Aniket is the son of Prem. Now, Nitesh is the father of Prem. Thus, Aniket is the grandson of Nitesh.

7. **(d)** As the gender of Q is not known, hence, data is inadequate.

8 - 10. The relation diagram is as shown below:

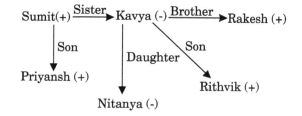

8. **(c)** From the above diagram, it is clear that Priyansh is cousin to Rithvik.

9. **(a)** From the above diagram, it is clear that Nitanya is niece to Rakesh.

10. **(c)** There are two nephews of Rakesh i.e. Priyansh and Rithvik.

11. **(b)** The man in the photograph is son of Anusha's grandfather's son i.e., the son of Anusha's father. Hence, the boy is the brother of Anusha.

12. **(c)** Father of Praveen's daughter's father → Praveen's father.
    Hence, the person in the brother of Praveen's father.
    Therefore, the person is the uncle of Praveen.

13. **(d)** P is the mother of K
    K is the sister of D
    D is the father of J.
    Therefore, J is the nephew or niece of K and P is the grandmother of J.

14. **(b)** Nalni is the daughter of the only son of Gopi's grandfather. Hence, it's clear that Nalni is the sister of Gopi.

15. **(b)** C – A + B means C is the mother of A who is the father of B. This clearly implies that A is male and hence the son of C.

16. **(a)** P + R – Q means P is the son of R who is the wife of Q i.e. Q is the father of P.

17. **(c)** P × R ÷ Q means P is the brother of R who is the mother of Q i.e. P is the uncle of Q.

18. **(b)** P = R + Q means P is the sister of R who is the son of Q i.e. P is the daughter of Q.

19. **(a)** P = R ÷ Q means P is the sister of R who is the mother of Q i.e. P is the aunt of Q.

20. **(c)** Since E is the brother of B

    Therefore, A is the father of E

    But D is the wife of E.

    Hence, D is the daughter-in-law of A.

21.-25: The relation diagram can be drawn as follows:

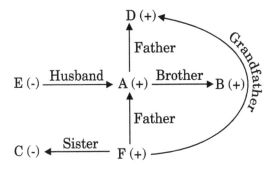

21. **(d)** From the above diagram, E is the mother.

22. **(c)** From the above diagram, A is E's husband.

23. **(d)** There are four male members in the group.

24. **(c)** From the above diagram, F is the son of E.

25. **(a)** From the above diagram, B and A are brothers. F is the brother of C. So, three brothers are A, B, F.

26. **(d)** Without knowing the sex of C, we can't be determined whether B is sister of C or B is brother of C. Similarly without knowing the sex of B we can't be determined whether C is sister of B or C is brother of B. Therefore, both (1) and (2) are necessary.

27. **(c)**

28. **(c)**

CHAPTER 6

Direction Sense Test

OBJECTIVE
- Students will develop the ability to trace and follow the logical path correctly and sense of direction correctly as well.

INTRODUCTION

Direction is a measurement of position of one thing with respect to another thing.

Displacement is the measurement of distance between initial and the final point. Direction and distance test mainly deal with two types of directions i.e. main directions and cardinal directions.

MAIN DIRECTIONS

There are four types of directions, viz, East, West, North and South as shown below. The word 'NEWS' stands for all the four directions, i.e. North, East, West and South.

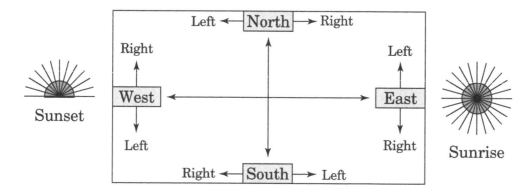

CARDINAL DIRECTIONS

A direction between two main directions is called cardinal direction. Clearly, there are four cardinal directions.

(i) N-E (North-East)
(ii) N-W (North-West)
(iii) S-E (South-East) and
(iv) S-W (South-West)

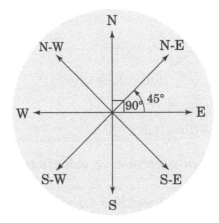

Note: Angle formed between two main directions is 90 and angle formed between a cardinal direction and main direction is 45 as shown in the above diagram.

ROTATION OF ANGLES

To solve angle movement questions, it is necessary to know about the rotations of angles which are given below.

(i) For right direction movement (Clockwise)

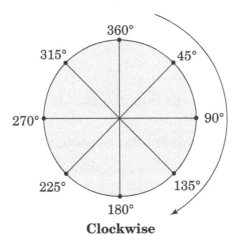

Clockwise

(ii) For left direction movement (Anti-clockwise)

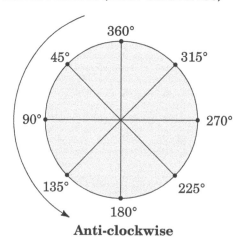

Left turn Anti-clockwise direction

Right turn Clockwise direction

The change in direction when a person or vehicle takes a right or a left turn

Direction before taking the turn	Direction in which the person or vehicle will be moving after taking turn	
	Right	Left
North	East	West
South	West	East
East	South	North
West	North	South

SHADOW CASE

In Morning/Sunrise time

(a) If a person is facing towards Sun, the shadow will be towards his back or in west.

(b) If a person is facing towards South, the shadow will be towards his right.

(c) If a person is facing towards West, the shadow will be towards his front.

(d) If a person is facing towards North, the shadow will be towards his left.

In Evening/Sunset time

(a) If a person is facing towards Sun, the shadow will be towards his back or in East.

(b) If a person is facing towards North, the shadow will be towards his right.

(c) If a person is facing towards East, the shadow will be towards his front.

(d) If a person is facing towards South, the shadow will be towards his left.

Note: At 12:00 noon there is no shadow because the rays of the Sun are vertically downward.

Types of Direction and Distance

Type 1: Final Direction Based

In these types of questions, we have to ascertain the final direction with respect to the initial point or the directional relations between two points/things.

Example 1:

Harish is facing North and turns through 90 clockwise, again 180 anticlockwise. In which direction is he facing now?

(a) South   (b) East

(c) West   (d) North

Ans. (c)

Explanation: The direction diagram of Harsh is as shown below:

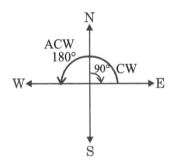

So, he faces the West direction.

Type 2: Distance (Displacement) Based

In these types of questions, we deal with the final distance between starting and final point or between two points/persons/things. There are various formats/patterns of displacement.

Example 2:

Sidharth walks 30 m West. Then, he turns left and walks 20m. Now, he turns left and walks 30 m. Finally he turns right and walks 40 m. How far is he from his original position?

(a) 40 m (b) 30 m
(c) 50 m (d) 60 m

Ans. (d)

Explanation: The direction diagram of Sidharth is as follows:

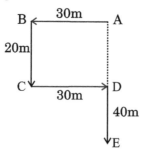

Here, required distance = AD = BC = 20 m and DE = 40m

Now, = AD + DE = 20 + 40 = 60 m.

Type 3: Distance (Displacement) and Direction Based

In these types of questions, we deal with the final distance between starting and final point of any person/object/thing. There are various formats/patterns of distance and direction.

Example 3:

A tourist drives 10 Km towards East and turns to the right hand and drives 3 Km. Then, he drives towards West (turning to his right) 10 Km. He, then turns to his left and drives 2 Km. How far is he from his starting point and in which direction would he be?

(a) 10 Km, East (b) 5 Km, North (c) 8 Km, West (d) 5 Km, South

Ans. (d)

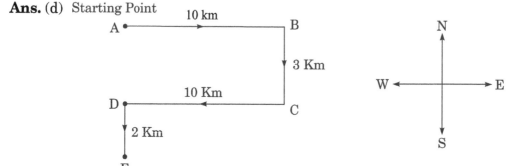

Here, AD = BC = 3 Km

∴ Required distance AE = AD + DE = 3 + 2 = 5 Km

His final point is E which is in South direction from starting point A.

Example 4:

Sunny is facing the temple. If he turns to his left, he will face the Mall. He turns _____ to his left.

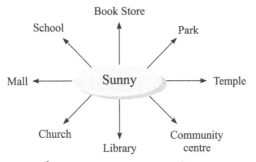

(a) $\frac{1}{4}$ turn (b) $\frac{1}{3}$ turn (c) $\frac{1}{2}$ turn (d) $\frac{3}{4}$ turn

Ans. (c)

Explanation:

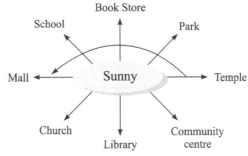

So, Sunny turns $\frac{1}{2}$ turn to his left.

Example 5:

Which point is east of B?

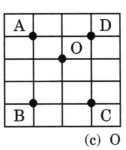

(a) A (b) D (c) O (d) C

Ans. (d)

Explanation:

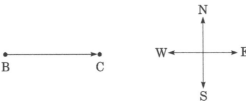

So, point C is east of B.

LEVEL-1

1. Ruhi is moving towards North. She takes right turn. After this, she takes right turn. In which direction, she is moving now?

   (a) South (b) North (c) West (d) East

2. Carefully observe the following figure.

   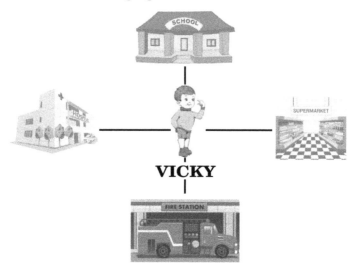

   In the above figure, Vicky is facing the school. If he turns 90 to his right, then in which direction will he face?

   (a) Hospital (b) Fire Station (c) Market (d) School

3. A man walks 5 km towards south and then turns to the right. After walking 3 km he turns to the left and walks 5 km. Now in which direction is he from the starting place?

   (a) South (b) South-West (c) North-West (d) West

4. Akhil rode his bicycle northward, then turned left and rode 1 km and again turned left and rode 2 km. He found himself 1 km west of his starting point. How far did he ride northward initially?

   (a) 1 km (b) 2 km (c) 3 km (d) 5 km

5. Six friends Shalini, Megha, Avni, Roy, Jay and Kavya are standing in six different directions as shown below. In which direction is Avni standing?

(a) South (b) West (c) North-East (d) South-West

6. Vishal started to walk straight towards south. After walking 5 m he turned to the left and walked 3 m. After this he turned to the right and walked 5 m. Now to which direction Vishal is facing?

(a) South (b) North-East (c) South-West (d) East

7. Deepika is facing the Mall. What will she be facing if she turns 270 clockwise?

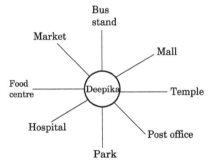

(a) Food Centre (b) Market (c) Bus stand (d) Hospital

8. Which point is south-west of A?

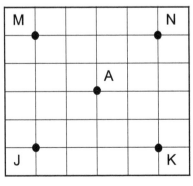

(a) M (b) N (c) J (d) K

9. Manav facing the mall now. If he make 180 turn to his left, he will be facing the_____.

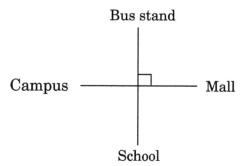

   (a) School   (b) Bus stand   (c) Campus   (d) Mall

10. Surbhi turns anticlockwise 180 and faces north-east in the end. Which direction was Surbhi facing at first?

    (a) West
    (b) South-west
    (c) South
    (d) South-east

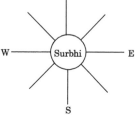

11. After walking 5 km, Shweta turned to the right and then walked 2 km. After this, she turned to the left and walked 8 km. In the end, she was moving towards the north. Form which direction did she start her journey?

    (a) North   (b) East   (c) West   (d) South

12. Jay is delivering mattresses. He goes 2 miles north, 3 miles east, 2 miles south, and 2 miles east. Which direction must Jay go to get back to his starting point?

    (a) South-west   (b) North   (c) West   (d) North-east

13. Gavin decides to drive around and visit some friends. Leaving home, he drives 5 kms east, 1 km south, and 1 km north. How far and in which direction must Gavin go to get back to his home?

    (a) 5 km east   (b) 5km west   (c) 5 km south   (d) 5 km north

14. Reena leaves home and begins skating. She skates 3 blocks north, 5 blocks east, 6 blocks south, and 5 blocks west. In which direction must Reena go to get back to her home?

    (a) South   (b) North   (c) East   (d) West

15. Study the following map carefully and find out which point is North-East of point O.

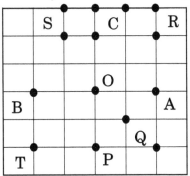

(a) P (b) A (c) B (d) R

16. Kavya is facing south-west. When she turns 3 right angles clockwise in which place does she face now?

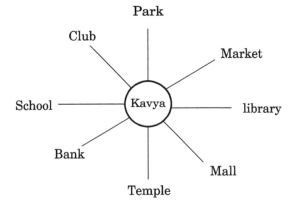

(a) Library (b) Market (c) Mall (d) Temple

17. Neela is delivering packages. She goes 2 miles south, 2 miles east, 1 mile north, and 2 miles west. Which direction must Neela go to get back to her starting point?

(a) South (b) North (c) East (d) South-west

18. Badri is facing south-east. If he turns clockwise through 135, which direction will he face in the end?

(a) South-west (b) North-east (c) West (d) South

19. If South becomes East, then what will South-west be?

(a) West
(b) North-east
(c) North-west
(d) South-east

20. Vijay traveled 12 km southward, then turned right and travelled 10 km, then turned right and travelled 12 km. How far was Vijay from the starting point?

(a) 10 km (b) 22 km (c) 12 km (d) None of these

21. Yakshi goes to market from home along the indicated path. How many times she will turn left?

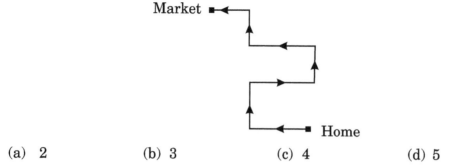

   (a) 2 (b) 3 (c) 4 (d) 5

DIRECTIONS (Qs. 22-26): Study the information carefully and answer the questions.

I am standing at a major crossroads as shown below in the image below.

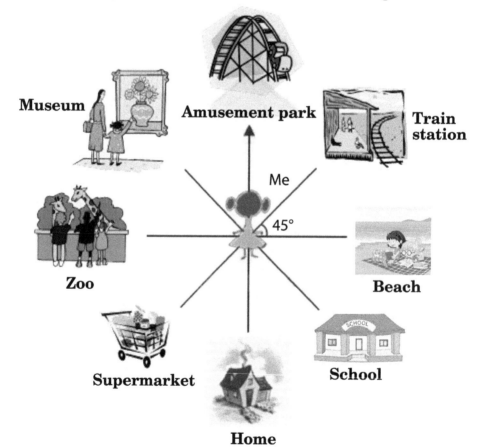

22. I am facing north. Which place is to my east?
    (a) Zoo (b) Home (c) School (d) Beach
23. I am looking south. If I turn 45 in the clockwise direction, what will I be facing?
    (a) Supermarket (b) Museum
    (c) Train Station (d) Amusement Park

24. I am facing the zoo. How many degrees in the anti-clockwise direction must I turn to face the school?
    (a) 45　　　(b) 90　　　(c) 135　　　(d) 180

25. I am facing south-west. Which place will I be facing if I turn 180 ?
    (a) Museum　　(b) Train Station　　(c) School　　(d) Amusement Park

26. After a three-quarter turn in the clockwise direction, I end up facing the super-market. Which direction was I facing at the start?
    (a) Amusement Park　　　　(b) Zoo
    (c) Museum　　　　　　　　(d) Beach

DIRECTIONS (Qs. 27-30): Fill in the blanks based on the image below.

27. The _____ is north-west of the basketball.
    (a) Basketball　　　　　　(b) Skates
    (c) Soccer ball　　　　　　(d) Swimming goggles

28. The _____ is south-east of the soccer ball.
    (a) Skates　(b) Basketball　(c) Soccer ball　(d) None of these

29. The boxing gloves are west of the _____.
    (a) Skates　(b) Basketball　(c) Soccer ball　(d) None of these

30. The soccer ball is south of the _____.
    (a) Skates　　　　　　　　(b) Swimming goggles
    (c) Boxing gloves　　　　　(d) Basketball

LEVEL-2

1. A police officer leaves headquarters to patrol the city. He drives 3 km east, 4 km. south, and 4 km north. In which direction must the police officer go to get back to headquarters?
    (a) East　　　(b) West　　　(c) North　　　(d) South

2. Jacky leaves the pizza parlour to deliver pizzas. He goes 3 miles north, 1 mile west, and 3 miles south. How many miles is Jacky from the pizza parlour?

   (a) 1 mile (b) 4 miles (c) 3 miles (d) 5 miles

3. Sheetal is 30 m south-west of Bannu. Kanu is 30 m southeast of Bannu. Kanu is in which direction of Sheetal?

   (a) North-east (b) East (c) North-west (d) North

4. Vivek is facing super market. What will he facing if he turns 315 clockwise?

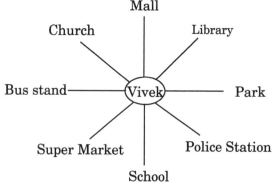

   (a) Library (b) Park (c) Police Station (d) School

5. Sahil walks 5 km towards East and then turns left and walks 6 km. Again he turns right and walks 9 km. Finally he turns to his right and walks 6 km. How far is he from the starting point?

   (a) 9 km (b) 12 km (c) 14 km (d) 21 km

DIRECTIONS (Qs. 6-7): Observe the given diagram carefully and answer the following questions.

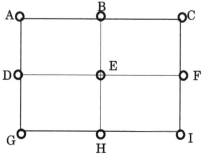

6. Ruhi is at position G facing D. She walks forward and makes a 90 turn to the right. She walks on the next position where she makes another 90 turn to the right to reach the next and final position. What is her final position?

   (a) E (b) I (c) H (d) F

7. Geet is at position I facing H. She walks forward and makes 90 turn to the right. She walks on the next position where she makes another 90 turn to the left to reach the next and final position. What is her final position?

   (a) F (b) D (c) B (d) A

DIRECTIONS (Qs. 8-10): Study the given diagram carefully and answer the following questions.

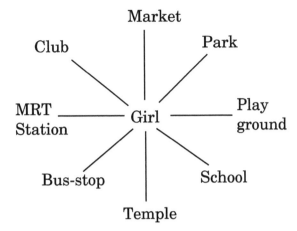

8. If the girl is facing MRT Station and turns 270 in a anticlockwise direction, what will she be facing?
   (a) Park (b) Club (c) Market (d) Playground
9. If the girl is facing Temple and turns 135 in a clockwise direction, what will she be facing?
   (a) MRT Station (b) Club (c) Playground (d) School
10. If the girl is facing School and turns 45 in a clockwise direction and then 90 anticlockwise direction, what will she be facing?
    (a) Temple (b) Bus-stop (c) Playground (d) School
11. Ritesh is facing North-west. He turns 90 in the clockwise direction and then 135 in the anticlockwise direction. Which direction is he facing now?
    (a) South (b) East (c) North (d) West
12. Which point is south west of K?

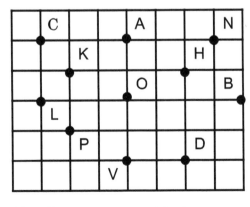

   (a) L (b) C (c) A (d) B

13. Sohan was facing the Basketball court at the beginning. He turned clockwise to face North. What angle did he turn through?

    (a) 90
    (b) 45
    (c) 180
    (d) 270

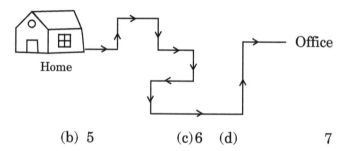

14. Rishab goes to office from home along the indicated path. How many times he will turn right?

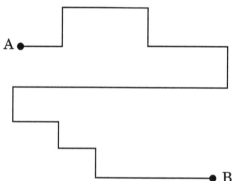

    (a) 4   (b) 5   (c) 6   (d) 7

DIRECTIONS (Qs. 15-16): As shown in the figure given below, Molik walked from A to B. Answer the following questions.

15. How many times did Molik take turns?
    (a) 16   (b) 15   (c) 13   (d) 12

16. How many times did Molik walk towards the East?
    (a) 4   (b) 5   (c) 6   (d) 8

17. Ronak started from his office, walked straight 6 km west, then turned right and walked straight 4 km, then again turned right and walked straight 8 km. In which direction is he from his office?
    (a) North-west   (b) South-west   (c) North-east   (d) South-east

18. Riya made a $\frac{3}{4}$ clockwise turn first followed by an anti clockwise $1\frac{1}{2}$ turn; She now faces south. Which direction was she facing first?
    (a) North   (b) East   (c) West   (d) South

19. If the given clock rotates 270 anticlockwise, then the hands will be in _____ direction.
    (a) North
    (b) West
    (c) East
    (d) South

20. A cab driver leaves his passenger to the city. He drives 6 km west, 8 km south, 6 km east and 8 km west. In which direction he is facing now?
    (a) North   (b) West   (c) East   (d) South

21. P is facing Basketball court. If he returns 180 clockwise and then 270 anticlockwise, then he will be facing _____ . **(Olympiad)**

    (a) Pond   (b) Basketball court   (c) Park   (d) Library

22. Mohit is facing the railway station. What will he be facing, if he turns 315 anticlockwise? **(Olympiad)**

    (a) Hospital   (b) Park   (c) Temple   (d) Hotel

23 Kushal started from his home, walked straight 5km West, then turned left and walked straight 3 km, then again turned left and walked straight 7 km. In which direction is he from his home? **(Olympiad)**
    (a) North-East   (b) South-West   (c) South-East   (d) North-West

24. Rehan travelled 4 km straight towards South. He turned left and travelled 6 km straight, then he turned left and travelled 4 km straight. How far is he from the starting point? **(Olympiad)**
    (a) 8 km   (b) 10 km   (c) 6 km   (d) 18 km

25. If the given clock rotates 270 clock-wise, then the hands will be in _____ direction. **(Olympiad)**

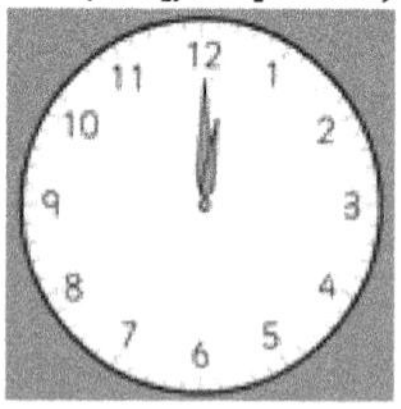

(a) North

(b) East

(c) West

(d) South

26. Garima goes to school from home along the indicated path. How many times she will turn right? **(Olympiad)**

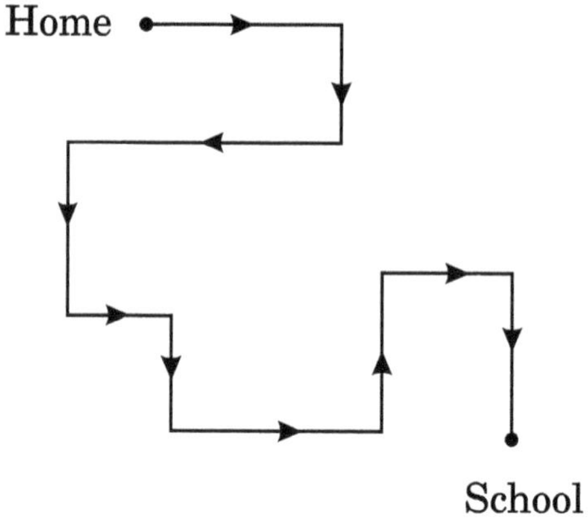

(a) 5 (b) 6 (c) 7 (d) 8

27. _______ will replace P, Q, R, S respectively in given below matrix, if the turns will be clockwise. **(Olympiad)**

Shape	After 1/8 turn	After 1/4 turn
N	P	R
E	S	Q

(a) 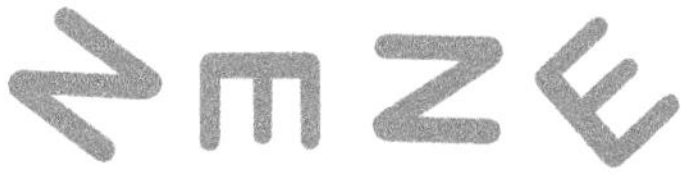

(b) 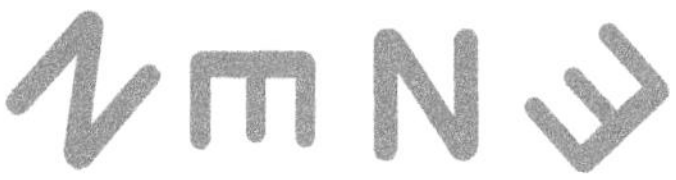

(c) 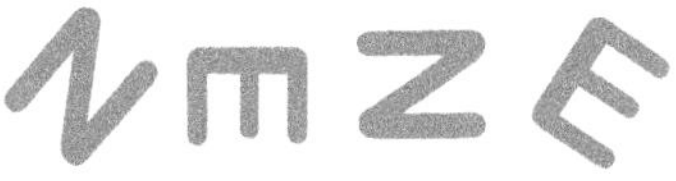

(d) 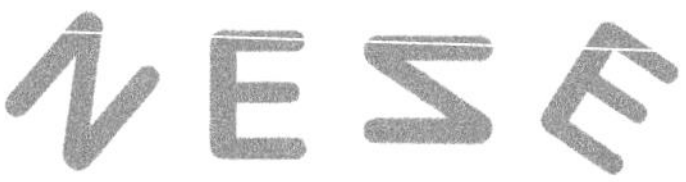

28. What will be the direction of P and Q respectively, if Figure (X) is rotated 6 anticlockwise? **(Olympiad)**

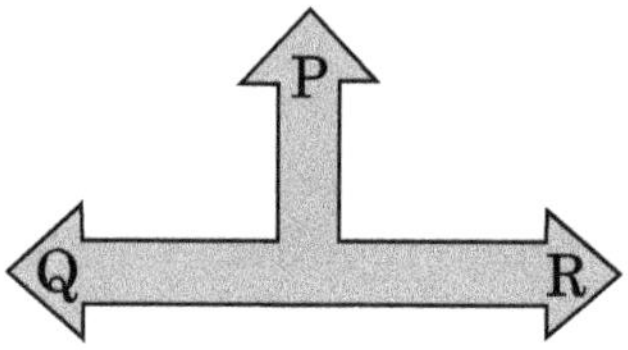

(a) South, North (b) East, West (c) West, South (d) West, East

29. Beena was facing the library in the beginning. She turned anti-clockwise to face south-east. What angle did she turn through? **(Olympiad)**

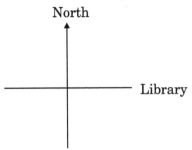

(a) 130 (b) 315 (c) 225 (d) 230

30. If Mohit is facing the sports club and turn in an anticlockwise direction to face the Airport, what angle did he turn through? **(Olympiad)**

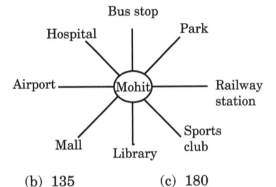

(a) 225 (b) 135 (c) 180 (d) 270

31. Which of the following will be the view of the given figure after $3\frac{1}{4}$ clockwise rotation? **(2018)**

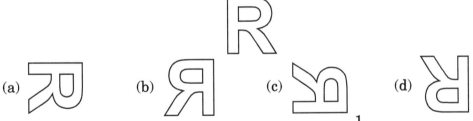

32. Yash is facing towards the Bus Stop now. If he takes $3\frac{1}{8}$ turn anti-clockwise, then he will be facing the **(2018)**

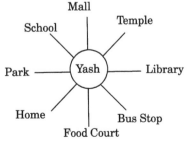

(a) Temple (b) Library
(c) Food Court (d) Home

33. Shubham is facing the Bank. What would he be facing, if he turns 225 clockwise? **(2019)**

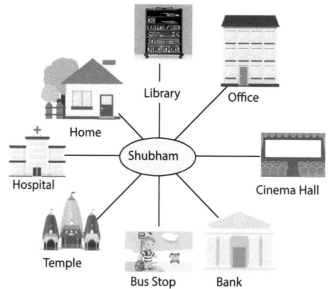

(a) Office (b) Temple (c) Hospital (d) Library

34. Rashi is facing the garden. If she turns 45' in anti-clockwise direction and then 270 in the clockwise direction, then what will she be facing? **(2020)**

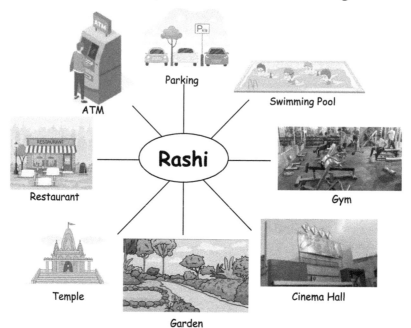

(a) Swimming Pool (b) ATM
(c) Temple (d) Restaurant

35. Radha is facing South-West. She turns 90 anticlockwise and then 225 clockwise. In which direction will she be facing now? **(2020)**

    (a) North-East (b) East
    (c) North-West (d) North

36. If Palak is facing the Parking, then what will she be facing if she turns 180 anticlockwise and then 135 clockwise? **(2021)**

    (a) Institute (b) Bus stop
    (c) Bank (d) School

37. Sakshi is facing towards North-East direction. She turns 45 anti-clockwise and then 135 clockwise. Which direction will she be facing now?

    (a) North-West (b) Sout
    (c) East (d) South-East

38. Karan walks 8 m towards North and then turn left and walks 7 m. Again he turns to right and walks 3 m. Finally, he turns right and walks 7 m. In which direction is he now with respect to the starting point? **(2022)**

    (a) East (b) West
    (c) North (d) South

39. Which one of the following statements is correct for the diagram shown below?
(2022)

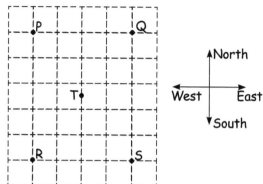

(a) Point R is in North-East of T.
(b) Point S is in North-West of T.
(c) Point P is in South-East of T.
(d) None of these

40. The picture given below presents Raj's route to school from his house. Which set of directions Raj has to follow to return home from school? **(2022)**

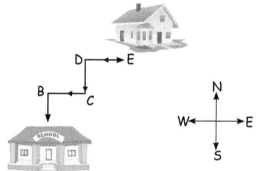

(a) North, East, North, East
(b) West, South, West, North
(c) West, North, East, South
(d) West, South, West, South

Answers and Explanation

Level-1

1. **(a)** The direction diagram is as shown below:

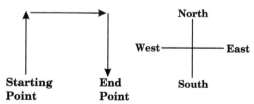

So, Ruhi is moving towards South.

2. **(c)** The direction diagram can be shown as below:

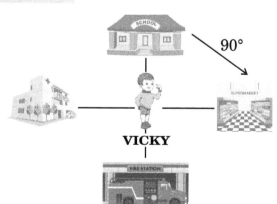

In the above diagram, Vicky turns 90 degree to his right. After turning, he faces market.

3. **(b)** The direction diagram is as follow:

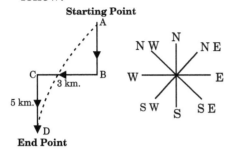

4. **(b)** The direction diagram of Akhil is as follow:

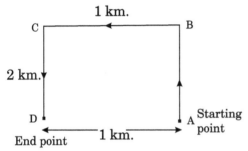

So, Akhil rode 2 km northward.

5. **(d)** According to the given diagram, Avni is standing in South-West direction.

6. **(a)** The direction diagram of Vishal is as follows:

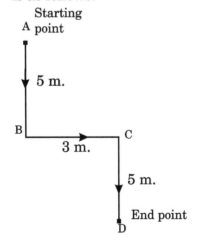

Hence, Vishal will face in the end towards South.

7. **(b)** 270 clockwise means 3 right angles. After three right angles she will be facing market.

8. **(c)**

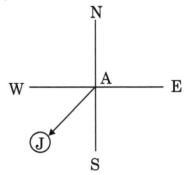

So, point J is south-west of A.

9. **(c)**

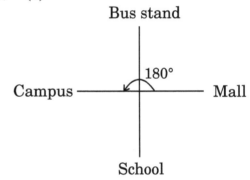

Manav will be facing the campus.

10. **(b)**

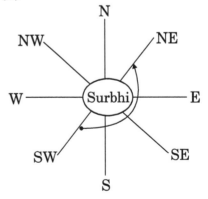

So, Surbhi was facing south-west at first.

11. (a) The direction diagram of Shweta is as follows:

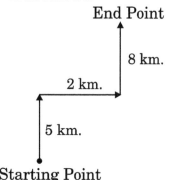

So, Shweta starts her journey from North direction.

12. (c) The direction diagram of Jay is as follows:

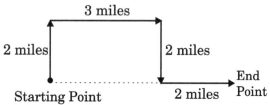

So, Jay must go west direction to get back to his starting point.

13. (b) The direction diagram of Gavin is as follows:

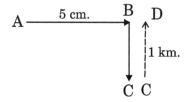

So, Gavin must go 5 km west direction to get back to his home.

14. (b) The direction diagram of Reena is as follows:

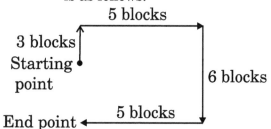

So, Reena must go North direction to get back to her home.

15. (d)

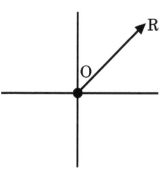

So, point R is North-East of point O.

16. (c) Kavya is facing south-west. When she turns 3 right angles clockwise then she faces Mall.

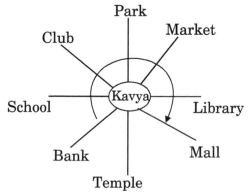

17. (b) The direction diagram of Neela is as shown below:

Starting point

2 miles End point 1 mile
2 miles
2 miles

So, Neela must go North direction to get back to her starting point.

18. (c) Badri is facing south-east. If he turns clockwise through 135,

108

then he will face west direction in the end.

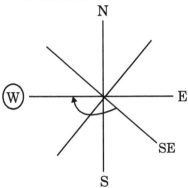

19. **(d)** The diagrammatic representation of direction is as shown below:

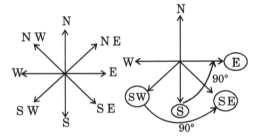

Clearly, directions are moving 90 anticlockwise. Hence, South-west will becomes South-east.

20. **(a)** The direction diagram of Vijay is as follows:

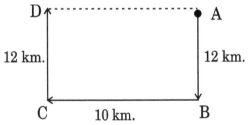

∴ Required distance from starting point = AD = BC = 10 km

21. **(b)**

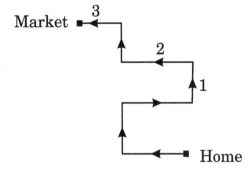

So, from the above path, she will turn left 3 times.

22. **(d)** Beach is to my east.
23. **(a)** If I turned 45 in the clockwise direction then I will be facing supermarket.
24. **(c)** 135 in the anticlockwise direction must I turn to face the school.
25. **(b)** I will be facing Train Station if I turn 180.
26. **(d)** I was facing beach at the start.
27. **(c)** The Soccer ball is north-west of the basketball.
28. **(b)** The basketball is south-east of the soccer ball.
29. **(c)** The boxing gloves are west of the soccer ball.
30. **(a)** The soccer ball is south of the skates.

Level-2

1. **(b)** The direction diagram of police officer is as follows:

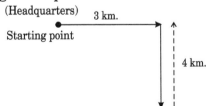

So, the police officer must go in the west direction to get back to headquarters.

2. (a) The direction diagram of Jacky is as follows:

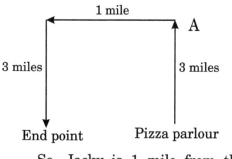

So, Jacky is 1 mile from the pizza parlour.

3. (b) The direction diagram is as follows:

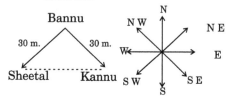

So, Kanu is in east direction of Sheetal.

4. (d) 315 clockwise means 3 right angles and one 45 angle. After right angles, he will be facing police station and after a 45-turn, he will be facing school.

5. (c) The direction diagram of Sahil is as follows:

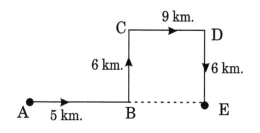

Therefore, required distance
= AE = 5 + 9 = 14 km.

6. (c) According to the given diagram, Ruhi's final position is H.

7. (b) According to the given diagram, Geet's final position is D.

8. (c)

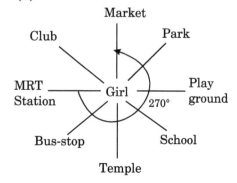

So, she will be facing Market.

9. (b)

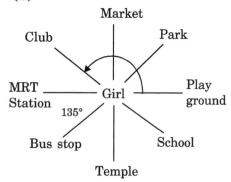

So, she will be facing Club.

10. (c)

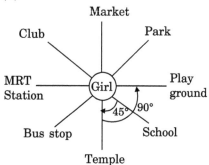

So, she will be facing Playground.

11. **(d)**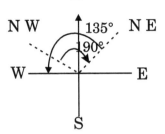

So, Ritesh is facing West direction.

12. **(a)** L point is south-West of K.
13. **(d)** He turned through an angle of 270°.
14. **(b)** 5 times he will turn right.
15. **(d)** Total number of lines in the figure − 1 = Total number of turns.

    The figure has 13 lines. So, Molik took (13 − 1 =) 12 turns.
16. **(c)** 6 times Molik walked towards the East.
17. **(c)** The direction diagram of Ronak is as follows:

    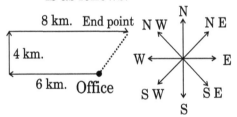

    So, he is in the North-east direction from his office.
18. **(b)** The direction diagram of Riya is as follows:

    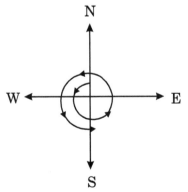

    So, she was facing east direction at first.
19. **(d)** If the given clock rotates 270° anticlockwise, then the hands will be in south direction.
20. **(b)** The direction diagram of cab driver is as follows:

    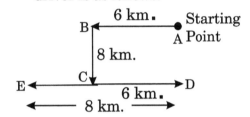

    So, now he is facing west direction.
21. **(a)** He will be facing Pond.
22. **(a)** Mohit is facing Hospital, if he turns 315° anticlockwise.
23. **(c)** The direction diagram of Kushal is as follows:

    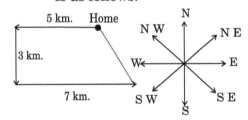

    So, Kushal is south-east direction from his home.
24. **(c)** The direction diagram of Rehan is as follows:

    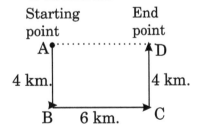

    From the above diagram,

    AD = BC = 6 km.

    So, Rehan is 6 km. far from his starting point.

25. (c)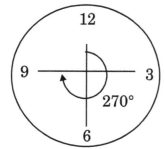

The hands will be in West direction.

26. (a)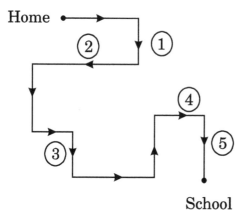

So, 5 times she will turn right.

27. (c) Option (c) will replace P, Q, R, S respectively, if the turns will be clockwise.

28. (c) West and South will be the direction of P and Q respectively.

29. (b)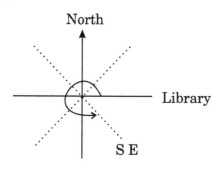

She turned through 315° angle.

30. (a)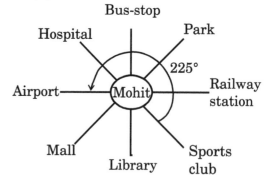

So, he turned through an angle of 225°.

31. (a) Total rotation = $3\frac{1}{4} = 3 + \frac{1}{4}$

1 rotation = 360°

$\frac{1}{4}$ rotation = 360° $\frac{1}{4}$ = 90°

On rotating the figure $3\frac{1}{4}$ clockwise, we get the figure given in option A.

32. (b) Total rotation = $3\frac{1}{8} = 3 + \frac{1}{8}$

1 rotation = 360°

$\frac{1}{8}$ rotation = 360° $\frac{1}{8}$ = 45°

On rotation the figure $3\frac{1}{8}$ anti-clockwise, he will be facing the Library.

33. (d) When Shubham turns 225° in clockwise direction, he will be facing towards Library.

34. (a) When Rashi turns 45° in anti-clockwise direction, she will be facing towards Cinema Hall. Then on turning 270° in clockwise direction, she will be facing towards swimming pool.

35. (d) North

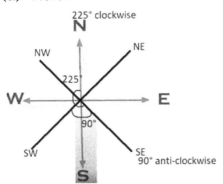

36. (d) When Palak turns 180 in anti-clockwise direction, she will be facing towards Metro station. Then on turning 135 in clockwise direction, she will be facing towards School.

37. (d) When Sakshi turns 45 in anti-clockwise direction, she will be facing towards North. Then on turning 135 in clockwise direction, she will be facing towards South-East direction.

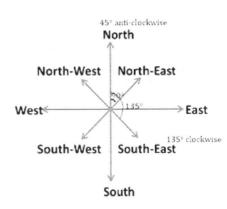

38. (c) North

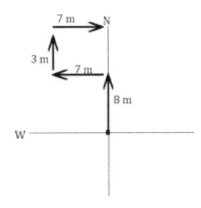

39. (d)

40. (a)

CHAPTER 7

Number, Ranking & Time Sequence Test

OBJECTIVES

- Students will be able to identify the position of an object/a person from left end or right end.
- They will be able to identify interchanging positions of two persons.

INTRODUCTION

In this chapter generally the ranks of a person from both sides left or right or from top and from bottom are mentioned and total numbers of persons are asked.

TYPES OF QUESTIONS

1. Total number of persons and positions of one person (either from left or right) are given.
2. Position of more than one person is given.
3. Ascending/Descending order – according to age, height, weight, marks etc.

FORMULAS FOR ORDER AND RANKING

Finding rank either from left or from right

Total – (given rank – 1) = required rank

Finding total numbers

Case 1

When ranks of one person are given from both sides of the row.

Ranks of common person from both sides (R1 + R2) – 1

Case 2

When ranks of two persons and numbers of the persons who are sitting between these two persons are given.

(R1 + R2) + number of middle persons

Finding the numbers of persons who are sitting between any two persons

Total – (Rank from left + Rank from the right)

Finding Rank of Middle Person

Step 1: Convert both ranks from the same side.

Step 2: Find the average of both ranks.

Example 1:

Here is a table

Name	Rank from top	Rank from bottom
Rahul	5	1
Kavita	4	2
Chetan	3	3
Aryan	2	4
Raj	1	5

Let us discuss about 'Raj'

Raj's rank from top = 1 and from bottom = 5

Total number of persons in the row = 5

- Means total rank = (rank from top + rank from bottom) – 1

    = (1 + 5) – 1 = 5

- Rank from top = total rank – (rank from bottom – 1)

    = 5 – (5 – 1) = 1

- Rank from bottom = total rank – (rank from top – 1)

    = 5 – (1 – 1) = 5

Example 2:

In a class of 52 students, Ankur's rank is 18th from the bottom. What is his rank from the top?

(a) 34   (b) 35   (c) 36   (d) 38

Ans. (b)

Explanation: Number of students ahead of Ankur = 52 – 18 = 34

Now, Ankur's rank from the top = 34 + 1 = 35.

Example 3:

Shweta is eighth from left and Rishabh is thirteenth from right. If there are nine students between them then how many students are there in a row?

(a) 12   (b) 16   (c) 25   (d) 30

Ans. (d)

Explanation:

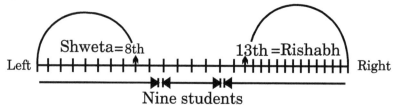

∴ Total number of students in a row = 8 + 13 + 9 = 30

Example 4:

Jyoti is seventh from left end and is fourth to the left of Manya who is seventh from right end. Then how many students are there in a row?

(a) 17   (b) 18   (c) 16   (d) 14

Ans. (a)

Explanation:

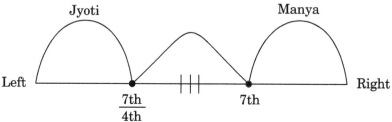

Total students in a row = 7 + 3 + 7 = 17

Example 5:

Jai is 15th from left and Vijay is 14th from right. When they interchange their positions respectively then Vijay becomes 21st from right end. What will be Jai's position from left after interchanging?

(a) 25   (b) 22   (c) 27   (d) 28

Ans. (b)

Explanation:

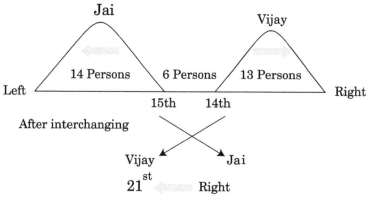

Jai's position from the left after interchanging = 15 + 6 + 1 = 22.

Example 6:

Among five persons, Raja secured more marks than only Kapil. Ashok and Jagdish secured less marks than only Nikhil. Who among them secured third least marks?

(a) Nikhil (b) Raja
(c) Jagdish (d) Cannot be determined

Ans. (d)

Explanation:

Nikhil > Ashok / Jagdish > Raja > Kapil

Third least marks = Either Ashok or Jagdish

Hence, it cannot be determined who secured third least marks.

Example 7:

If yesterday was Sunday, what day will it be the sixth day from today?

(a) Sunday (b) Friday (c) Saturday (d) Monday

Ans. (c)

Explanation:

If yesterday was Sunday. So today is Monday. Then, sixth day from Monday will be Saturday.

Example 8:

Prem correctly remembers that Riya's birthday was after Monday but before Thursday. Vinit correctly remembers that Riya's birthday was after Tuesday but before Saturday, on which day of the week does Riya's birthday definitely fall?

(a) Thursday (b) Wednesday (c) Friday (d) Tuesday

Ans. (b)

Explanation:

According to Prem, Riya's birthday falls = Tuesday or Wednesday

According to Vinit Riya's birthday falls = Wednesday, Thursday or Friday

So, Riya's birthday falls on Wednesday.

LEVEL-1

1. Nikhil ranked 8th in a class of 50 students from the top. What is his rank from the bottom in the class?

   (a) 42nd (b) 43rd (c) 44th (d) 45th

2. In a garden there is a row of trees, one tree is fifth from the either ends of this row. How many trees are there in the row?

   (a) 5 (b) 8 (c) 10 (d) 9

3. Among Sheetal, Ronit, Kavya and Deepu, Ronit is heavier than Sheetal and Kavya. Kavya is not heavy as Sheetal. Deepu is heavier than Ronit. Who is the lightest?

   (a) Ronit (b) Sheetal (c) Deepu (d) Kavya

4. Asha ranks sixth from the top and fourteenth from the bottom in class. How many students are there in the class?

   (a) 20 (b) 18 (c) 19 (d) 25

5. Reeta spent 25 minutes on her homework last night. She started at 5 : 50 p.m. What time did she finish her work?

   (a) 6 : 15 p.m. (b) 5 : 10 p.m. (c) 5 : 15 p.m. (d) 6 : 10 p.m.

6. How many weeks are there in 1 year?

   (a) 55 (b) 53 (c) 51 (d) 52

7. Eight friends are sitting in a row. Rochelle is 3rd from the left. What is her position from the right?

   (a) 11th (b) 6th (c) 4th (d) 2nd

8. How many '8' are followed by even number in following set figures?

   1 8 4 3 8 1 4 8 3 2 8 7 8 4 8 5 6 8 7 8 4 1 8 6

   (a) 3 (b) 2 (c) 4 (d) 6

9. Samant remembers that his brother's birthday is after 13th but before 16th of January, while, his sister remembers that her brother's birthday is after 14th but before 17th of January. On which date of January is Samant's brother's birthday?

   (a) 16th (b) 18th (c) 19th (d) 15th

10. Among five children P, Q, R, S and T each having a different height, P is taller than only S and R is shorter than only T. Who among them is the third in order of height?

    (a) T (b) Q (c) R (d) S

11. Ramesh is 9th from downwards in a class of 31 students. What will be his position from upwards?

    (a) 21st (b) 22nd (c) 23rd (d) 24th

12. Some girls are sitting in a line. Meeta is on 10th place from left and Simran is on 11th place from right. There are 4 girls between them. How many girls are there in the line?

    (a) 25 (b) 26 (c) 28 (d) 24

13. It takes 12 minutes to bathe a dog at Dr. Rishi's Dog home. How long would it take to bathe 10 dogs?

    (a) 60 minutes (b) 100 minutes (c) 120 minutes (d) None of these

14. The month with neither 31 nor 30 days is?

    (a) April (b) November (c) February (d) March

15. The positions of how many digits in the number 351462987 will remain unchanged after the digits are rearranged in ascending order within the number?

    (a) None (b) one (c) Two (d) Three

16. How many letters are there between 8th letter from left and 7th letter from right in the English alphabet?

    (a) 7 (b) 11 (c) 8 (d) 9

17. In the given letter series, which letter is exactly midway between M and J?

    Z A B C Y X L M N D E F G H O P Q R S T I J K U V W

    (a) H (b) P (c) O (d) G

18. Shruti wanted to travel around the world. She worked it out that the trip would take her five years. How many months would that be?

    (a) 15 months (b) 65 months (c) 60 months (d) 52 months

19. If Anika finds that she is 10th from the right in a line of girls and fourth from the left. How many girls should be added to the line such that there are 28 girls in the line?

    (a) 11 (b) 12 (c) 13 (d) 15

20. If Payal is behind Ratna, Meena is last in the queue and Prabha is not behind Ratna, then who will be the first person in the queue?

    (a) Payal (b) Prabha (c) Ratna (d) Meena

21. In a queue, Raina is 12th from the front and Pratiksha is 19th from the end, while Dally is in between Raina and Pratiksha. There are 38 persons in the queue, how many persons are in between Raina and Pratiksha?

    (a) 5 persons (b) 6 persons (c) 4 persons (d) 7 persons

22. Siya is elder than Swapna. Lavanya is elder than Swapna but younger than Siya. Survana is younger than both Harry and Swapna, Swapna is elder than Harry. Who is the youngest?

    (a) Survana (b) Siya (c) Lavanya (d) Harry

23. Answer the following question based on the letter-number sequence given below:

    A 3 L G 5 P E 7 9 F S H I M T 6 Y Z Q 3 U 2 B

    Which of the following letter/number is exactly in the middle between the 7th letter/number from the left end and 5th letter/number from the right end?

    (a) H (b) S (c) M (d) I

24. Study the following arrangement carefully and answer the question given below.

    F @ 3 9 H © A D I % 4 E * $ M K 2 U R P 5 W ¥ 8 1 T J V 7

    Which letter is 6th to the right of 14th letter from the left?

    (a) R (b) P (c) % (d) 4

25. How many 5s are there in the following number sequence which are immediately preceded by 7 and immediately followed by 6?

    Terms: 7 5 5 9 4 5 7 6 4 5 9 8 7 5 6 7 6 4 3 2 5 6 7 8

    (a) 1 (b) 2 (c) 3 (d) 4

DIRECTION (Qs. 26-28): Study the following arrangement and answer the questions given:

    81   47   56   38   79   67

26. If the positions of first and second digits are changed in each number, which is the lowest number?

    (a) 47 (b) 81 (c) 56 (d) 38

27. If in each number 1 is added to first digit, then which is the largest number?

    (a) 38 (b) 81 (c) 56 (d) 47

28. If all numbers are arranged in ascending order, then what is the difference between the numbers which is second from the left and third from the right?

    (a) 36 (b) 9 (c) 12 (d) 20

29. Priti scored more than Rahul. Yogita scored as much as Divya. Lokita scored less than Manju. Rahul scored more than Yogita. Manju scored less than Divya. Who scored the highest?

    (a) Lokita (b) Divya (c) Manju (d) Priti

30. Sohan ranks 7th from the top and 26th from the bottom in a class. How many students are there in the class?

    (a) 32 (b) 33 (c) 34 (d) 35

31. Five boys Sam, Rahul, Monu, Rohit and Raj took part in a race. Sam finished before Monu, Monu finished after Rohit. Rohit and Raj both finished after Rahul and Rahul finished after Sam. Who won the race? **(2018)**

    (a) Sam (b) Monu (c) Raj (d) Rohit

32. Akshi is taller than Reena who shorter than Kirti. Aanya is shorter than Akshi but taller than Kirti. Two other girls are taller than Akshi. Who is the shortest? **(2019)**

    (a) Kirti (b) Aanya (c) Reena (d) Can't be determined

33. Find the missing number which will complete the given number pattern. **(2020)**

    | 9 | 23 | 51 | 107 | ? | 443 |

    (a) 219 (b) 175 (c) 231 (d) 305

34. Arrange the given words as they occur in a dictionary and select the correct option **(2020)**

    1. Rotate   2. Resolve   3. Ration   4. Revolve
    5. Result

    (a) 3, 2, 5, 4, 1 (b) 2, 5, 3, 4, 1 (c) 3, 5, 2, 1, 4 (d) 2, 3, 4, 5, 1

35. Chetna ranked 19th from the bottom in a class of 25 students. What is her rank from the top in the class? **(2020)**

    (a) 6th (b) 7th (c) 5th (d) 8th

36. If Mohit is shorter than Sahil but taller than Rohit. Rishi is the tallest. Anuj is shorter than Sahil but taller than Mohit. Who is the shortest? **(2022)**

    (a) Sahil (b) Anuj (c) Rohit (d) Mohit

LEVEL-2

1. Kathir is senior of Gagan. Gagan is senior of Appu. Appu is junior of Raj. Raj is junior of Gagan. Who is the senior most?

    (a) Gagan (b) Raj (c) Kathir (d) Appu

2. Some girls are sitting in a row. M is sitting 12th from the left and N is 8th from the right. If there are four girls between M and N, how many girls are there in row?

    (a) 20 (b) 22 (c) 24 (d) 26

3. Aakriti and Akansha are ranked fourth and fifth respectively from the top in a class of 25 students. What will be their respective ranks from the bottom in the class?

    (a) 22nd and 21st (b) 23rd and 21st
    (c) 22nd and 24th (d) 25th and 22nd

4. If today is Friday and Anita's birthday is on 3rd day after today, then on which day she will celebrate her birthday?

    (a) Sunday (b) Tuesday (c) Monday (d) Friday

5. If today is Monday, then what day will be 8th day?

   (a) Thursday (b) Monday (c) Friday (d) Saturday

6. If the positions of the first and third digits of each number are interchanged, which of the following will be the lowest number?

   5 1 9   3 6 4   2 8 7   1 5 8   8 3 5

   (a) 8 3 5 (b) 2 8 7 (c) 3 6 4 (d) 1 5 8

7. In a line, Shreya is 8th from the left and Bhavna is 17th from the right. If they interchange their positions, Shreya becomes 14th from the left. How many girls are there in the row?

   (a) 25 (b) 27 (c) 28 (d) 30

8. Jack remembers that his brother Paresh's birthday falls after 20th May but before 28th May, while Tripti remembers that Paresh's birthday falls before 22nd May but after 12th May. On what date Paresh's birthday falls?

   (a) 26th May (b) 18th May (c) 20th May (d) 21st May

9. Nisha leaves her house at 20 minutes to seven in the morning, reaches Pooja's house in 25 minutes, they finish their breakfast in another 15 minutes and leave for their office. What time do they leave Pooja's house to reach their office?

   (a) 7 : 20 a.m. (b) 7 : 25 a.m. (c) 7 : 40 a.m. (d) 7 : 55 a.m.

10. How many odd numbers are there in the following series of numbers, each of which if preceded by an odd number?

    5 3 4 8 9 7 1 6 5 3 2 9 8 7 3 5

    (a) 5 (b) 6 (c) 7 (d) 8

11. Some boys are sitting on a bench.
    - Raj and Vijay are sitting at one of the ends.
    - There are three persons between Vijay and Ankur.
    - Aryan is sitting midway between Vijay and Ankur.
    - Ankur is sitting just next to Raj

    How many people are sitting on the bench?

    (a) 4 (b) 5 (c) 6 (d) 7

12. In a row of 10 girls, when Poonam was shifted by two places towards the left, she became sixth from the left end. What was her earlier position from the right end of the row?

    (a) First (b) Second (c) Third (d) Fourth

13. Meghna was born on April 8, 1985. How old will she be on her birthday in 2016?

    (a) 29 (b) 30 (c) 31 (d) 35

14. Miss Kapoor is taking a Maths test. The marks (out of 50) scored by each student are given below.

Priya	Jatin	Poonam	Dev	Manav	Tanu	Komal	Amit	Raj	Latika
30	15	25	45	42	47	12	20	49	10

Who scored the highest and who scored the lowest marks respectively?

(a) Raj, Jatin   (b) Tanu, Latika   (c) Dev, Jatin   (d) Raj, Latika

15. Some boys are sitting in a row. P is sitting fourteenth from the left and Q is seventh from the right. If there are four boys between P and Q, how many boys are there in the row?

(a) 25   (b) 23   (c) 21   (d) 19

16. Four runners Simran, Rohit, Latika and Anuj took part in a 100m race.

Simran : I was faster than Rohit.

Rohit : I was the second.

Latika : I was neither at the first nor at the last place.

Who stood last in the race?

(a) Simran   (b) Rohit   (c) Anuj   (d) Latika

Direction (Qs. 17-18): Read the following information and answer the following questions. Five boys participated in a competition.

Rohit : I was ranked lower than Sanjay.

Vikas : I was ranked higher than Dinesh.

Kamal : I was between Rohit and Vikas.

17. Who was ranked highest?

(a) Sanjay   (b) Vikas   (c) Dinesh   (d) Kamal

18. Who was ranked lowest?

(a) Sanjay   (b) Kamal   (c) Dinesh   (d) Vikas

19. Which of the following letter/number is exactly in the middle of 7th letter/number from the right end and 9th letter/number from the left end in the given below arrangement? **(Olympiad)**

3 D 8 J H 5 K V T 2 P 1 W Q C 7 A N S 4 Z R 9

(a) 1   (b) Q   (c) 5   (d) W

20. Among a group of six boys. Tarun is taller than Samay but not as tall as Rohit. Aakash is the tallest. Arun is shorter than Rohit but taller than Rehan. Rehan is taller than Tarun. If the boys are arranged in ascending order of height, who is the third tallest? **(Olympiad)**

(a) Arun   (b) Rehan   (c) Rohit   (d) Samay

21. If the following numbers are arranged in the descending order, what will be the middle digit of the number which will be exactly in the middle? **(Olympiad)**

   317, 493, 283, 269, 875, 423, 725

   (a) 2 (b) 3 (c) 6 (d) 7

22. Tarun ranked 6th in the class of 35 students from top. What is the rank from the bottom of the class? **(Olympiad)**

   (a) 39th (b) 30th (c) 28th (d) 31st

23. Read the information given below and answer the question that follows:

   (i) There is a group of five girls.

   (ii) Garima is second in height.

   (iii) Priya is taller than Latika and shorter than Garima.

   (iv) Manha is the tallest.

   (v) Megha is shorter than Latika. **(Olympiad)**

   Who is shorter than Manha but taller than Priya?

   (a) Priya (b) Latika (c) Megha (d) Garima

24. Mohit remembers that his brother's birthday is after the 15th, but before 18th of February, while his sister remembers that her brother's birthday is after the 16th, but before 19th of February. On which date in February, is Mohit's brother's birthday? **(Olympiad)**

   (a) 16th February (b) 18th February
   (c) 19th February (d) 17th February

25. If Raj finds that he is 10th from the left end in a line of boys and 6th from the right end, then how many boys should be added to the line such that there are 28 boys in the line? **(Olympiad)**

   (a) 12 (b) 14 (c) 20 (d) 13

26. Manha remembers that her father's birthday is after 10th, but before 15th of October, Her sister remembers that her father's birthday is before 20th, but after 13th of October. On which day is her father's birthday? **(Olympiad)**

   (a) 15th (b) 13th (c) 14th (d) 16th

27. 21 students are standing in a line. Deepak is in the middle. What is his position from left as well as from right? **(Olympiad)**

   (a) 12th (b) 10th (c) 11th (d) 9th

28. _____ is exactly in the middle of 4th letter from the left end and 15th letter from the right end in English alphabetical series. **(Olympiad)**

   (a) I (b) J (c) K (d) H

29. In the given letter series, which letter is exactly midway between F and R? **(Olympiad)**

   Y A C B E D F I J H K M N O Q P R U V X T Z

   (a) N   (b) K   (c) M   (d) H

30. Study the following arrangement carefully and answer the question given below. **(Olympiad)**

   M4ET%J9IB@U8©N#F1V7*2AH3Y5$6K

   Which of the following is ninth to the right of the seventeenth from the right end of the above?

   (a) A   (b) %   (c) I   (d) Y

31. Ruhani is sitting 12th from the left end in a row facing North. Ridhan is sitting 3rd from the right end in the row. If there are only two students between Ridhan and Ruhani, then find the total number of students in the row. **(2021)**

   (a) 19   (b) 17   (c) 18   (d) 16

32. In a row of 35 students, Rashi is eighth from the left end. What is the position of Rashi from the right end, if five students from the right end left the row? **(2021)**

   (a) 21st (b) 22nd (c) 23rd (d) 24th

33. Kaushal celebrates his daughter's birthday on two days after the second thursday of September 20XX. **(2022)**

SEPTEMBER 20XX						
Sun	Mon	Tue	Wed	Thu	Fri	Sat
	1	2	3	4	5	6
7	8	9	10	11	12	13
14	15	16	17	18	19	20
21	22	23	24	25	26	27
28	29	30				

   On which day will he celebrate his daughter's birthday? **(2022)**

   (a) 13th September   (b) 11th September
   (c) 15th September   (d) 14th September

34. In a row of boys, if A, who is tenth from the left, and B, who is ninth from the right, interchange their positions, A becomes fifteenth from the left. How many boys are there in the row? **(2022)**

   (a) 21   (b) 23   (c) 27   (d) 28

Answers and Explanation

Level-1

1. **(b)** Rank of Nikhil from the bottom = (Total number of students in a row – Rank of Nikhil from the top) + 1

    So, rank of Nikhil from the bottom = (50 – 8) + 1 = 43rd

2. **(d)** Tree 1, Tree 2, Tree 3, Tree 4 _ (Tree 5) _ Tree 6, Tree 7, Tree 8, Tree 9
    Total trees = 4 + 1 + 4 = 9.

3. **(d)** The order of weights is shown below:

    Deepu > Ronit > Sheetal > Kavya

    So, Kavya is the lightest.

4. **(c)** Total students in the class = (rank from top + rank from bottom) – 1 = (6 + 14) – 1 = 19.

5. **(a)** 5 : 50 + 25 minutes = 6 : 15.

6. **(d)** There are 52 weeks in a year.

7. **(b)** Position of Rochelle from the right = (Total number of friends in the row – Position of Rochelle from the left) + 1 = (8 – 3) + 1 = 6th.

8. **(c)** There are 4 such 8's which are followed by even number.

    18**4**3814832878**4**8568784**1**86

9. **(d)** Auording to Samant the birth date : 14   15

    Auording to Samant's sister 15   16

    Here, 15th is common to both. So, Samant's brother's birthday is on 15th of January.

10. **(b)** P > only S and R < only T.

    Descending order of is

    T > R > (Q) > P > S
    1   2   3   4   5

    Hence, Q is third in order of height.

11. **(c)** Ramesh's position from upwards = (Total students – Ramesh's position from down) + 1

    = (31 – 9) + 1 = 23rd

12. **(a)** (Meeta's place from left + Simran's place from right) + (Girls between them)

    = (10 + 11) + (4) = 25 girls.

13. **(c)** Time taken for 1 dog = 12 Minutes

    Time taken for 10 dogs

    = 12 × 10 = 120 minutes

14. **(c)** The month with neither 31 nor 30 day is February.

15. **(c)** Given number 3 5 1 4 6 2 9 8 7

    After rearrangement 1 2 3 4 5 6 7 8 9

    So, there are two numbers, 4 and 8 remain unchanged after the rearrangement.

16. **(b)** Total number of letters in the English alphabet = 26

    Total number of letters in English alphabet – (letter from the left + letter from the right)

    So, required number of letters = 26 – (8 + 7) = 11.

17. **(c)** The given letter series:

    Z A B C Y X L M N D E F G H O P Q R S T I **J** K U V W

18. **(c)** 12 × 5 = 60 months
19. **(d)** Number of girls in the line
 = (10 + 4) − 1 = 13
 Number of girls to be added
 = 28 − 13 = 15 girls.
20. **(b)** Sequence in queue:
 I. Prabha
 II. Ratna
 III. Payal
 IV. Meena
 Hence, Prabha is the first person in the queue.
21. **(d)** Number of persons between Raina and Pratiksha
 = 38 − (12 + 19) = 38 − (31)
 = 7 persons
22. **(a)** The order of age is as follows:
 Siya > Lavanya > Swapna > Harry > Survana
 So, Survana is the youngest.
23. **(d)** The 7th letter/number from the left end = E
 The 5th letter/number from the right end = Q
 A 3 L G 5 P **E** 7 9 F S H I M T 6 Y Z **Q** 3 U 2 B
 So, the middle letter/number is I.
24. **(b)** The series is:
 14th from left
 F @ 3 9 H © A D I % 4 E * $ M K 2 U R **P** 5 W ¥ 8 1 T J V 7
 14 + 6 = 20th from left
25. **(a)** Sequence we are looking 756
 Number Sequence 7 5 5 9 4 5 7 6
 4 5 9 8 $\boxed{7\ 5\ 6}$ 7 6 4 3 2 5 6 7 8
 Preceded by 7 and followed by 6 So, there is only one such 5.
26. **(b)** Rearrangement:
 18 74 65 83 97 76
 Number 81 is the lowest.
27. **(b)** Rearrangement:
 91 57 66 48 89 77
 Number 81 is the largest.
28. **(d)** Ascending Order:
 38 47 56 67 79 81
 2nd from left   third from right
 ∴ Difference = 67 − 47 = 20.
29. **(d)** The arrangement is as follows:
 Priti > Rahul > Yogita
 = Divya > Manju > Lokita
 Therefore, Priti scored the highest.
30. **(a)** Total number of students in the class = (7 + 26) − 1 = 32
31. **(a)** Sam won the race. Sam > Rahul > Rohit > Raj > Monu
32. **(c)** Reena is the shortest. Reena<Kirti<Aanya<Akshi< 2 other girls.
33. **(a)** (9 × 2) + 5 = 23
 (23 × 2) + 5 = 51
 (51 × 2) + 5 = 107
 (107 × 2) + 5 = 219
34. **(a)** 3, 2, 5, 4, 1; Ration, Resolve, Result, Revolve, Rotate.
35. **(b)** Her rank = 25 − 19 + 1 = 7th
36. **(c)** Rohit is the shortest.
 Rohit<Mohit<Anuj<Sahil<Rishi

Level-2

1. **(c)** The arrangement is as follows:

   Kathir > Gagan > Raj > Appu

   So, Kathir is the most senior.

2. **(c)** Number of girls in the row = Number of girls up till M + Number of girls between M and N + Number of girls including N.

   = 12 + 4 + 8 = 24 girls

3. **(a)** Number of students behind Aakriti in rank = (25 – 4) = 21

   Aakriti is 22nd from the bottom.

   Number of students behind Akansha in rank = (25 – 5) = 20

   So, Akansha is 21st from the bottom.

4. **(c)**

Today	Next day	Second day	Third day
Friday	Saturday	Sunday	Monday

   So, she will celebrate her birthday on Monday.

5. **(b)** If today is Monday, then the 8th day will be Monday.

6. **(c)** Given that

   5 1 9   3 6 4   2 8 7   1 5 8   8 3 5

   After Arrangement

   9 1 5   **4 6 3**   7 8 2   8 5 1   5 3 8

   So, it is clear that, 3 6 4 is the lowest number.

7. **(d)** Shreya and Bhawna inter-change their positions. So, Shreya's new position is the same as Bhawna's earlier position. This position is 14th from the left and 17th from the right is Bhawna's new position.

   Number of girls in the row = (13 + 1 + 16) = 30

8. **(d)** According to Jack, Paresh's birthday falls on, ㉑st 22nd, 23rd, 24th, 25th, 26th and 27th of May.

   According to Tripti, Paresh's birthday falls = 13th, 14th, 15th, 16th, 17th, 18th, 19th, 20th and ㉑st May.

   The common day is 21st.

   Paresh's birthday falls on 21st.

9. **(a)** Nisha leaves her house 6 : 40 a.m.

   Reaches Pooja's house = 6.40 + 25 minutes = 7.05 a.m.

   Finish their breakfast = 7.05 + 15 minutes = 7.20 a.m.

10. **(b)** The given series:

    5 3 4 8 <u>9 7</u> 1 6 5 3 2 9 8 <u>7 3</u> 5

    So, the numbers are 5 3, 9 7 , 7 1 , 5 3 , 7 3 and 3 5.

11. **(c)** Raj   Ankur   Aryan   Vijay

    Total persons = 4 + 2 = 6.

12. **(c)** Row Arrangement

Poonam's position after shifting by two places towards left

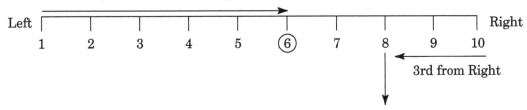

13. **(c)** Meghna on April 8, 1985

    Her age is = 2016
    ───────
    = 31 years

14. **(d)** Raj scored the highest marks = 49

    Latika scored the lowest marks = 10

15. **(a)** Number of boys in the row = number of boys upto P + number of boys between P and Q + number of boys including Q and those behind Q

    = 14 + 4 + 7 = 25.

16. **(c)** Simran > Rohit > Latika > Anuj.
        (1)   (2)   (3)   (4)

    Hence, Anuj stood last in the race.

(Qs. 17 & 18) Ranking from high to low

Sanjay > Rohit > Kamal > Vikas > Dinesh

17. **(a)** Sanjay ranked highest.
18. **(c)** Dinesh ranked lowest.
19. **(d)** 7th letter/number from the right end = A

    9th letter/number from the left end = T

    So, the middle letter/number is W.

    T 2 P 1 **W** Q C 7 A

20. **(a)** The order of their heights is as follows:

    Aakash > Rohit > Arun > Rehan > Tarun > Samay

    So, Arun is the third tallest.

21. **(a)** The numbers are arranged in the descending order as:

    875   725   493   317

    283   269

    middle digit

    So, the middle digit is 2.

22. **(b)** The rank of Tarun from the bottom of the class =

    (35 - 6) + 1 = 30th

23. **(d)** The order of their heights is as follows:

    Manha > Garima > Priya > Latika > Megha

    So, Garima is shorter than Manha but taller than Priya.

24. (d) Birth date according to Mohit : 16 ⑰

Birth date according to his sister : ⑰ 18

Here, 17th is common to both.

So, Mohit's brother's birthday is on 17th of February.

25. (d) Here, $(10 - 6) + 1 = 5$ (Raj's position)

Now, $(28 - 5) = 13$, So, there are 13 boys should be added to the line.

26. (c) Birth date according to Manha : 11 12 13 ⑭

Birth date according to her sister : 12 13 ⑭ 15
16 17 18 19

Here, 14 is common date to both.

So, Manha's father's birthday date is 14th of October.

27. (c) Left $\xrightarrow{10\text{th}}$ Deepak $\xleftarrow{10\text{th}}$ Right

So, $10 + 1 + 10 = 11$th

His position from left as well as from right is 11th.

28. (d)

A B C D E F G [H] I J K L M N O P Q R S T U V W X Y Z
4th from left ↑ middle   15th from Right

So, H is exactly in the middle.

29. (c)

Y A C B E D **F** I J H K [M] N O Q P **R** U V X T Z
↑ middle

30. (a) 17th from the right end = © and 9th from the right of © is A.

31. (b) Total students
$= 12 + 2 + 3 = 17$

North
↑ (Left)   1 2 3 4 5 6 7 8 9 10 11 12 13 14 15 16 17
                                        ↓   ↓   (Right)
                                   (Ruhani)   (Ridhan)

32. (c) If five students from the right end left the row, then remaining total number of students
$= 35 - 5 = 30$.

Now, position of Rashi from right end $= 30 - 8 + 1 = 23$rd.

33. (a) Date on which he celebrate his daughter's birthday = Second Thursday of September + 2 days

Date on which he celebrate his daughter's birthday
= 11th September + 2 days
= 13th September.

34. (b)

CHAPTER 8

Arithmetical Reasoning

OBJECTIVE

- This test measures student's ability to perform basic arithmetic operations and to solve problems that involve fundamental arithmetic concepts.

INTRODUCTION

Arithmetic reasoning focuses on word problems and delivers mathematical questions and equations in a format that must be synthesized.

Examples 1:

After buying 5 ice-creams at ₹20 each, Shanaya has Rs.5 left. How much amount did she have at first?

(a) 100 (b) 102 (c) 105 (d) 110

Ans. (c)

Explanation:

Cost of one ice-cream = ₹20

Cost of five ice-creams = 20 × 5 = ₹100

After buying 5 ice-creams, Shanaya is left with = ₹5

Total amount he had first = 100 + 5 = ₹105

Examples 2:

Sania has 12 chocolates. Suraj has one fourth as many chocolates as Sania. Ridhima has 8 more chocolates than Suraj. How many total chocolates are there?

(a) 12 (b) 14 (c) 26 (d) 28

Ans. (c)

Explanation:

Total number of chocolates Sania has = 12

Suraj has = 12 × 1/4 = 3

Ridhima has = 3 + 8 = 11

Total chocolates = 12 + 3 + 11 = 26

3. One pan can fry 2 pieces of meat at one time. Every piece of meat takes two minutes to be cooked (one minute for each side). Using only one pan, what is the least possible time to cook 1000 pieces of meat?
   (a) 1000 minutes   (b) 1500 minutes   (c) 2000 minutes   (d) 2500 minutes

Ans. (a)

Explanation:
One pan can fry at one time = 2 pieces of meat
Every piece of meat takes time = 2 minutes
Possible time to cook 1000 pieces = 1000 × 2 = 2000 minute
but 2 pieces can be fried at one time = 2000/2 = 1000 minutes

4. Manav wrote the number sentences below,
   20 = ☐ × 4
   ☐ × $ = 15

The value of ☐ is the same in both the sentences. Both of Manav's number sentences are true. What is the value of $?
   (a) 1   (b) 2   (c) 3   (d) 5

Ans. (c)

Explanation:
Value of ☐5☐ is = 5
Value of $ is = 3
20 = ☐5☐ × 4
☐5☐ × 3 = 15

5. Shorya is 10 years younger than Vishal. Vishal is 5 years older than Rithvik. Rithvik is twice as old as Jai. Jai is 5 years old. What is the combined age of these four people?
   (a) 50 years   (b) 55 years   (c) 25 years   (d) 35 years

Ans. (d)

Explanation:
Jai's age = 5 years
Rithvik's age = 5 × 2 = 10 years
Vishal's age = 10 + 5 = 15 years
Shorya's age = 15 − 10 = 5 years
Total combined age = 5 + 10 + 15 + 5 = 35 years

LEVEL-1

1. In a garden, Shanu saw 52 Roses and Sunflowers. There are 27 more Roses than Sunflowers. How many were Sunflowers?
   (a) 20   (b) 25   (c) 30   (d) 35

2. Gaurav has 96 sheeps in his farm. He has 12 times as many sheeps as he has cows. The number sentence below can be used to find the number of cows, c, he has $96 \div c = 12$
   How many cows, c, does Gaurav have?
   (a) 10 cows (b) 12 cows (c) 8 cows (d) 6 cows

3. A tailor had a number of shirt pieces to cut from a roll of fabric. He cut each roll of equal length into 10 pieces. He cut at the rate of 45 cuts in a minute. How many rolls would be cut in 24 minutes?
   (a) 30 rolls (b) 58 rolls (c) 120 rolls (d) 150 rolls

4. Tom scored 4 more points in the basket ball game than Mary. Lindy scored 22 points, which was twice as many as Tom. How many points did Mary score?
   (a) 7 (b) 8 (c) 11 (d) 14

5. If you write 1 to 80 counting, then how many times do you write 4?
   (a) 8 (b) 16 (c) 9 (d) 18

6. Priya cuts a cake into two halves and cuts one half into six smaller pieces of equal size. Each of the small pieces is twenty grams in weight. If she has seven pieces of cake in all with her. What is the weight of cake in all?
   (a) 220 gm (b) 250 gm (c) 240 gm (d) 225 gm

7. Sara is 2 years older to Bina and 2 years younger to Diya, while Bina and Kiran are twins. How many years older is Diya to Kiran?
   (a) 4 years (b) 6 years (c) 2 years (d) 5 years

8. Shivam had 23 candies. He puts the same number in each of the two bags, seven candies are left after this. How many did he put in each bag?
   (a) 6 (b) 7 (c) 8 (d) 9

9. A shepherd had 27 sheep. All but 10 died. How many was he left with?
   (a) 27 (b) 10 (c) 17 (d) 8

10. What is the smallest number of ducks that could swim in this formation- two ducks in front of a duck, two ducks behind a duck and a duck between two ducks?
    (a) 9 (b) 7 (c) 5 (d) 3

11. Isha wants to buy dog treats for her 5 dogs. At the pet store she sees the boxes of treats. Which box of dog treats should Isha buy so that each of her dogs can receive an equal number of treats with 2 treat left over?

    (a) 25 DOG TREATS (b) 20 DOG TREATS (c) 17 DOG TREATS (d) 15 DOG TREATS

12. Wilson is buying curd for a party.
    - He needs to buy 50 kg of curd.
    - Curd is sold only in 8 and 12 kg packages.

    Which choice shows the least amount of curd Wilson can buy to have enough for a party?
    (a) Five 12 kg packages
    (b) Three 12 kg packages and two 8 kg packages
    (c) Two 12 kg packages and three 8 kg packages
    (d) Six 8 kg packages

13. A bird shooter was asked how many birds he had in the bag. He replied that there were all sparrows but 6, all pigeons but 6 and all ducks but 6. How many birds he had in the bag in all?
    (a) 36 (b) 18 (c) 27 (d) 9

14. Use the picture to answer the question.

    Row 1: Red, Blue, Red, Pink
    Row 2: Blue, Black, Red, Red
    Row 3: Pink, Red, Pink, Red

    Himanshu will use one marker to colour half of the triangles. What is the colour of the marker Himanshu will use?
    (a) Black (b) Pink (c) Red (d) Blue

15. At the end of fresher party in the college, 15 friends present all shakes hands with each other once. How many handshakes will there be altogether?
    (a) 95 (b) 85 (c) 100 (d) 75

16. Patrick has a set of green, white and black marbles.
    - The green marbles make up exactly $\frac{1}{2}$ of the set.
    - The set has 2 black marbles.
    - The number of white marbles is twice the number of black marbles.

    How many marbles are in Patrick's set?
    (a) 6 (b) 4 (c) 8 (d) 12

17. Simran has 6 carrots. Sara has 3 more carrots than Simran. Denny has 3 times as many carrots as Sara. How many carrots does Denny have?
    (a) 6 (b) 9 (c) 18 (d) 27

18. On Friday, Mary was a referee at 3 soccer games. She arrived at the soccer field 20 minutes before the first game. Each game lasted for $1\frac{1}{2}$ hours. There were 5 minutes break between each game. Mary left 15 minutes after the last game. How long, in minutes, was Mary at the soccer field?
    (a) 300 minutes (b) 305 minutes (c) 315 minutes (d) 320 minutes

19. A pouch contains 6 blue marbles, 3 red marbles, 1 green marble, and 2 pink marbles.

What is the probability that Tom will select, without looking, a blue marble in the first try?

(a) $\frac{6}{12}$ (b) $\frac{3}{12}$ (c) $\frac{1}{12}$ (d) $\frac{2}{12}$

20. Shekhar wanted to use his calculator to subtract 2743 and 169. He entered 2643 + 169 by mistake. Which of these could he do to correct to mistake?

    (a) Subtract 100   (b) Add 100   (c) Subtract 400   (d) Add 400

21. How many minutes are there in 1/8 of a day?

    (a) 120 minutes   (b) 140 minutes   (c) 160 minutes   (d) 180 minutes

22. In Aporva's class there are twice as many girls as boys. There are 9 boys in the class. What is the total number of boys and girls is the class?

    (a) 9   (b) 18   (c) 24   (d) 27

23. A number machine takes a number and operates on it. When the input number is 6, the output number is 11, as shown below,

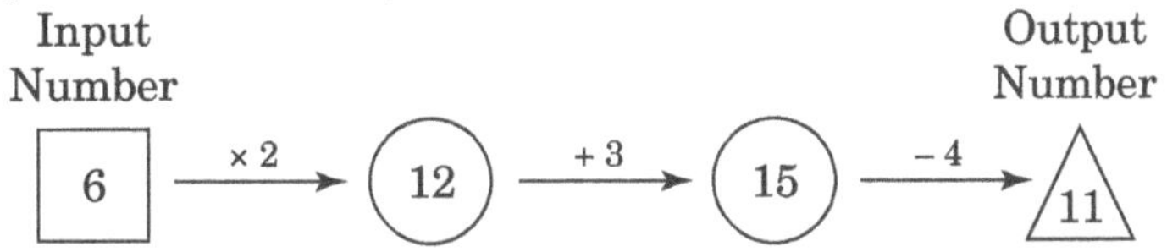

    Input Number: 6 ×2→ 12 +3→ 15 −4→ 11 Output Number

    When the input number is 8, which of these is the output number?

    (a) 14   (b) 13   (c) 15   (d) 19

24. Tell the numbers that will replace ▲, ■ and ★ in the given square so that the sum of numbers from every side is 105.

32	39	■
▲	35	33
36	★	38

    (a) ■ 34, ▲ = 37, ★ 31
    (b) ■ 31, ▲ = 34, ★ 37
    (c) ■ 37, ▲ = 31, ★ 34
    (d) ■ 30, ▲ = 31, ★ = 34

25. Kartik had 45 sweets. He put the same number in each of three boxes and had six sweets left over. How many did he put in each box?

    (a) 10   (b) 12   (c) 13   (d) 8

26. A group of 1200 persons including captains and soldiers are travelling in a train. For every 15 soldiers, there is one captain. The number of captains in the group is

    (a) 70   (b) 75   (c) 80   (d) 85

27. Raj bought 12 plums and ate $\frac{1}{3}$ of them. Shivam bought 12 plums and ate $\frac{1}{4}$ of them. Which statement is true?

    (a) Raj ate 4 plums and Shivam ate 3 plums.

    (b) Raj ate 3 plums and Shivam ate 4 plums.

    (c) Raj and Shivam ate the same number of plums.

    (d) Raj had 9 plums remaining.

28. When Pinocchio lies, his nose gets 5 cm longer. When he tells the truth, his nose gets 3 cm shorter. When his nose was 10 cm long, he told three lies and made two true statements. How long was Pinocchio's nose now?

    (a) 18 cm (b) 19 cm (c) 21 cm (d) 22 cm

29. The product of all numbers in the dial of a telephone is _____?

    (a) 1,58,480 (b) 1,00,000 (c) zero (d) None of these

30. A man wears socks of two colours- white and grey. He has altogether 20 white socks and 20 grey socks in a drawer. Supposing he has to take out the socks in the dark, how many must he take out to be sure that he has a matching pair?

    (a) 39 (b) 20 (c) 3 (d) None of these

31. How many possible combinations of 1 key and 1 key chain each can be formed from the given keys and key chains? **(2020)**

    (a) 10 (b) 12 (c) 18 (d) 24

32. How many different possible combinations of 1 notebook and 1 pen each can be formed from the given notebooks and pens? **(2021)**

    (a) 15 (b) 18 (c) 8 (d) 20

LEVEL-2

1. Vishal got twice as many sums wrong as he got right. If he attempted 48 sums in all, how many did he solve correctly?

    (a) 18 (b) 24 (c) 16 (d) 14

2. The number of boys in a class is three times the number of girls. Which one of the following numbers cannot represent the total number of children in the class?

   (a) 48   (b) 44   (c) 40   (d) 42

3. If every 2 out of 3 readymade shirts need alterations in the collar, every 3 out of 4 need alterations in the sleeves and every 4 out of 5 need it in the body, how many alterations will be required for 60 shirts?

   (a) 88   (b) 133   (c) 123   (d) 143

4. A farmer built a fence around his plot. He used 27 fence poles on each side of the square plot. How many poles did he need altogether?

   (a) 108   (b) 100   (c) 104   (d) None of these

5. For every soft drink bottle that Tom collected, Maria collected 4. Tom collected a total of 8 soft drink bottles. How many bottles did Maria collect?

   (a) 4   (b) 16   (c) 24   (d) 32

6. The top shelf held 27 books. The bottom shelf held 43 books. 11 books from the top shelf were checked out. 6 books from the bottom shelf were missing. How many total books are left on both shelves?

   (a) 51   (b) 52   (c) 53   (d) 54

7. Nina joined a short term course in art and craft on 20th April. The course classes got over on 9th June. What is the total duration of the class?

   (a) 30 days   (b) 45 days   (c) 51 days   (d) 100 days

8. I have a few sweets to be distributed. If I keep 2, 3 or 4 in a pack, I am left with one sweet. If I keep 5 in a pack. I am left with none. What is the minimum number of sweets I have to pack and distribute?

   (a) 54   (b) 65   (c) 37   (d) 25

9. Rishika's exam started on 2nd March and the last exam was on 3rd April. What was total duration of her exams?

   (a) 30 days   (b) 33 days   (c) 44 days   (d) 60 days

10. In a garden, there are 10 rows and 12 columns of mango trees. The distance between the two trees is 2 metres and a distance of one metre is left from all sides of the boundary of the garden. The length of the garden is

    (a) 24 m   (b) 20 m   (c) 22 m   (d) 26 m

11. A school coach just announced that by the end of the quarter, all students should run the 10 miles in less than 70 minutes. There are 15 students in the goup.
    - 6 of them ran 10 miles in 1 hour + 5 minutes
    - 4 of them ran 10 miles in 1 hour + 3 minutes
    - 2 of them ran 10 miles in 1 hour + 9 minutes
    - 3 of them ran 10 miles in 1 hour and 10 minutes.

    How many students made the goal?

    (a) 3   (b) 10   (c) 4   (d) 12

12. A pizzeria caters parties and just finished baking 60 pizzas. The Indian group just picked up their order of 1/4 of the pizzas baked. A school graduation party is picking up 1/3 of the pizzas baked. A smart arts club bought 1/20 of the pizzas baked.
    How many pizzas are left out of the 60 that were baked?
    (a) 20 (b) 15 (c) 18 (d) 22
13. A certain number of horses and an equal number of men are going somewhere. Half of the owners are on their horses' back, while the remaining ones are walking along leading their horses. If the number of legs walking on the ground is 70, how many horses are there?
    (a) 10 (b) 12 (c) 14 (d) 16
14. The total of the ages of Amar, Anaya and Ashish is 80 years. What was the total of their ages three years ago?
    (a) 72 years (b) 74 years (c) 71 years (d) 77 years
15. 30 members of a club decided to play a badminton singles tournament. Every time a member loses a game he is out of the tournament. There are no ties. What is the minimum number of matches that must be played to determine the winner?
    (a) 61 (b) 15 (c) 29 (d) None of these
16. A motorist knows four different routes from Bristol to Birmingham. From Birmingham to Sheffield, he knows three different routes and from Sheffield to Carlisle, he knows two different routes. How many routes does he know from Bristol to Carlisle?
    (a) 8 (b) 12 (c) 24 (d) 46
17. A monkey climbs 30 feet at the beginning of each hour and rests for a while when he slips back 20 feet before he again starts climbing in the beginning of the next hour. If he begins his ascent at 8.00 a.m., at what time will he first touch flag at 120 feet from the ground?
    (a) 4 p.m. (b) 5 p.m. (c) 6 p.m. (d) None of these
18. Mrs. Kapoor ordered 3 different colours of markers.
    - She ordered 20 of each colour markers.
    - She also ordered some pencils.
    - She ordered 2 times as many pencils as markers.
    How many pencils did Mrs. Kapoor order?
    (a) 20 (b) 60 (c) 100 (d) 120
19. In a chess tournament, each of the six players will play every other player exactly once. How many matches will be played during the tournament?
    (a) 12 (b) 15 (c) 30 (d) 36
20. Riya is twice as old as Siya. Three years ago, she was three times as old as Siya. How old is Riya now?
    (a) 16 years (b) 14 years (c) 12 years (d) 6 years

21. When Rahul was born, his father was 32 years older than his brother and his mother was 25 years older than his sister. If Rahul's brother is 6 years older than him and his mother is 3 years younger than his father, how old was Rahul's sister when he was born?

    (a) 10 years (b) 7 years (c) 14 years (d) 20 years

22. Raja and Ritu collect baseball cards. Each has the same number of cards. If John gives Raja and Ritu 6 more baseball cards each, who will have the greater number of baseball cards, Raja or Ritu?

    (a) Raja
    (b) Ritu
    (c) Raja and Ritu will have the same number of baseball cards.
    (d) None of the above

23. Shorya has Rs. 480 in the denominations of one-rupee notes, five-rupee notes and ten-rupee notes. The number of notes of each denomination is equal. What is the total number of notes he has?

    (a) 90 (b) 45 (c) 75 (d) 60

24. If a clock takes seven seconds to strike seven, how long will it take to strike ten?

    (a) 5 seconds (b) 7 seconds (c) 9 seconds (d) None of these

25. In a class, 20% of the students own only two cars each, 40% of the remaining own three cars each and the remaining members own only one car each. Which of the following statements is definitely true from the given statements?

    (a) Only 20% of the total members own three cars each.
    (b) 48% of the total members own only one car each.
    (c) 60% of the total members own at least two cars each.
    (d) 80% of the total members own at least one car.

26. Manav's mother prepares sandwiches with two slices of bread each. A packet of bread has 24 slices. How many sandwiches can she prepare from two and half packets of bread?

    (a) 12 (b) 24 (c) 30 (d) 34

27. The number of red frogs exceeded the number of blue frogs by 50. The number of green frogs was 20 less than the number of blue frogs. If there were 100 blue frogs, what was the sum of the reds, the blues, and the greens?

    (a) 250 (b) 80 (c) 330 (d) 230

28. Suzen had 81 chickens. He sold an equal number of chickens to each of 3 customers and had 54 chickens left. How many chickens did Suzen sell to each customer?

    (a) 8 (b) 9 (c) 10 (d) 11

29. The hour hand of a watch rotates 30 degrees every hour. How many complete rotations does the hour hand make in 6 days?

    (a) 6 (b) 12 (c) 14 (d) 18

30. If Jill needed to buy 9 bottles of soda for a party in which 12 people attended, how many bottles of soda will she need to buy for a party in which 8 people are attending?
    (a) 6   (b) 10   (c) 12   (d) 8

31. How many different pairs of 1 girl and 1 boy each can possibly be formed from 4 girls and 3 boys? **(2019)**
    (a) 7   (b) 14   (c) 12   (d) None of these

32. Vishal starts his guitar classes from 1st Wednesday of July 20XX. If he takes leaves on odd number of days, then for how many days does he go for guitar classes in that month? (Assume that every Sunday is a holiday.) **(2019)**

July 20XX						
Sun	Mon	Tue	Wed	Thu	Fri	Sat
1	2	3	4	5	6	7
8	9	10	11	12	13	14
15	16	17	18	19	20	21
22	23	24	25	26	27	28
29	30	31				

    (a) 14   (b) 15   (c) 16   (d) 12

33. Find the missing number, if same rule is followed in all the three Figures. **(2022)**

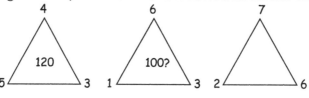

    (a) 100   (b) 110   (c) 180   (d) 150

34. If Puneet went to park everyday in March 20XX except the dates which are multiples of 3, then for how many days did he go to the park? **(2022)**

MARCH 20XX						
S	M	T	W	T	F	S
					1	2
3	4	5	6	7	8	9
10	11	12	13	14	15	16
17	18	19	20	21	22	23
24	25	26	27	28	29	30
31						

    (a) 21   (b) 20   (c) 10   (d) 18

35. If in each of the following numbers, all digits are written in reverse order, then which of the following will be the greatest? **(2022)**

| 184 | 567 | 764 | 408 | 715 |

   (a) 184   (b) 764   (c) 408   (d) 567

36. Find the missing number, if same rule is followed in all the three figures. **(2022)**

   (a) 6
   (b) 7
   (c) 15
   (d) 8

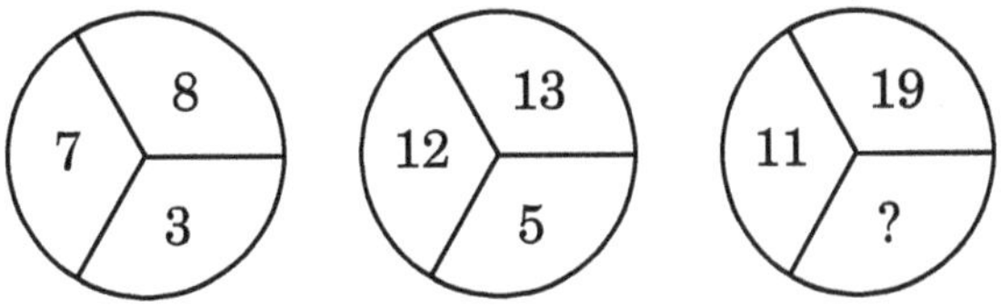

37. Find the missing number. **(2022)**

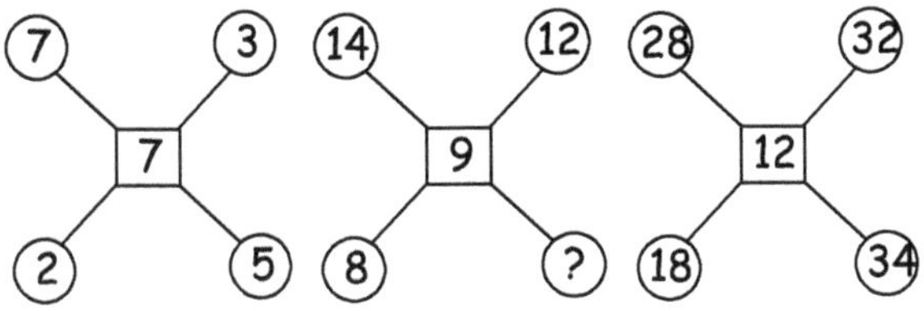

   (a) 12   (b) 13
   (c) 14   (d) 15

38. Find the missing number if the same rule is followed in all the three figures. **(2022)**

| 13 | 8 |
| 108 | |

| 16 | 9 |
| 148 | |

| 18 | 8 |
| ? | |

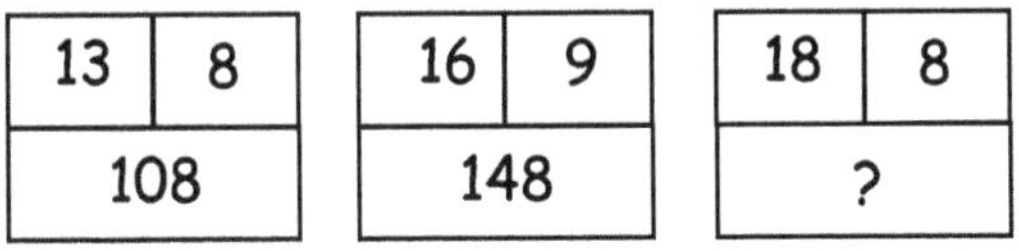

   (a) 196   (b) 184   (c) 138   (d) 148

Answers and Explanation

Level-1

1. **(b)** Total number of roses = 52
   Total number of sunflowers
   = 52 − 27 = 25
2. **(c)** 96 ÷ c = 12
   c = 96 ÷ 12 = 8
   So, Gaurav has 8 cows.
3. **(c)** Number of cuts made to cut a roll into 10 pieces = 9
   ∴ Required number of rolls
   = 45 × 24/9 = 120.
4. **(a)** Lindy scored = 22 points
   Tom scored = 22/2 = 11 points
   Mary scored = 11 − 4 = 7 points
5. **(d)** Clearly from 1 to 80, there are numbers with 4 as the unit's digit −
   4, 14, 24, 34, 44, 54, 64, 74 and ten number with 4 as tens digit −
   40, 41, 42, 43, 44, 45, 46, 47, 48, 49.
   So, required number = 8 + 10 = 18.
6. **(c)**

   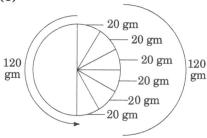

   The weight of cake is 240 gm.
7. **(a)** Diya > Sara > Bina = Kiran
   (2 yrs) (2 yrs) (Twins)
   Diya is = 2 + 2 = 4 years older to Kiran.
8. **(c)** Total candies = 23
   Candies leftover = 7
   Candies in each bag
   = 23 − 7 = 16
   = 16/2 = 8
9. **(b)** "All but 10 died" means all except 10 died i.e. 10 sheep remained alive.
10. **(d)** Three ducks can be arranged as shown below to satisfy all the three given conditions.

    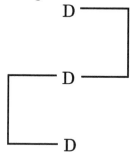

11. **(c)** By observing the options:
    Option (a),
    5 + 5 + 5 + 5 + 5 = 25 Dog Treats + No left over
    Option (b),
    4 + 4 + 4 + 4 + 4 = 20 Dog Treats + No left over
    Option (c),
    3 + 3 + 3 + 3 + 3 = 15 Dog Treats + 2 left over
12. **(b)** Three 12 kg packages
    = 12 × 3 = 36 kg
    Two 8 kg packages = 8 × 2
    = 16 kg
    Total curd = 36 + 16 = 52 kg

13. **(d)** Number of sparrows + Number of ducks = 6 and number of sparrows + Number of pigeon = 6. This is possible when there are 3 sparrows, 3 pigeons and 3 ducks i.e. 9 birds in all.

14. **(c)** Total number of triangles = 12
    Number of Red triangles = 6
    Number of Blue triangles = 2
    Number of Pink triangles = 3
    Number of Black triangles = 1
    It is clear that, Red triangles are the half of the total. So, Himanshu will use Red marker.

15. **(a)** Clearly,
    The total number of handshakes
    = (14 + 13 + 12 + 11 + 10 + 9 + 8 + 7 + 6 + 5 + 4 + 3 + 2 + 1) = 95.

16. **(d)** Number of black marbles = $\boxed{2}$
    Number of white marbles = 2 × 2 = 4
    Total number of black and white marbles = 4 + 2 = 6
    Total marbles (n) = $n = \frac{1}{2} \times n + 6$
    n = 6 × 2 = 12
    Number of green marbles = $12 \times \frac{1}{2} = 6$.

17. **(d)** Number of carrots Simran has = 6
    Number of carrots Sara has = 6 + 3 = 9
    Number of carrot Denny has = 9 × 3 = 27.

18. **(c)**
    - Mary arrived at soccer field = 20 minutes before the first game.
    - Each game duration = $1\frac{1}{2}$ hours = 90 minutes

    Three games duration = 90 × 3 = 270 minutes
    - Minutes brake between each game = 5 minutes

    Total minutes among games = 5 × 2 = 10 min.
    - Mary left soccer field after 15 minutes of last game.

    Total minutes = 20 + 270 + 10 + 15 = 315 minutes

19. **(a)** Total marbles = 12
    Blue marbles = 6
    Probability of selecting blue marbles = $\frac{6}{12}$.

20. **(b)** Actual calculation = 2743 + 169 = 2912
    Calculation done by mistake = 2643 + 169 = 2812
    Therefore, Difference = 2912 – 2812 = 100.

21. **(d)** One day has 24 hours
    1/8 of a day = 24 × 1 = 3 hours
    1 hour = 60 minutes
    3 hours = 3 × 60 = 180 minutes.

22. **(d)** Number of boys in the class = 9
    Number of girls in the class = 9 × 2 = 18
    Total number of boys and girls = 18 + 9 = 27.

23. **(c)**
    Input Number → ×2 → 8 → 16 → +3 → 19 → −4 → 15   Output Number

    The Output Number will be 15.

24. (a) ☐ 34, ▲ = 37, ★ 31

32	39	34	= 105
37	35	33	= 105
36	31	38	= 105

= 105   105   105

25. (c) Total sweets = 45
Sweets left over = 6
Sweets in each box
= 45 − 6 = 39
= 39 / 3 = 13

26. (b) Out of every 15 persons, there is one captain.
So, number of captains = 1200 / 16 = 75.

27. (a) Raj ate = $12 \times \dfrac{1}{3}$ = 4 plums
Shivam ate
= $12 \times \dfrac{1}{4}$ = 3 plums

So, Raj ate 4 plums and Shivam ate 3 plums.
Hence, statement (a) is correct.

28. (b) Pinnocchio's nose length
= 10 cm
Pinnocchio's nose length after three lies = 10 + (5 x 3) = 10 + 15 = 25 cm
Pinnocchio's nose length after two true statements
= 25 − (2 × 3)
25 − 6 = 19 cm.

29. (c) Since one of the number on the dial of a telephone is 0, so the product of all the numbers on it is 0.

30. (c) There are socks of only two colours, so two out of any three socks must always be of the same colour.

31. (d) Possible combinations
= 4 × 6 = 24

32. (a) 5 × 3 = 15

Level-2

1. (c) Suppose the boy got x sums right and 2x sums wrong.
Then, x + 2x = 48 ⇒ 3x = 48
⇒ x = 16.

2. (d) Let number of girls = x and Number of boys = 3x
Then, 3x + x = 4x = Total number of students.
Thus, to find exact value of x, the total number of students must be divisible by 4.

3. (b) Number of alterations required in 1 shirt
= $\dfrac{2}{3} + \dfrac{3}{4} + \dfrac{4}{5} = \dfrac{133}{60}$
Therefore, Number of alterations required in 60 shirt
= $\dfrac{133}{60} \times 60 = 133$

4. (c) Since each pole at the corner of the plot is common to its two sides, so we have
Total number of poles needed
= 27 × 4 − 4 = 108 − 4 = 104

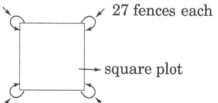

27 fences each

square plot

5. (d) Total soft drink bottles collected by Tom = 8

Total soft drink bottles collected by Maria
= 8 × 4 = 32.

6. (c) Number of books on top shelf = 27

Number of books on bottom shelf = 43

Total missing books
= 11 + 6 = 17

Number of books left on both shelves
= 27 + 43 − 17 = 53

7. (c) Number of days left in April
= 30 − 19
= 11 days
(Since April has 30 days)
Number of days in May = 31 days
(Since May has 31 days)
Number of days in June = 9 days
So, the total duration of the class = 11 + 31 + 9 = 51 days

8. (d) The required number will be such that it leaves a reminder of 1 when divided by 2, 3 or 4 and no reminder when divided by 5. Such a number is 25 among options.

9. (b) Number of days left in March = 31 − 1 = 30 days
Number of days in April = 3 days
Total duration of her exams = 30 + 3 = 33 days.

10. (a) Each row contains 12 plants.
There are 11 gaps between the two corner trees (11 × 2) metres and 1 metre on each side is left.
∴ Length = (22 + 2) m = 24 m.

11. (d) Express 70 minutes in the form of hours + minutes since most of the figures given were in that form, hence:
70 minutes = 60 minutes + 10 minutes = 1 hour + 10 minutes
This means that for students to pass, they must run the 10 miles distance in less than this time set by the coach. Checking the students' time one by one, only 3 out of 15 students were not able to run the 10 miles in less than 1 hour + 10 minutes.
15 − 3 = 12 students made the goal

12. (d) Compute the number of pizzas picked up:
Number of pizzas picked up by Indian group = 1/4(60) = 15
Number of pizzas picked up by School = 1/3(60) = 20
Number of pizzas picked up by Smart arts = 1/20(60) = 3
The total number of pizzas picked up = 15 + 20 + 3 = 38
The number of pizzas left = 60 − 38 = 22

13. (c) Let number of horses
= number of men = x.
Then, number of legs = 4x + 2 x (x/2) = 5x.
So, 5x = 70 or x = 14.

14. (c) Required sum = (80 − 3 × 3) years
= (80 − 9) years
= 71 years.

15. (c) Clearly, every member except one (i.e. the winner) must lose one game to decide the winner.
So, minimum number of matches to be played
= 30 − 1 = 29.

16. (c) Total number of routes from Bristale to Carlisle = $(4 \times 3 \times 2)$ = 24.

17. (c) Net ascend of monkey in 1 hr = $(30 - 20)$ = 10 feet

So, the monkey ascends 90 feet in 9 hrs i.e. till 5 p.m. Clearly, in the next 1 hour i.e. till 6 p.m. the monkey ascend remaining 30 feet to touch the flag.

18. (d) Total order of markers = $3 \times 20 = 60$

Total order of pencils = 60×2 = 120.

19. (b) I. matches of first player with other 5 players

II. matches of second player with 4 players other than the first player

III. matches of third player with 3 players other than the first player and second player.

IV. matches of fourth player with 2 players other than the first player, second player and third player.

V. matches of fifth player with 1 player other than the first player, second player, third player and fourth player.

So, total matches will be 5 + 4 + 3 + 2 + 1 = 15

20. (c) Let Siya's present age = x years
Then Riya present age = 2x years
Three years ago
$(2x-3) = 3(x-3)$
$2x - 3 = 3x - 9$
or x = 6
So, Riya's age = 2x = 2×6 = 12 years.

21. (a) When Rahul was born, his brother's age = 6 yrs
His father's age = $(6 + 32)$ yrs = 38 yrs.
His mother's age = $(38 - 3)$ yrs = 35 yrs
His sister's age = $(32 - 25)$ yrs = 10 yrs.

22. (c) As both has the same number of card John also gives both 6 more baseball cards. So, Raja and Ritu will have the same number of baseball cards.

23. (a) Let number of notes of each denomination be x.
Then, x + 5x + 10x = 480
16x = 480
x = 30
Hence, total number of notes = 3x = 90.

24. (d) Here, seven strike of a clock have 6 intervals while 10 strikes have 9 intervals.
Therefore, required time = 7 / 6 × 9 seconds = 10 ½ seconds.

25. (b) Let total number of members be 100.
Then, Number of members owning only 2 cars = 20
Number of members owning 3 cars = 40% of 80 = 32
Number of members owning only 1 car = 100 − (20 + 32) = 48
Thus, 48% of the total members own one car each.

26. (c) A package of bread has = 24 slices
Sandwiches made by one packages of bread = 12

Sandwiches made by two packages of bread
= 12 × 2 = 24
Sandwiches made by half packages of bread = 6
Total sandwiches = 24 + 6 = 30.

27. (c) Number of blue frogs = 100
Number of red frogs = 100 + 50 = 150
Number of green frogs = 100 − 20 = 80
Total frogs = 100 + 150 + 80 = 330.

28. (b) Total chickens = 81
Chickens left = 54
Chickens sold = 81 − 54 = 27
Chickens sold to each customer = 27 / 3 = 9 Chickens.

29. (b) There are 360 degrees in a complete circle.
So, 360 / 30 = 12 hours to make one full circle.
In 6 days there are 24 hours × 6 = 144 hours total.
The total number of rotations will be 144/12 = 12.

30. (a) Here, 9 bottles / 12 people = x bottles / 8 people
Cross- multiply to solve a proportion
9 × 8 = x × 12
72 = 12x
x = 6.
So, 6 bottles of soda will she need to buy for a party.

31. (c) Total possible combinations = 4 × 3 = 12

32. (d) Vishal starts his class from 4th July (1st Wednesday of July 20XX).
Total number of days he go for guitar classes in that month = 12

July 20XX						
Sun	Mon	Tue	Wed	Thu	Fri	Sat
1	2	3	4	5	6	7
8	9	10	11	12	13	14
15	16	17	18	19	20	21
22	23	24	25	26	27	28
29	30	31				

33. (d) 150
(4 + 5 + 3) × 10 = 120
(6 + 3 + 1) × 10 = 100
(7 + 2 + 6) × 10 = 150

34. (a) Days which are multiple of three in March 20XX = 3, 6, 9, 12, 15, 18, 21, 24, 27, 30
Number of days for which he go to the park = 31 − 10 = 21

35. (c) Reverse order of the given numbers are: 184 − 481, 567 − 765, 764 − 467, 408 − 804, 715 − 517. So, reverse order of 408 will be greatest.

36. (a) (7 + 8) ÷ 5 = 15 ÷ 5 = 3
(12 + 13) ÷ 5 = 25 ÷ 5 = 5
(11 + 19) ÷ 5 = 30 ÷ 5 = 6

37. (d)
38. (d)

CHAPTER 9

Logical Venn Diagram

OBJECTIVES

- Students will be able to find out the relation between some items of a group by diagrams.
- They will be able to compare and contrast groups of things.

INTRODUCTION

A Venn Diagram is a visual brainstorming tool used to compare and contrast two (sometimes three) different things. Comparing is looking at traits that things have in common, while contrasting is looking at how they differ from each other.

A Venn Diagram is made up of two large circles that intersect with each other to form a space in the middle. Each circle represents something that you want to compare and contrast. Where the two circles intersect, you would write traits that the two things have in common. In either side of the intersecting space, you would write the differences among the two things.

TYPE-I : Different Types of Questions Based on Venn Diagrams

CASE 1:

When one group of items is completely included in the second group of items and the second, again completely belongs to the third group, they are represented as shown.

Example 1:

Seconds, Minutes, Hours
Explanation: Venn diagram would be as follows:

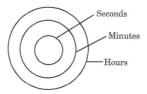

Clearly, seconds are a part of minutes and minutes are a part of hours.

CASE 2:

If the items evidently belong to three different groups, i.e., they are not correlated with each other in any way. They are represented as shown.

Example 2:

Whale, Crocodile, Bird

Explanation:

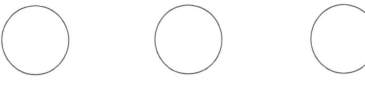

Whale   Crocodile   Bird

They all belong to different categories.

CASE 3:

If the three items are partly related to each other, they are represented as shown.

Example 3:

Human, Carnivorous, Animal

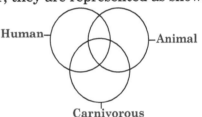

Explanation: Venn diagram would be as given.

Clearly, all three are related to each other.

Case 4:

If two separate groups of items are completely unrelated to each other, but they are completely included in the third group, then the relationships can be diagrammatically shown as:

Example 4:

Hospital, Nurse, Patient

Explanation:

Nurse and Patient are entirely different. But both are parts of Hospital.

Case 5:

When two groups of items have some common relationship and both of them are completely included in the third group, the relationship is shown by two smaller intersecting circles in a third large circle.

Example 5:

Animal, Cat, Pet

Explanation:
Some Cats are Pets and some pets are cats but all Cats and Pets are Animals.

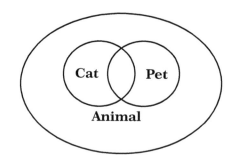

Case 6:

If one item belongs to the class of second while, third item is entirely different from the two and they may be represented by the following diagram.

Example 6:

Engineers, Human Being, Rats

Explanation: Venn diagram is as follows :

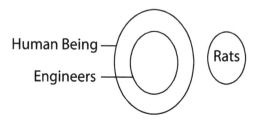

As we know that, all engineers are human beings but rats are entirely different to both of these.

Case 7:

If one group of items is partly included in the second group of items and the third group is completely unrelated to these two groups, their relationship is diagrammatically shown as:

Example 7:

Wire, Copper, Rubber

Explanation:

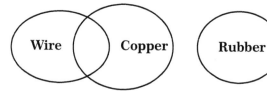

Some Wires are made of Copper but Rubber is entirely different.

Case 8:

If one item belongs to the class of second and the third item is partly related to these two, they are represented as shown:

Example 8:

Females, Mothers, Doctors

Explanation: Venn diagram is as follows :

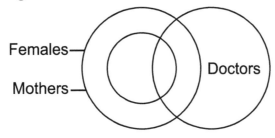

Case 9:

If one item belongs to the class of second and the third item is partly related to the second, they are represented as shown.

Example 9:

Females, Mothers, Children

Explanation:

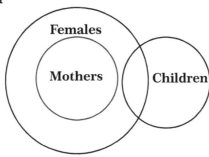

All Mothers are Females. This would be represented by two concentric circles but some females are Children but Children cannot be Mothers.

TYPE–II : Venn Diagrams formed by using different Geometrical Figures

We have used only circles to represent different relationships. Here, we will use different figures to show different relationships.

Example 10:

Which of the regions marked 1-7 represent the urban educated who are not hard working?

(a) 2 (b) 1
(c) 4 (d) 5

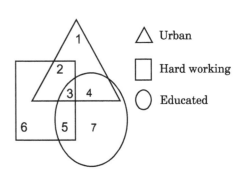

Ans: (c)

Explanation: The region which represents the urban educated who are not hard working lies outside the square but common to triangle and circle i.e. '4'.

Direction (Examples 11 and 12): Study the diagram given below and answer each of the following questions.

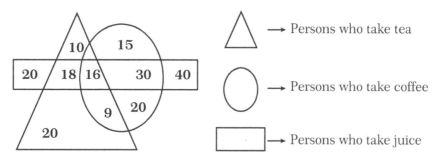

Example 11:

How many persons who take both tea and juice but not coffee?

    (a) 20   (b) 18   (c) 25   (d) 15

Ans: (b)
Explanation: 18 persons take both tea and juice but not coffee.

Example 12:

How many persons are there who take both tea and coffee but not juice?

    (a) 22   (b) 17   (c) 9   (d) 20

Ans: (c)
Explanation: Number of persons who take both tea and coffee but not juice is 9.

LEVEL-1

1. Which of the following diagrams indicates the best relation between Women, Mothers and Engineers ?

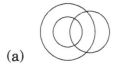 

2. Which of the following diagrams indicates the best relation between India, Haryana and World ?

3. In the figure given below, square represents doctors, triangle represents ladies and circle represents surgeon. By which letter the ladies who doctor and surgeon both are represented ?

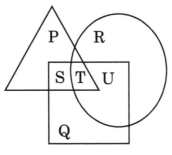

(a) U (b) T (c) S (d) P

4. Which Venn diagram represents the relation between Boys, Students, Athletes?

(a) (b) (c) (d)

5. Which Venn Diagram correctly shows the relationship between A and B?
Whereas:
A = (even numbers less than 10),
B = (odd numbers less than 10)

(a) A: 2 4 6 8   B: 5 3 1 9 7
(b) A: 1 4 6 2   B: 3 5 8 9
(c) A B: 1 2 / 3 / 4 5
(d) 5 (1 2 4 6 8 7) 3

6. In the following figure, triangle represents Boys, square represents Players and circle represents Coach. Which part of the diagram represents the Boys who are Players but not Coach?

(a) P
(b) R
(c) Q
(d) T

7. In the given figure, if Triangle represents healthy people, Rectangle represents old persons and Circle represents men. What is the number of those men who are healthy but not old?

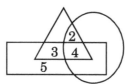

(a) 3 (b) 4 (c) 2 (d) 6

8. Select from four alternative diagrams, the one that best illustrates the relationship among the three classes : Pigeons, Birds, Dogs.

DIRECTIONS (Qs. 9 &10): Study the following diagram to answer the given questions.

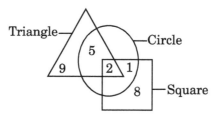

9. Find out the number, that lies inside all the figures.

   (a) 2
   (b) 5
   (c) 9
   (d) No such number is there

10. What are the numbers that lie inside any two figures only?

    (a) 2, 1   (b) 5, 1   (c) 5, 9   (d) 9, 1

DIRECTIONS (Qs. 11-13): Shivam asked a group of students which brand of cola they like: Lime or Pepsi. The results can be seen in the given Venn Diagram. Use the diagram to answer the questions.

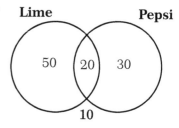

11. How many students like only Lime?

    (a) 50   (b) 20   (c) 30   (d) 10

12. How many students like both Lime and Pepsi?

    (a) 50   (b) 30   (c) 20   (d) 10

13. How many students like neither Lime nor Pepsi?

    (a) 20   (b) 10   (c) 50   (d) 30

14. Which Venn diagram best illustrates the relationship among Sea, Island and Mountain?

    (a)   (b)   (c)   (d)

15. Identify the diagram that best represents the relationship among classes given below.

    Sportsmen, Cricketers, Batsmen

    (a)   (b)   (c)   (d)

16. Given below are three figures that represent graduates, post graduates and officers. Which part represents all the officers who are graduates and post graduates?

    (a) G   (b) D   (c) B   (d) C

17. Identify the diagram that best represents the relationship among the classes given below

    Police, Thief, Criminal

    (a)   (b)   (c)   (d)

18. Read the clues to find the secret number.
    - It is not an even number
    - It is in the triangle
    - It is in the rectangle

    What number is it?

    (a) 2   (b) 4   (c) 3   (d) 5

19. In the given Venn-diagram, what does the red circle represent?

    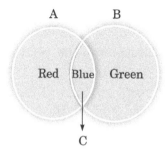

    (a) Set A (b) Set B (c) Set C (d) None of these

20. The diagram given below represents those students who play Basketball, Kho-Kho and Cricket. Study the diagram and identify the students who play all the three games.

    (a) T
    (b) S
    (c) V
    (d) S + T + V

    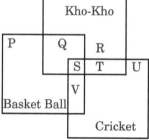

21. Study the diagram and identify the people who can speak only one language.

    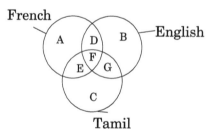

    (a) D + E + G
    (b) C + B + A
    (c) A
    (d) C

22. Which of the following statements is correct with regard to the given figure?

    (a) A and B are all in three shapes
    (b) E, A, B, C are all in three shapes
    (c) F, C, D, B, A are all in three shapes.
    (d) Only B is in all three shapes

    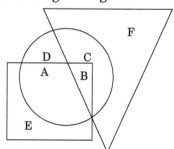

23. Identify the diagram that best represents the relationship among classes given below.
    Food, Curd, Spoons

    (a) ○○○   (b) ◯◯◯   (c) ⊚   (d) ○ ○

DIRECTIONS (Qs. 24-28): In a birthday party, pizzas, burgers and cakes are served and it is represented by the given Venn-diagram. Study the given diagram carefully and answer the following questions based on it.

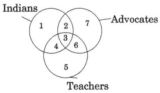

24. How many persons had cakes?
    (a) 6   (b) 6 + 3   (c) 6 + 4   (d) 6 + 2 + 3 + 4
25. How many persons had only pizzas?
    (a) 3   (b) 2   (c) 5   (d) 5 + 4
26. How many persons had both pizzas and burgers but not cakes.
    (a) 2   (b) 4   (c) 5   (d) 7
27. How many persons had cakes and pizzas but not burgers?
    (a) 3   (b) 2   (c) 4   (d) 6
28. How many persons had at least two items?
    (a) 2   (b) 3 + 2   (c) 3 + 4 + 2   (d) 3 + 4 + 2 + 4
29. Which number space indicates Indian teachers who are also advocates?

    [Venn diagram: Indians, Advocates, Teachers with numbers 1, 2, 7, 3, 4, 6, 5]

    (a) 2   (b) 3   (c) 4   (d) 6
30. In the following figure, how many educated people are employed?

    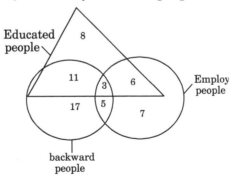

    (a) 18   (b) 20   (c) 15   (d) 9

31. Which of the following Venn diagrams best represents the relationship amongst, "Doctors, Teachers and Parents"? **(2018)**

32. Which of the following Venn diagrams best represents the relationship amongst. "Wild animals, Tiger and Wolf? **(2020)**

33. Which of the following Venn diagrams best represents the relationship amongst. "Year. Week and Month" **(2020)**

34. Which of the following Venn diagrams best represents the relationship amongst, "Furniture, Table and Wire"? **(2021)**

35. Which of the following Venn diagrams best represents the relationship amongst, "English, Hindi and Telugu"? **(2022)**

LEVEL-2

1. The diagram below shows the sports people watched. How many people watched Tennis match?
   (a) 10
   (b) 15
   (c) 20
   (d) 25

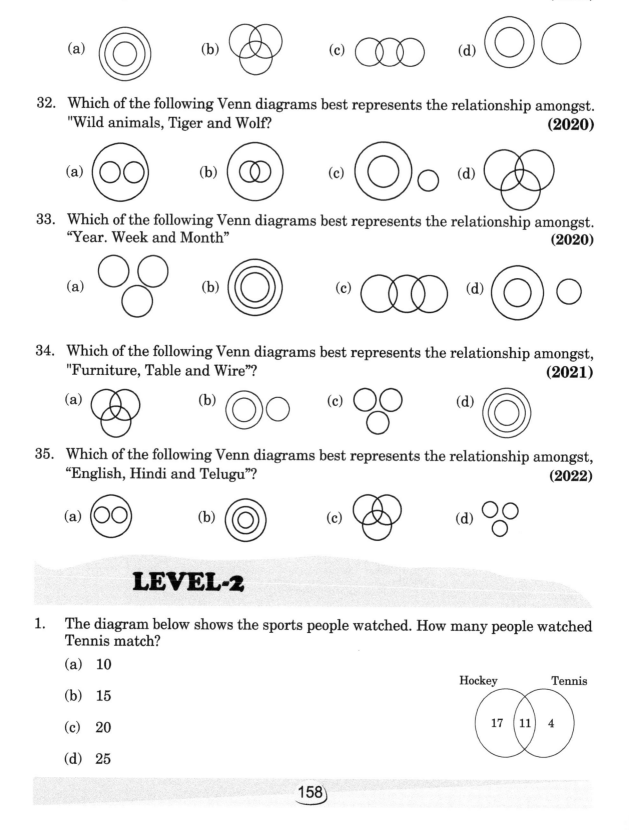

DIRECTIONS (Qs. 2 & 3): The diagrams below represent a class of children. G is the set of girls and F is the set of children who like football.

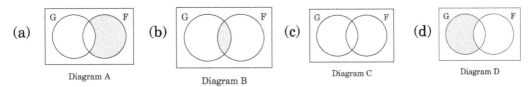

2. Which diagram has the shading which represents girls who like football?

   (a) Diagram A (b) Diagram B (c) Diagram C (d) Diagram D

3. Which diagram represents girls who dislike football?

   (a) Diagram A (b) Diagram B (c) Diagram C (d) Diagram D

4. Find out which of the diagrams given in the alternatives correctly represents the relationship stated in the question.

   Sharkes, Whales, Turtles

5. In the given diagram, Circle represents strong men, Square represents short men and Traingle represents military officers. Which region represents military officers who are short but not strong?

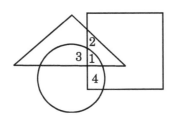

   (a) 2 (b) 3 (c) 4 (d) 1

6. Which one of the following diagrams represents the relationship among Delhi, Lucknow, Uttar Pradesh?

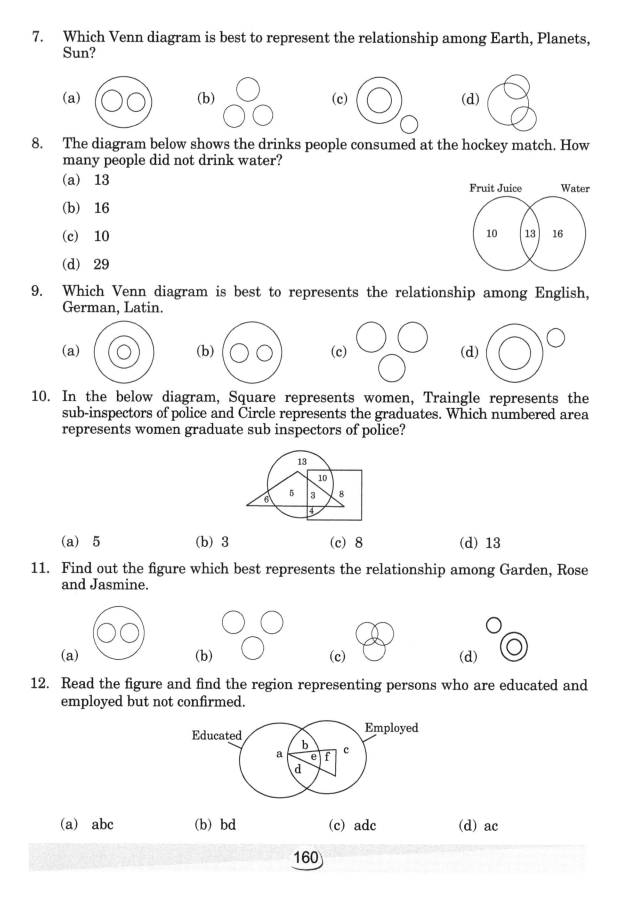

13. The Triangle stands for Hindi, Circle for French, Square for English and Rectangle for German.

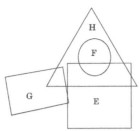

On the basis of above diagram, which of the following statements is true?

(a) All French speaking people speak German

(b) All French speaking people speak English

(c) All German speaking people speak English and Hindi

(d) All French speaking people speak Hindi also

14. The diagram below shows the pet of students in a class. How many students had a dog?

(a) 28
(b) 32
(c) 38
(d) 42

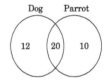

15. Which Venn diagram represents the best relation among Paper, Stationery, Ink?

16. In the given figure, circle represent students studying three different subjects. How many students study all the three subjects?

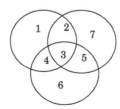

(a) 2   (b) 3   (c) 4   (d) 1

17. Identify the diagram that best represents the relationship among the classes given below:

    Liquids, Milk, River Water

    (a) 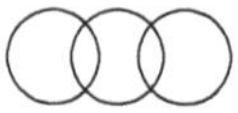   (b) 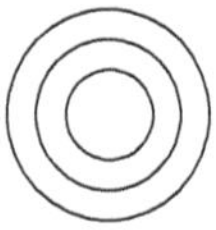   (c)    (d)

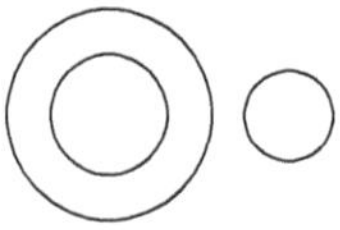

18. How many students are taking singing classes in Summer Camp?

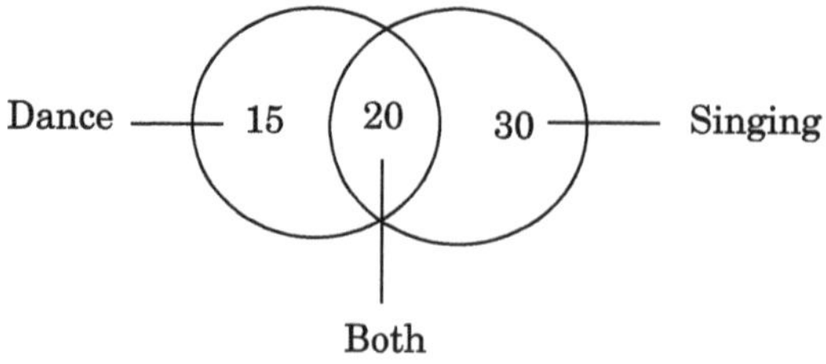

    (a) 15   (b) 20   (c) 30   (d) 50

DIRECTIONS (Qs. 19-23): Study the diagram given below and answer the following questions.

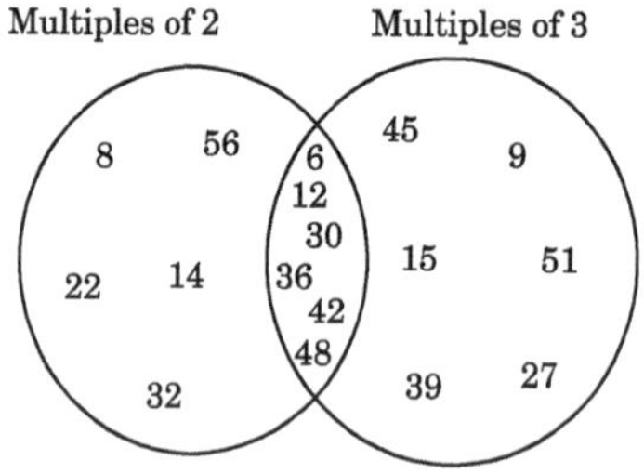

19. How many numbers are multiple of 2 only?

    (a) 5   (b) 11   (c) 6   (d) 4

20. How many numbers are multiple of 3?

    (a) 6   (b) 5   (c) 12   (d) 11

21. How many numbers are multiple of 2 and 3 both?

    (a) 5   (b) 6   (c) 11   (d) 4

22. How many numbers are not multiples of both 2 and 3?

    (a) 5   (b) 6   (c) 10   (d) 11

23. How many numbers are multiple of only 3?

    (a) 11   (b) 12   (c) 5   (d) 6

24. The diagram below show how many children took Pastries and Chocolates from a bakery shop. How many children have only chocolates?

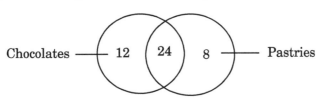

(a) 8 (b) 12 (c) 32 (d) 36

25. The diagram below shows number of men and women watching a Hockey match. How many persons are watching Hockey match?

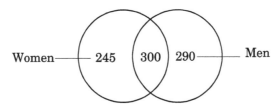

(a) 245 + 290 (b) 245 + 300 (c) 245 + 300 + 290 (d) 290 + 300

26. The diagram below shows the attributes of flowers in a flower shop. How many flowers are only Pink?

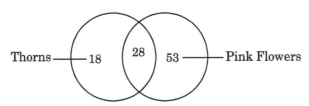

(a) 18 (b) 18 + 28 (c) 28 + 53 (d) 53

DIRECTIONS (Qs. 27 & 28): Observe the diagram carefully and answer the questions.

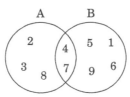

27. What are the elements of Set A?
    (a) (2, 3, 8)
    (b) (2, 3, 8, 4)
    (c) (2, 3, 8, 4, 7)
    (d) (5, 1, 9, 6)

28. What are the elements of both Set A and Set B?
    (a) (2, 3, 8, 4) (b) (4, 7)
    (c) (5, 1, 9, 6, 4, 7) (d) (2, 3, 8, 4, 7)

29. The triangle represents teachers, the circle represents singers, and the rectangle represents the guitarists. Which number in the diagram represents teachers who are also singers and guitarists?

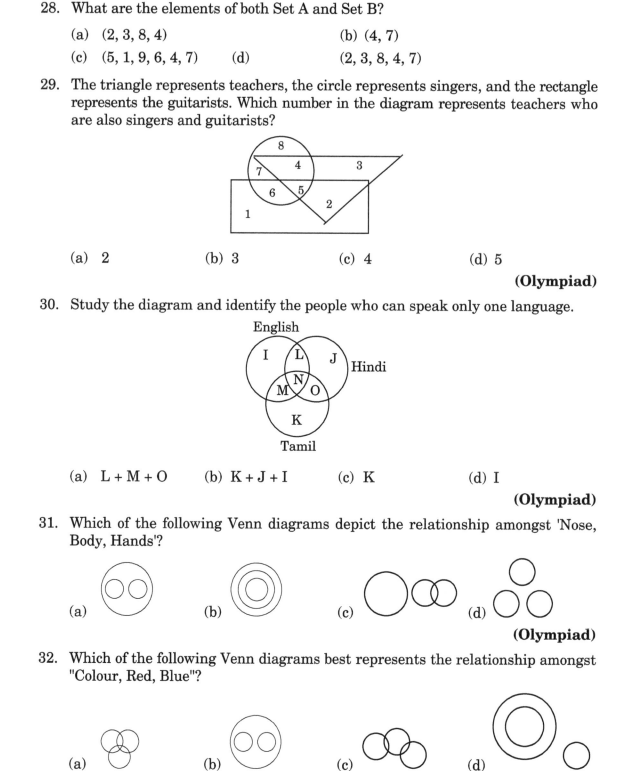

    (a) 2 (b) 3 (c) 4 (d) 5

    (Olympiad)

30. Study the diagram and identify the people who can speak only one language.

    (a) L + M + O (b) K + J + I (c) K (d) I

    (Olympiad)

31. Which of the following Venn diagrams depict the relationship amongst 'Nose, Body, Hands'?

    (a) (b) (c) (d)

    (Olympiad)

32. Which of the following Venn diagrams best represents the relationship amongst "Colour, Red, Blue"?

    (a) (b) (c) (d)

    (Olympiad)

Answers and Explanation

Level-1

1. **(a)** All mothers are women and some mothers and some women may be engineers.

   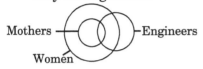

2. **(d)** Haryana is in India and India is in the World.

3. **(b)** The ladies who are both doctor and surgeon are represented by better 'T'.

4. **(c)**

   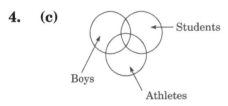

   Some boys are students.
   Some students are athletes.
   Some athletes are boys.

5. **(a)** In option (a) A represents even Numbers less than 10 and B represents odd numbers less than 10. But both are entirely different.

6. **(c)** Q is the part of the figure that represents those boys who are players but not coach.

7. **(c)** '2' is the number of those men who are healthy but not old.

8. **(a)** All Pigeons are Birds. But, Dogs are entirely different.

9. **(a)** There is only one number i.e. 2 that lies inside all the three figures.

10. **(b)** Such numbers are 5 and 1.

11. **(a)** 50 students like only lime.

12. **(c)** 20 students like both lime and Pepsi.

13. **(b)** 10 students like neither Lime nor Pepsi.

14. **(d)**

    Island is a part of sea. But Mountain is entirely different.

15. **(c)** All the batsmen are cricketers and all the cricketers are sportsmen.

    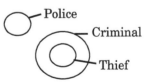

16. **(a)** The figure representing officers, who are graduates and post graduates should be covered by all three circles i.e. 'G'.

17. **(a)** Thieves are criminal but police is different.

18. **(c)** Number 3 is an odd number which lies inside both triangle and rectangle.

165

19. **(a)** Set A represents the red circle.
20. **(b)** S indicates those students who play all the three games.
21. **(b)** The regions represented by the letters C, B and A denote such people who can speak only one language.
22. **(d)** Only B is in all three shapes.
23. **(d)** Curd is a type of food but spoon is different.
24. **(d)** 6 + 2 + 3 + 4 = 15 persons had cakes.
25. **(c)** 5 persons had only pizzas.
26. **(b)** 4 persons had both pizzas and burgers but not cakes.
27. **(a)** 3 persons had cakes and pizzas but not burgers.
28. **(d)** 3 + 4 + 2 + 4 = 13 persons had at least two items.
29. **(b)** The number '3' space represents Indian teachers, who are also advocates as this number is common to given condition.
30. **(d)** 3 + 6 = 9
    So, 9 educated people are employed.
31. **(b)**
32. **(a)** Tiger and wolf both are wild animals.
33. **(b)**
34. **(b)** Table is included in furniture and wire is different from furniture.
35. **(d)** English, Hindi and Telugu all are different languages.

Level-2

1. **(b)** 11 + 4 = 15 people watched Tennis Match.
2. **(b)** In the diagram, shading region represents girls who like football.
3. **(d)** Diagram D represents girls who dislike football.
4. **(c)** Sharks belong to class Pisces. Whale is a Mammal and Turtle belongs to class Reptilia.
5. **(a)** Darken portion in below diagram represents that there are 2 military officers who are short but not strong.

   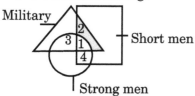

6. **(c)** Delhi is separate state while Lucknow is part of Uttar Pradesh.

   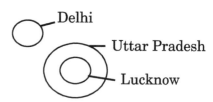

7. **(c)**

   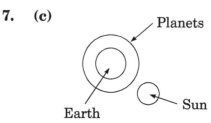

   Earth is a planet. But, Sun is entirely different.
8. **(c)** 10 people did not drink water.
9. **(c)**

   English, German and Latin are entirely different from each other.

10. **(b)** Women graduate sub-inspectors of police can be represented by the region common to all the three geometrical figures. Such region is marked as '3'.

11. **(a)** Best representation of the relationship is:

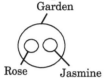

12. **(b)** The letters 'b' and 'd' are present in both the circles.

13. **(d)** Since the circle lies inside the triangle, so, all the French speaking people speak Hindi also.

14. **(b)** 12 + 20 = 32 students have dog.

15. **(d)**

Paper and Ink are entirely different. But both are items of stationery.

16. **(b)** The number '3' common to all the three subjects.

17. **(c)**

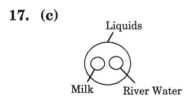

18. **(d)** Students are taking singing classes in Summer Camp = 20 + 30 = 50.

19. **(a)** 5 numbers (8, 56, 14, 22, 32) are multiples of 2.

20. **(c)** 12 numbers are multiple of 3. 12 numbers are 6, 12, 30, 36, 42, 48, 45, 9, 15, 51, 39, 27.

21. **(b)** 6 numbers (6, 12, 30, 36, 42, 48) are multiples of 2 and 3 both.

22. **(d)** Multiple of 2 only = 5 numbers (8, 14, 22, 32, 56)
Multiple of 3 only = 6 numbers (9, 15, 27, 39, 45, 51)
5 + 6 = 11 numbers are not multiples of both 2 and 3.

23. **(d)** 6 numbers are multiples of only 3.

24. **(b)** 12 children have only chocolates.

25. **(c)** 245 + 300 + 290 persons are watching Hockey match.

26. **(d)** 53 flowers are only Pink.

27. **(c)** 2, 3, 8, 4, 7 are the elements of Set A.

28. **(b)** 4, 7 are the elements of both Set A and Set B.

29. **(d)** Number '5' represent teachers who are also singers and guitarists.

30. **(b)** K, J and I the people who can speak only one language.

31. **(a)**

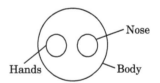

Nose and hands both are the body parts.

32. **(b)**

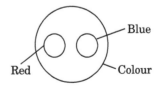

Both red and blue are colours.

CHAPTER 10

Problem Solving

OBJECTIVES

- Students will develop the ability to understand what the goal of the problem is and what rules could be applied that represent the key to solving the problem.
- They will develop abstract thinking and creative approach.

INTRODUCTION

The process of working through details of a problem to reach a solution is called problem solving. It may include mathematical or systematic operations and can be a gauge of an individual's critical thinking skills.

FOUR STAGES OF PROBLEM SOLVING

Stage 1 : Understand and explore the problem;

Stage 2 : Find a strategy;

Stage 3 : Use the strategy to solve the problem;

Stage 4 : Look back and reflect on the solution.

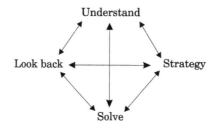

Example 1:

Four families P, Q, R and S are living in houses in a row. Q has P and S as neighbours. S has Q and R as heighbours. Who lives next to P?

   (a) P   (b) Q   (c) R   (d) S

Ans. (b)

Explanation: The information can be represented as:

P   Q   S   R

So, Q lives next to P.

DIRECTIONS (Examples 2 & 3) : Read the given information and answer the following questions.

Four friends Ronit, Akhil, Manan and Sanam like to play four different sports namely Hockey, Tennis, Cricket and Football but not in the same order. Ronit likes neither Tennis nor Hockey. Akhil likes to play Cricket. Manan does not like to play Tennis.

2. Which sport is played by Ronit?
   (a) Hockey   (b) Football   (c) Cricket   (d) Tennis
3. Who plays Tennis as it is his favourite sport?
   (a) Sanam   (b) Manan   (c) Ronit   (d) Akhil

Ans. (Qs. 2-3)

Explanation: The arrangement of four friends is as following :

Friends	Ronit	Akhil	Manan	Sanam
Sports	Football	Cricket	Hockey	Tennis

2. (b) Ronit plays Football.
3. (a) Tennis is Sanam's favourite sport.

Example 4:

Four people are standing in a queue outside the ATM for cash withdrawal. The two persons standing at the extreme ends are Ritesh and Abhay. Anisha is front of Abhay. Ritu is standing behind Ritesh.

Counting from the front, at which place is Anisha?

(a) First   (b) Second
(c) Third   (d) Fourth

Ans. (a)

Explanation: The arrangement of four people in a queue is as follows :

ATM

1 → Ritesh

2 → Ritu

3 → Anisha

4 → Abhay

So, Anisha is at third place counting from front.

DIRECTIONS (Examples 5-8): Read the information given below carefully and answer the following questions. A, B, C, D, E, F and G are sitting in a row facing north.

- A is sitting at the right end and G is sitting at the left end.
- F is at the immediate right of E.
- E is 4th to the right of G.
- C is the neighbour of B and D.
- D is third to the left of A.

Example 5:
Who is/are to the left of C?

(a) Only B   (b) G, B and D   (c) G and B   (d) D, E, F and A

Ans. (c)

Explanation:

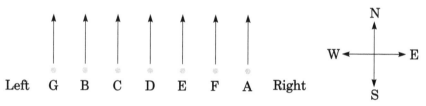

G and B are to the left of C.

Example 6:
Which of the following statements is not true?

(a) A is at one of the ends.
(b) E is to the immediate left of D.
(c) G is at one of the ends.
(d) F is sitting between E and A.

Ans. (b)

Explanation:

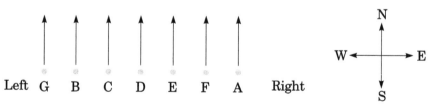

Option (b) is not correct as,
E is to the immediate right of D.

Example 7:
Who are the neighbours of B?

(a) C and D   (b) G and F   (c) C and G   (d) C and E

Ans. (c)

Explanation:

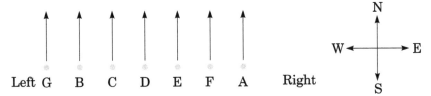

C and G are the neighbours of B.

Example 8:

What is the position of D?

(a) Between B and C (b) Extreme left
(c) Centre (d) Extreme right

Ans. (c)

Explanation:

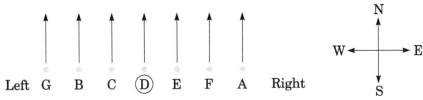

D is in Centre.

LEVEL-1

1. Four friends in the sixth grade were sharing a pizza. They decided that the oldest friend would get the extra piece. Roshni is two months older than Garima, who is three months younger than Niya. Karisma is one month older than Garima. Who should get the extra piece of pizza?

    (a) Garima (b) Niya (c) Karisma (d) Roshni

2. The high school Math department needs to appoint a new chairperson, which will be based on seniority. Ms. Sunita has less seniority than Mr. Rakesh, but more than Ms. Babita. Mr. Suresh has more seniority than Ms. Sunita, but less than Mr. Rakesh. Mr. Rakesh doesn't want the job. Who will be the new Math deparment chairperson?

    (a) Ms. Babita (b) Mr. Rakesh (c) Mr. Suresh (d) Ms. Sunita

3. A blacksmith has three iron articles A, B and C, each having a different weight.
    - A weighs twice as much as C.
    - B weighs half as much as C.

Which of the following represents the descending order of weighs of the articles?

(a) A, B, C (b) B, A, C (c) A, C, B (d) C, A, B

4. Tanni broke half as many balloons as Ritika. Altogether they broke 18 balloons. Ritika broke 12 balloons. How many balloons did Tanni break?

(a) 9 (b) 8 (c) 10 (d) 6

5. There are five buses M,N,O,P and Q in a row on a road. Bus M is standing at the front and Q is standing at the back end. Bus N stands between M and O. Bus P stands between O and Q. Which bus is in the middle of the five?

(a) M (b) P (c) N (d) O

DIRECTIONS (Qs. 6 & 7): Study the given information carefully and answer the questions.

- There are four friends A, B, C and D.
- Each one is proficient in one of the games, namely: Badminton, Volleyball, Cricket and Hockey.
- D Plays Hockey.
- C does not play either Badminton or Cricket.
- A does not play Cricket.

6. Who plays cricket?

(a) A (b) B (c) C (d) D

7. Which game is played by C?

(a) Hockey (b) Badminton (c) Cricket (d) Volleyball

8. There are three separate large black boxes, and inside each large box there are two separate small red boxes, inside each of these small boxes, there is one smaller blue box. How many boxes are there altogether?

(a) 9 (b) 12 (c) 15 (d) 18

9. There are five friends- Sachin, Kamal, Mohan, Arun and Raj. Sachin is shorter than Kamal, but taller than Raj. Mohan is the tallest. Arun is a little shorter than Kamal and a little taller than Sachin. Who is the second tallest?

(a) Raj (b) Sachin (c) Kamal (d) Arun

10. Five students are standing in a circle. Abhinav is between Alok and Ankur. Apurva is on the left of Abhishek. Alok is on the left of Apurva. Who is sitting next to Abhinav on his right?

(a) Apurva (b) Ankur (c) Abhishek (d) Alok

DIRECTIONS (Qs. 11-13): Read the given information carefully and answer the following questions.

Five children are standing in line waiting for the ice-cream shop to open.

- Shivam is in the exact middle of the line.
- Raj is directly behind Shubam.

- Abhay is not first or last.
- Kavya is on the first.

11. Who is standing at last?
    (a) Abhay (b) Raj (c) Shivam (d) Kavya
12. Who is standing between Shivam and Raj?
    (a) Kavya (b) Abhay (c) Shubam (d) None of these
13. What is the correct order of line?
    (a) Kavya ← Shubam ← Shivam ← Raj ← Abhay
    (b) Kavya ← Abhay ← Shivam ← Shubam ← Raj
    (c) Kavya ← Raj ← Shivam ← Abhay ← Shubam
    (d) Kavya ← Raj ← Shivam ← Shubam ← Abhay

DIRECTIONS (Qs. 14 & 15) Read the following information carefully to answer the questions given below.

(i) Kapil, Mohit and Happy are intelligent.
(ii) Kapil, Ravi and Jitesh are hard-working.
(iii) Ravi, Happy and Jitesh are honest.
(iv) Kapil, Mohit and Jitesh are ambitious.

14. Which of the following persons is neither hard-working nor ambitious?
    (a) Kapil (b) Mohit (c) Happy (d) Jitesh
15. Which of the following persons is neither honest nor hard-working but is ambitious?
    (a) Jitesh (b) Mohit (c) Happy (d) Ravi
16. Paresh started with 32 baseball cards. He sold 8 cards. Then he bought 12 more. How many cards does he have now?
    (a) 36 (b) 40 (c) 24 (d) 30
17. Rani's desk is in the third row from the front and the second row from the back of classroom. The desks in the classroom are lined up in straight rows. Her desk is also the third from the left and first from the right. How many desks are there?
    (a) 9 desks (b) 12 desks (c) 15 desks (d) 16 desks

DIRECTIONS (Qs. 18 & 19): Four boys took part in a race. Raj finished before Mohit but behind Gaurav. Ashish finished behind Mohit.

18. Who won the race?
    (a) Raj (b) Mohit (c) Gaurav (d) Ashish

19. Who was on the second position?
    (a) Raj (b) Gaurav (c) Mohit (d) Ashish
20. If A * B means A and B are of the same age; A – B means B is younger than A; then Vijay * Saurabh – Reena means?
    (a) Reena is the youngest
    (b) Reena is the oldest
    (c) Reena is younger than Saurabh
    (d) None of these

DIRECTIONS (Qs. 21-22): Read the information given below carefully and answer the following questions.

Six students A, B, C, D, E and F are sitting in the field. A and B are form Nehru House while the rest belong to Gandhi House. D and F are tall while the others are short. A, C and D are wearing glasses while the others are not.

21. Which two students, who are not wearing glasses are short?
    (a) A and F (b) C and E (c) B and E (d) E and F
22. Which short student of Gandhi House is not wearing glasses?
    (a) F (b) E (c) B (d) A

LEVEL-2

DIRECTIONS (Qs. 1-3): Study the information carefully to answer the questions given below.

In a school, there were five teachers P,Q,R,S and T. P and Q were teaching Hindi and English. R and Q were teaching English and Geography. S and P were teaching Mathematics and Hindi. T and Q were teaching History and French.

1. Who among the following teachers was teaching maximum number of subjects?
    (a) P (b) Q (c) R (d) T
2. Which subject/subjects was/were taught by more than two teachers?
    (a) English
    (b) History
    (c) Hindi
    (d) Both (a) and (c)
3. S,Q and P were teaching which of the following common subject/subjects?
    (a) Hindi only
    (b) English only
    (c) Hindi and English
    (d) English and Geography
4. Six friends Ansh, Raj, Dev, Vinay, Raghav and Amit met up to go bowling together and then split into 2 teams, three in each. If Ansh, Dev and Amit were in one team, who did they play against?
    (a) Ansh, Raj and Vinay
    (b) Dev, Vinay and Raghav
    (c) Dev, Raghav and Ansh
    (d) Raj, Vinay and Raghav

5. There are five different houses A to E in a row. A is right of B and E is to the left of C and right to A, B is to the right of D. Which of the houses is in the middle?
    (a) C (b) B (c) A (d) E
6. Five boys took part in a race. Raj finished before Mehul but behind Garv. Ashish finished before Shabd but behind Mehul. Who won the race?
    (a) Raj (b) Mehul (c) Garv (d) Shabd
7. Five men A, B, C, D and E read newspaper. The one who reads first gives it to C. The one who reads last had taken from A. E was not the first or last to read. There were two readers between B and A.

    Who read the newspaper last?

    (a) A (b) D (c) E (d) C

DIRECTIONS (Qs. 8-10) : Read the given information carefully and answer the following questions.

Five boys are sitting on a bench facing north. Avi is to the left of Aarav and right of Nikunj. Vipul is sitting on the right end. Atul is between Aarav and Vipul.

8. Who is in sitting in the middle?
    (a) Avi (b) Aarav (c) Nikunj (d) Vipul
9. Who is second from right?
    (a) Avi (b) Vipul (c) Aarav (d) Atul
10. What is the position of Avi in sitting arrangement?
    (a) Second form left (b) Second from right
    (c) Fourth from left (d) In the middle
11. Four girls Rishima, Manvi, Piyali and Shifali are standing in a single line facing north. Manvi and Rishima are standing to the left of Piyali and there are two girls standing between Manvi and Shifali. Who is standing at the extreme right position?
    (a) Piyali (b) Shifali (c) Rishima (d) Manvi
12. In a shop, the items were arranged in a shelf consisting of six rows. Biscuits are arranged above the tins of chocolates but below the rows of packets of chips, cakes are at the bottom and the bottles of peppermints are below the chocolates. The topmost row had the display of jam bottles.

    Where exactly are the bottles of peppermints? Mention the place from the top.

    (a) 2nd (b) 3rd (c) 4th (d) 5th

DIRECTIONS (Qs. 13-15): Study the following information to answer the questions.

There are six cities A, B, C, D, E and F.

A is not a hill station.

B and E are not historical places.

D is not an industrial city.

A and D are not historical cities.

A and B are not alike.

13. Which two cities are industrial centres?
    (a) A and B   (b) E and F   (c) C and D   (d) B and F
14. Which city is a hill station and an industrial centre but not a historical places?
    (a) E   (b) F   (c) A   (d) B
15. Which two cities are neither historical places nor industrial centres?
    (a) A and B   (b) D and E   (c) F and C   (d) B and D
16. On a trip there are 11 children and 1 adult per boat. If a total of 96 people went on this boat trip, how many children were there?
    (a) 85   (b) 86   (c) 88   (d) 90
17. Compare the knowledge of persons X, Y, Z, A, B and C in relation to each other. X knows more than A, Y knows as much as B. Z know less than C. A knows more than Y. The best knowledgeable person amongst all is:
    (a) C
    (b) X
    (c) A
    (d) Cannot be determined
18. I-Gmail runs faster than Yahoo.
    II-Hotmail runs faster than Gmail.
    III-Yahoo runs faster than Hotmail.
    If the first two statements are true, the third statement is _____.
    (a) True   (b) False   (c) Uncertain   (d) None of these
19. I. Preeti is taller than Megha.
    II. Meet is taller than Megha.
    III. Preeti is taller than Meet.
    If the first two statements are true, the third statement is _____.
    (a) True   (b) False   (c) Uncertain   (d) None of these

DIRECTIONS (Qs. 20-23): Read the given statements carefully and answer the following questions.

Seven boys A, B, C, D, E, F, and G live on seven floors – Ground, 1st, 2nd, 3rd, 4th, 5th and 6th (Top), not necessarily in that order. A lives just above B's floor. F lives at top floor. E lives in between B's and C's floor. D lives just above the A's floor. G lives on the ground floor and E lives on the second floor.

20. Who lives on the first floor?
    (a) B   (b) C   (c) E   (d) D

21. Who lives on the second floor?
    (a) F   (b) C   (c) E   (d) A
22. Who lives on the third floor?
    (a) B   (b) C   (c) F   (d) G
23. Who lives on the fourth floor?
    (a) D   (b) F   (c) A   (d) E
24. If Rohan works on all Saturday and the dates which are multiples of 5 considered as holiday, then how many days are working? (Assume that Sunday is holiday.) **(Olympiad)**

February						
S	M	T	W	T	F	S
					1	2
3	4	5	6	7	8	9
10	11	12	13	14	15	16
17	18	19	20	21	22	23
24	25	26	27	28		

    (a) 24   (b) 21   (c) 19   (d) 20
25. Mohit is taller than Rohit but shorter than Samay. Rohit is shorter than Anil but taller than Raghu. Who among them is the shortest with respect to height? **(Olympiad)**
    (a) Anil   (b) Rohit   (c) Raghu   (d) Mohit
26. Latika forgets the code of three alphabets (A, I, T) to open her locker. How many different combinations of letters, she could try to unlock her locker? **(Olympiad)**
    (a) 8   (b) 12   (c) 6   (d) 9
27. Amit celebrates his birthday on third Saturday of July 20XX. The date after birthday will be _____ **(Olympiad)**

August 20XX						
S	M	T	W	T	F	S
			1	2	3	4
5	6	7	8	9	10	11
12	13	14	15	16	17	18
19	20	21	22	23	24	25
26	27	28	29	30	31	

    (a) 19th (b) 21th (c) 22th (d) 20th

28. What is the product of all the numbers in the number pad of a telephone?

(Olympiad)
   (a) 362880   (b) 358420   (c) 294870   (d) None of these

29. Four darts were thrown at a dartboard as shown below. All four darts landed on the dartboard. Which of the following is NOT a possible score?

(Olympiad)

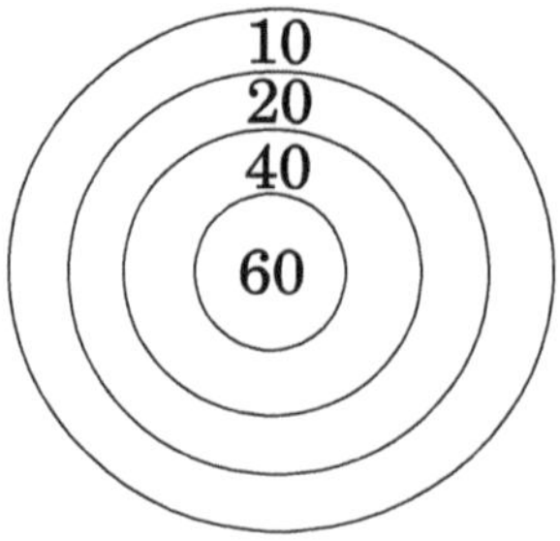

   (a) 80   (b) 90   (c) 130   (d) 210

30. Five girls took part in a race. Beena finished before Priya but behind Latika. Garima finished before Zarrin but behind Priya. Who won the race?

(Olympiad)
   (a) Beena   (b) Garima   (c) Latika   (d) Priya

31. Read the following information carefully and answer the question that follows.
   (i) Virat likes playing cricket and hockey.   **(2020)**
   (ii) Mohit likes playing football and hockey.
   (iii) Sandeep likes playing hockey, cricket and football.
   Which sport is liked by most number of boys?
   (a) Cricket   (b) Hockey
   (c) Football   (d) Can't be determined

32. Read the given information carefully and answer the question that follows.

   (2021)
   (i) Aanya likes chocolate and mango ice-creams but not butterscotch ice-cream.
   (ii) Shanaya likes mango and butterscotch ice-creams but not vanilla ice-cream.
   (iii) Manya likes mango and vanilla ice-creams but not chocolate ice-cream.
   (iv) Kavya does not like butterscotch ice-cream.
   Which ice-cream is liked by most of the girls among four?
   (a) Chocolate   (b) Mango   (c) Vanilla   (d) Butterscotch

Answers and Explanation

Level-1

1. **(b)** If Roshni is two months older than Garima, then Niya is three months older than Garima and one month older than Roshni. Karisma is younger than both Roshni and Niya. Niya is the oldest.

2. **(c)** Here, according to the given information,
   Mr. Rakesh > Mr. Suresh > Ms. Sunita > Ms. Babita
   So, Mr. Rakesh has the most seniority, but he does not want the job. Next in line is Mr. Suresh, who has more seniority than Ms. Sunita or Ms. Babita.

3. **(c)** Descending order of weight is A > C > B

4. **(d)** Number of balloons broken by Ritika and Tanni = 18
   Number of balloons broken by Tanni = $12 \times \dfrac{1}{2} = 6$

5. **(d)** Bus O is in the middle of the five as shown below.

(Qs. 6 & 7)

Friends	Games
A	Badminton
B	Cricket
C	Volleyball
D	Hockey

6. **(b)** B plays cricket.
7. **(d)** C plays volleyball.

8. **(c)** 3 + 6 + 6 = 15

   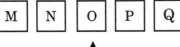

9. **(c)** According to the question,
   Mohan > Kamal > Sachin > Raj ....(i)
   Kamal > Arun > Sachin ....(ii)
   From equs. (i) and (ii),
   Mohan > Kamal > Arun > Sachin > Raj
   So, Kamal is the second tallest.

10. **(d)** On the basis of given information, the sitting arrangement is as following:

    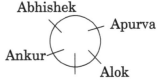

    So, Alok is sitting next to Abhinav on his right.

Solutions: (11-13)

```
          Ice-cream Shop
       ← Kavya   1
       ← Abhay   2
       ← Shivam  3
       ← Shubam  4
       ← Raj     5
```

11. **(b)** Raj is standing at last.
12. **(c)** Shubam is standing between Shivam and Raj.
13. **(b)**

179

SOLUTIONS (Qs. 14 & 15)
Table

	Intelligent	Hard working	Honest	Ambitious
Kapil	✓	✓	✗	✓
Mohit	✓	✗	✗	✓
Happy	✓	✗	✓	✗
Ravi	✗	✓	✓	✗
Jitesh	✗	✓	✓	✓

14. (c) From the above table, we find that Happy is neither hard-working nor Ambitious. Hence, option (c) is correct.

15. (b) From the above table, we find that Mohit is neither honest nor hard-working, but is ambitious. Hence, option (b) is correct.

16. (a) Total number of baseball cards = 32

Number of cards sold = 8

Number of cards after selling = 32 − 8 = 24

Number of cards Paresh bought = 12

Total number of cards Paresh has now = 24 + 12 = 36.

17. (b)

1	2	3
2		
3			→ Rani's Desk
Left 4			Right

Hence, there are 12 desks in the classroom.

Solutions (Qs. 18 & 19)

Gaurav > Raj > Mohit > Ashish
 (I)   (II)   (III)   (IV)

18. (c) Gaurav won the race.

19. (a) Raj was on the second position.

20. (a) Vijay and Saurabh are of the same age and Reena is younger than Saurabh.

SOLUTIONS (Qs. 21 & 22)

We may prepare a table as under :

	Nehru House	Gandi House	Tall	Short	Glasses	No glasses
A	X			X	X	
B	X			X		X
C		X			X	
D		X	X		X	
E		X		X		X
F		X	X			X

21. (c) B and E are short and not wearing glasses.

22. (b) E belongs to Gandhi House, is short and does not wear glasses.

Level-2

(Q.1-3): The arrangement is as follows:

Teachers → Subjects	P	Q	R	S	T
Hindi	✓	✓	✗	✓	✗
English	✓	✓	✓	✗	✗
Mathematics	✓	✗	✗	✓	✗
History	✗	✓	✗	✗	✓
French	✗	✓	✗	✗	✓
Geography	✗	✓	✓	✗	✗

1. **(b)** Q is teaching maximum number of subjects.
2. **(d)** Hindi and English are taught by more than two teachers.
3. **(a)** Teachers S, Q and P teach the Hindi subject only.
4. **(d)** Team 1 : Ansh, Dev, Amit
   Team 2 : Raj, Vinay, Raghav.
5. **(c)** Houses' sequence in a row:

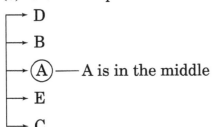

6. **(c)**

   Garv > Raj > Mehul > Ashish > Shabd.
   (1)   (2)   (3)   (4)   (5)

   So, Garv won the race.

7. **(b)** Readers, Position

Position	Readers
I	B
II	C
III	E
IV	A
V	D

So, D reads the newspaper last.

Solutions: (8-10)

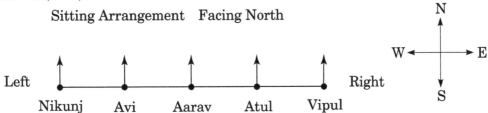

8. **(b)**
9. **(d)**
10. **(a)**

11. (b) The arrangement is as follows:

From the above arrangement it is clear that Shifali is standing at the extreme right position.

12. (d) The sequence from top to bottom is :

Jam bottles	Chips	Biscuits	Chocolates	Peppermint	Cakes
1	2	3	4	5	6

(Qs. 13-15)

The given information can be analysed as follows :

	A	B	C	D	E	F
Historical	✗	✗	✓	✗	✗	✓
Industrial	✓	✗	✓	✗	✓	✓
Hill Stations	✗	✓	✓	✓	✓	✓

13. (b) Since A and B are not alike and because A is industrial, B cannot be industrial but only a hill station. So, we put a cross for B across industrial.

Clearly, A, C, E, and F are industrial centres. So, the answer is (b).

14. (a) Since A and B are not alike and because A is industrial, B cannot be industrial but only a hill station. So, we put a cross for B across industrial.

E alone is a Hill station and an industrial centre but not a Historical place. So, the answer is (a).

15. (d) Since A and B are not alike and because A is industrial, B cannot be industrial but only a hill station.

So, we put a cross for B across industrial.

B and D are neither Historical places nor Industrial centres. So, the answer is (d).

16. (c) Total people per boat
= 11 + 1 = 12
Total people on trip = 96
Boats required for 96 people
= 96 ÷ 12 = 8
There were 8 adults
96 – 8 = 88 children.

17. (d) X > A, Y = B
C > Z, X > A > Y = B
But we do not know the position of C and Z in relation to others. So, (d) is the answer.

18. (b) Statement I:
Gmail > Yahoo,
Statement II:
Hotmail > Gmail
Combining I & II:
Hotmail > Gmail > Yahoo.
Therefore, the third statement is false.

19. (c) Statement I :
Preeti > Megha
Statement II :
Meet > Megha

Statement III :
Preeti > Meet (uncertain).

(Qs. 20-23):

Floor Arrangement

Floor	Owner
6th (Top)	F
5th	D
4th	A
3rd	B
2nd	E
1st	C
Ground	G

20. **(b)** C lives on the first floor.
21. **(c)** E lives on the second floor.
22. **(a)** B lives on the third floor.
23. **(c)** A lives on the fourth floor.

(Q. 24-30):

24. **(d)** If Rohan works on all Saturdays and the dates which are multiples of 5 are considered as holidays, then 20 days are working.

25. **(c)** According to the information:
    Samay > Mohit > Rohit ......(i)
    Anil > Rohit > Raghu .....(ii)
    From equations (i) and (ii), we get
    Samay > Mohit > Anil > Rohit > Raghu
    So, Raghu is the shortest with respect to hight.

26. **(c)** There are 6 combinations of letters A, I, T, ie,
    A I T   I A T   T I A
    A T I   I T A   T A I

27. **(c)**

July 20XX						
S	M	T	W	T	F	S
1	2	3	4	5	6	7
8	9	10	11	12	13	14
15	16	17	18	19	20	21 third saturday
22	23	24	25	26	27	28
29	30	31				

The date after his birthday will be 22nd.

28. **(d)** Since one of the numbers on the pad of a telephone is 0, so, the product of all the numbers on it is 0.

29. **(d)** As, 80 = 60 + 20
    90 = 60 + 20 + 10
    and 130 = 60 + 40 + 20 + 10.
    So, 210 is not a possible score.

30. **(c)** According to the given information:
    Latika > Beena > Priya ..... (i)
    and Priya > Garima > zarrin .....(ii)
    Combining both equations we get :
    Latika > Beena > Priya > Garima > Zarrin
    From the above equation, we can say that Latika won the race.

31. **(b)** Hockey is liked by all the three boys Virat, Mohit and Sandeep.

32. **(b)** Mango ice-cream is liked by all the girls.

CHAPTER 11

Estimation

OBJECTIVES
- Students will be able to generate a range of possible outcomes.
- They will be able to judge the size, amount and cost of given things.

INTRODUCTION

Estimation is a rough calculation of the value, number, quantity, or extent of something.

Example 1:

Mandeep walks the following distance each day of the week. Estimate the total distance that he walks.

Monday	Tuesday	Wednesday	Thurseay	Friday	Saturday	Sunday
4.5 km	3.5 km	1.5 km	2 km	4 km	5 km	6.5 km

  (a) 25   (b) 27   (c) 30   (d) 35

Ans. (b)

Explanation: The total distance = 4.5 + 3.5 + 1.5 + 2 + 4 + 5 + 6.5 = 27 km.

Example 2:

Estimate 2,342 + 738. Round to the hundred place.
  (a) 3180   (b) 3200   (c) 3100   (d) 3191

Ans. (c)

Explanation: Round each number to the nearest whole numbers

$$2{,}342 + 738$$
$$\downarrow \quad\quad \downarrow$$
$$2300 + 700 = 3100$$

Example 3:

How many 250 ml cartons of milk would it take to fill the 1 l carton?
  (a) 2   (b) 3   (c) 4   (d) 5

Ans. (c)

Explanation:

```
250 ml    +    250 ml      250 ml    +    250 ml
|_____|             |_____|
     500 ml         +            500 ml
     |_____|
              1000 ml  =   1 l
```

Example 4:

Mr. Gautam had 396 crayons left over at the end of the year. He's putting them in bags to send home with the kids. He has 20 students in his class. About how many crayons will each student get?

    (a) 20   (b) 30   (c) 40   (d) 25

Ans. (a)

Explanation: 396 is close to 400. 20 is already a friendly number.

$400 \div 20 = 20$, so each student will get about 20 crayons.

Example 5:

Ben had 2 boxes of blocks

- Each box had 50 blocks
- He built a tower with $\frac{1}{5}$ of the blocks out of each of the boxes.

How many blocks did Ben use to build the tower?

    (a) 50   (b) 40   (c) 30   (d) 20

Ans. (d)

Explanation: Each box had = 50 blocks

$$2 \text{ boxes had} = 50 \times 2 = 100 \text{ blocks}$$
$$\text{Ben used } \frac{1}{5} \text{ of blocks} = 100 \times \frac{1}{5} = 20 \text{ blocks.}$$

LEVEL-1

1. How many 500 mL cartons of water would it take to fill the 3.5 L carton?

    (a) 5   (b) 6   (c) 7   (d) 8

2. What is the probability of pulling a heart from a deck of 52 cards?

    (a) 2/3   (b) 1/4   (c) 3/8   (d) 3/4

3. Nimisha is learning metric unit of length. She wrote following sentences in her notebook. Write True/false (T/F) for the following sentences.
   - There are 100 centimeters in a metre.
   - There are 100 metres in a kilometre.
   - Centimetre is larger unit than kilometre.
   - Metre is smaller unit than centimetre.

   (a) TFTF   (b) FFFT   (c) TFFF   (d) FTFT

4. Mridula has written following statements about the metric unit she would use to measure the same objects. Find the incorrect sentence among the following sentences:

   P : Centimetre is used to measure the length of a pencil.
   Q : Kilometer is used to measure distance from one city to another.
   R : Kilogram is used to measure depth of a bucket.
   S : Metre is used to measure height of a tree.

   (a) Q   (b) R   (c) S   (d) P

5. If the cost of 1 litre of a cough syrup is ₹ 480.40, find the cost of 500 ml?

   (a) ₹ 240.40   (b) ₹ 280.40   (c) ₹ 240.10   (d) ₹ 240.20

6. What is the probability of picking a vowel from the word **EXPERIMENT**?

   (a) 3 / 10   (b) 1 / 5   (c) 1/ 10   (d) 2 / 5

7. Find the lightest set.

   250 grams   400 grams

   (a)   (b)   (c)   (d)

DIRECTIONS (Qs. 8-10): Balance the equation by choosing the correct estimated solution.

8. Each ▭ stands for 10g. Find the mass of three ▭.

   (a) 10g   (b) 30g   (c) 60g   (d) 120g

9.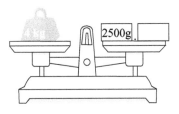

(a) 1kg (b) 2kg (c) 1500g (d) 1000g

10.

He bought _____ more apples than strawberries.
(a) 2 (b) 4 (c) 6 (d) 8

11. Rohit is comparing some objects. He wrote some sentences. Write true/false (T/F) for them.

    M : Sofa is heavier than chair.

    N : Towel is lighter than paper.

    O : Shoe box is heavier than shoes.

    P : Gas stove is lighter than gas cylinder.

    (a) TFFT (b) FTTF (c) TFFF (d) FFTF

12. Estimate the correct weight to balance the scale.

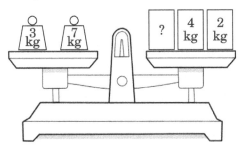

(a) 5 kg (b) 4 kg (c) 6 kg (d) 2 kg

13. Estimate the correct weight for balancing the weight/scale.

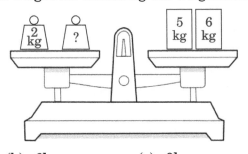

(a) 8kg (b) 6kg (c) 9kg (d) None of these

14. Find the value of 1 □ ?
    (a) 10 (b) 20 (c) 30 (d) 40

15. One circle weights _____
    (a) 3g (b) 2g (c) 4g (d) 1g

16. Estimate the product. Read each number to its greatest place value, then multiply
    8.8 × 52
    (a) 450 (b) 500 (c) 400 (d) 550

17. This comb is about 12 buttons long. About how many toothpicks long is this comb?
    (a) 4 (b) 6 (c) 8 (d) 10

18. If the cup is full, the coffee in the cup weighs as much as _____ marbles.
    (a) 8 (b) 9 (c) 16 (d) 18

19. Ratnakar has written some statements about length and height of some objects. Write true/false (T/F) for the sentences.
    M : Length of a bed is more than 1 litre.
    N : Height of a new born baby is more than 1 metre.
    O : Height of a sofa is less than 1 centimetre.
    P : Height of a school is less than 1 km.
    (a) FTTF (b) TFFT (c) FFFT (d) FFTF

20. A pineapple weighs 1 kg 200 g. How many pineapples would weigh 3 kg 600 g?
    (a) 1 (b) 2 (c) 3 (d) 4

21. Consider the statement which option must be true.
    Statement : R = L + H
    (a) H + L = R
    (b) H+ R = L
    (c) R – H = L
    (d) None of the above

22. If you roll a 6-sided dice, what is the probability of rolling a four?
    (a) 1/2 (b) 1/4 (c) 1/8 (d) 1/6

23. Diya's aunty has made a list of objects with their weights. Find the incorrect statement of the following:
    P : Weight of a mug full of coffee is about 450 gm.
    Q : Weight of a thread roll is about 2 kg
    R : Weight of a letter is about 5 g.
    S : Weight of a pair of Chappals is about 200 gm.
    (a) S (b) R (c) Q (d) P

24. Mitali bought a 50 litre container of oil. She used 44 litres 300 ml of it. How much oil is left?
    (a) 5L700 ml (b) 6L700 ml (c) 5L300 ml (d) None of these

25. What is the weight of big strawberry?
    (a) 3 g (b) 4 gm (c) 6 gm (d) 8 g

26. A bottle holds 1 litre of apple juice. Raj fills 5 glasses with apple juice. He puts 150 ml in each glass. How much apple juice is left in the bottle?
    (a) 150 ml (b) 250 ml (c) 350 ml (d) 750 ml

27. Balu's Toy Shop bought 91 bags of marbles. There were 314 marbles in each bag. About how many marbles did Balu's Toy Shop buy? Estimate the value.
    (a) 28500 (b) 26000 (c) 25000 (d) 27000

28. Tushar wrote some sentences about weight of some people. Write true/false for the following:

    M : Weight of new born baby is 100 kg.

    N : Weight of a man is about 7 g.

    O : Weight of a girl is about 1000 kg.

    P : Weight of a woman is about 55 kg.

    (a) TFFF (b) FFFT (c) FFTF (d) FTFF

29.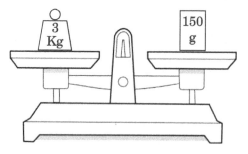

    The scales are to be balanced

    How many times 150 g weight does Simran need to put on the right side to balance these scales?

    (a) 10 (b) 15 (c) 20 (d) 25

30. Each fence post is five inches wide. How wide is the fence in the picture?

    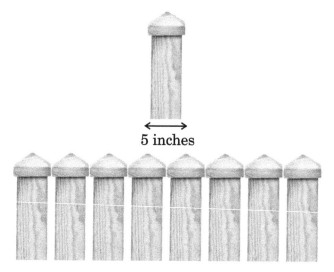

    (a) 35 inches (b) 40 inches (c) 45 inches (d) 50 inches

31. How many 5's are there in the given arrangement which are immediately preceded and immediately followed by an odd number? **(2021)**

    2 3 5 7 1 4 6 8 5 0 2 1 5 4 6 8 9 7 6 5 4 3 2 1 5 2 8 9

    (a) None (b) One (c) Two (d) Three

LEVEL-2

1. •>,>©and©>, then which of the following is definitely wrong.
   (a) •>   (b) •>©   (c) >   (d) >•

2. Estimate two cantaloupes weighs as much as _____ apples.

   $\frac{1}{2}$ Cantaloupe

   (a) 18   (b) 27   (c) 36   (d) 9

3. A university bookstore ordered 41 shipments of notebooks. There were 5,799 notebooks in each shipment. About how many notebooks did the bookstore order in all? Estimate the value.
   (a) 1,40,000   (b) 2,40,000   (c) 3,40,000   (d) 4,40,000

4.
   Balvinder brought

   How many less toffees than ice-creams did he buy?
   (a) 10   (b) 12   (c) 16   (d) 14

5. If @ > %, % > & , & > # and # > $, then which of the following is definitely true.
   (a) $ > @   (b) & > %   (c) % > $ (d) # > %

6. Which sign makes the given statement true? Estimate.

   1,489 ÷ 2 ? 145
   (a) >   (b) <   (c) =   (d) +

7. Which is the correct order of price (high to low) of the following products?
   (a) Tetra pack juice, pizza, Amul Full cream Milk, Mc puff
   (b) Mc puff, pizza, Tetra pack Juice, Amul Full cream Milk
   (c) Amul Full cream Milk, Tetra pack Juice, Mc puff, Pizza
   (d) Pizza, Amul Full cream Milk, Mc puff, Tetra pack Juice

8. Maya found a purse lying in the garden, near her house. Choose the best event that happens next.
   (a) She will throw a stone on it   (b) She will ignore
   (c) She will pick it up   (d) She will call the guard.

9.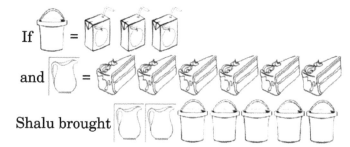

Shalu brought

How many more juices than pastries did she buy?

(a) 4 (b) 3 (c) 9 (d) 10

DIRECTIONS (Qs.10- 15): Study the information carefully to answer the questions.

There are 5 white balls, 8 red balls, 7 yellow balls and 4 green balls in a container. A ball is chosen at random.

10. What is the probability of choosing red?
    (a) 1/2 (b) 1/3 (c) 1/4 (d) 1/8
11. What is the probability of choosing green?
    (a) 1/2 (b) 1/4 (c) 1/6 (d) 1/8
12. What is the probability of choosing either red or white?
    (a) 13/24 (b) 1/24 (c) 5/8 (d) 0
13. What is the probability of choosing neither white nor green?
    (a) 1/8 (b) 13/24 (c) 1/6 (d) 5/8
14. What is the probability of choosing other than yellow?
    (a) 17/24 (b) 13/24 (c) 15/24 (d) None of these
15. What is the probability of choosing black?
    (a) 1/8 (b) 0 (c) 1 (d) 1/2

16.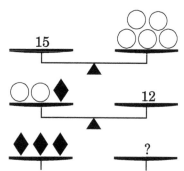

Find the value of ?

(a) 10 (b) 18 (c) 14 (d) 20

17.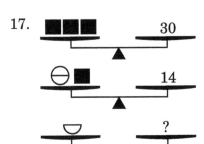

Find the value of ⌣ ?

(a) 1 (b) 8 (c) 4 (d) 2

DIRECTIONS (Qs. 18-20): Study the information carefully to answer the questions.
A score of 5 can appear in 4 ways on the throw of 2 dice.
1 + 4   2 + 3   3 + 2   4 + 1

Score is the sum of the 2 numbers that appear on the two dice. If two dice are thrown together, then answer the following questions.

18. In how many ways a score of 3 can appear.

    (a) 1 (b) 2 (c) 3 (d) 4

19. In how many ways a score of 6 can appear.

    (a) 2 (b) 7 (c) 5 (d) 3

20. In how many ways will have a score less than 5.

    (a) 3 (b) 4 (c) 5 (d) 6

21. Estimate the value.

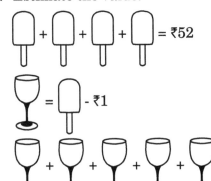

    (a) 58 (b) 59 (c) 60 (d) 62

22. 2 [◯] = 3 [◊ + ◊ + ◊] + 6. If ◊ = 2, then estimate the value of ◯?

    (a) 10 (b) 12 (c) 13 (d) 14

23. If you flip two coins 8 times, what is the best prediction possible for the number of times both coins will land on tails?

    (a) 4 (b) 1 (c) 2 (d) 5

24. Estimate the value.

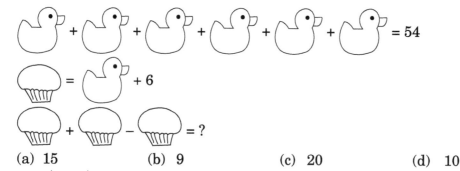

(a) 15   (b) 9   (c) 20   (d) 10

25.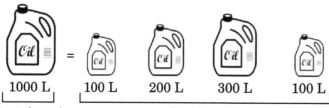

(a) 7   (b) 30   (c) 28   (d) 20

26.

[Container A: 1000 L | Container B: 100 L + 200 L + 300 L + 100 L]

Which of the following statements is true?
(a) Container B has 400 L oil more than container A.
(b) Container B has 100 L oil less than container A.
(c) Container B has 300 L oil less than container A.
(d) Container B has 100 L oil more than container A.

27. Which of the following is a reasonable estimate?
(a) A glass of water can hold about 10 liters of water.
(b) A swimming pool cannot hold about 15 liters of water.
(c) A bottle of juice has a capacity of 100 liters.
(d) A bucket can not hold about 5 liters of water.

28. A penny weighs 8 grams, A nickel weighs 7 grams, A dime weighs 4 grams. Estimate the value of 4 dimes, 6 nickels and 5 pennies weighs?
(a) 85 grams   (b) 90 grams   (c) 98 grams   (d) 100 grams

29. Estimate the total value?

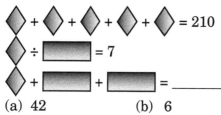

(a) 42   (b) 6   (c) 54   (d) 10

30. How many cubes will balance 2 spheres?

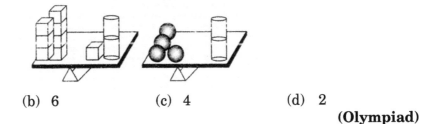

(a) 3   (b) 6   (c) 4   (d) 2

(Olympiad)

31. Shruti started going office from third Monday of March 20XX. How many days did she go to office in that month, if every Sunday is a holiday? **(2022)**

MARCH 20XX						
Sun	Mon	Tue	Wed	Thu	Fri	Sat
	1	2	3	4	5	6
7	8	9	10	11	12	13
14	15	16	17	18	19	20
21	22	23	24	25	26	27
28	29	30	31			

(a) 16   (b) 15   (c) 14   (d) 17

Answers and Explanations

Level-1

1. **(c)** As we know that,
   1L = 1000 mL
   So, 500 mL + 500 mL
   = 1000 mL
   500 mL + 500 mL = 1000 mL
   500 mL + 500 mL = 1000 mL
   500 mL = 500 mL
   Total = 3500 mL i.e., 3.5 L

2. **(b)** Total number of cards = 52
   Total number of hearts = 13
   So, the probability
   = 52 / 13 = 1 / 4

3. **(c)** TFFF

4. **(b)** The incorrect statement is, kilogram is used to measure depth of a bucket.

5. **(d)** Cost of 500 ml of a cough syrup
   = 480.40/2
   = ₹ 240.20.

6. **(d)** Given word- EXPERIMENT
   Total number of letters in the word = 10
   Total number of vowels in the word = 4
   So, the probability
   = 4 / 10 = 2 / 5

7. **(b)** 400 + 250 + 250 = 900 grams is lightest.

8. **(b)** Each ⬚ stands for = 10gm

Three ⬚ stands for = 3 × 10 gm

As ⬚ = ▢

Then three ▢ stands for
= 30g

9. **(c)** 1kg = 1000g
4kg = 4 × 1000 = 4000g
To balance the equance
4000 − 2500 = 1500g

10. **(c)** Step 1
The first statement tells us that one box contains 4 apples
Step 2
Therefore, 3 boxes = 3 × 4
= 12 apples
Step 3
The second statement tells us that one jar contains 2 strawberries.
Step 4
Therefore, 3 jars = 3 × 2
= 6 strawberries
Step 5
Thus, the difference between the number of apples and strawberries
= 12 − 6 = 6

11. **(a)** TFFT
12. **(b)** 4 kg
13. **(c)** 9 kg

14. **(a)** 1★ = 20
2★ = 20 + 20 = 40 = 4▢
1▢ = 10

15. **(c)** Here, one circle weighs 4g

16. **(a)** Round 8.8 to the nearest whole number = 9
Round 52 to the nearest ten = 50
8.8 × 52 = ?
9 × 50 = 450.

17. **(a)** 3 buttons = 1 toothpick
12 buttons = 12/3 = 4 toothpicks.

18. **(d)** Cup empty = 8 marbles
Cup 1/2 full = 17 marbles
1/2 coffee in the cup
= 17 − 8 = 9 marbles
Full coffee in the cup
= 9 × 2 = 18 marbles

19. **(c)** FFFT

20. **(c)** Weight of 1 Pineapple
= 1 kg 200 g = 1200 g
∴ Weight of 3 Pineapples
= 3 × 1200 g = 3600 g = 3 kg 600 g.

21. **(c)** R − H = L is correct.

22. **(d)** There are 6 possible outcomes: 1, 2, 3, 4, 5, 6.
There is 1 favorable outcome: 4.
The probability is 1 out of 6, or 1/6.

23. **(c)** Q

24. **(a)** 5L 700 ml

25. **(c)** Total weight of 4 strawberries
= 8 gm
Weight of a strawberry
= 8/4 = 2 gm
Weight of 5 strawberries
= 5 × 2 = 10 gm
Weight of a big strawberry
= 16 − 10 = 6 gm.

26. **(b)** 1 litre = 1000 ml
    5 glasses have
    = 150 × 5 = 750 ml
    Apple juice left in the bottle
    = 1000 − 750 = 250 ml

27. **(d)** Round the first factor to the nearest ten and the second factor to the nearest hundred.
    91 × 314 = ?
    ↓   ↓
    90 × 300 = 27,000

28. **(b)** FFFT

29. **(c)** 3 kg = 3000 gm
    Number of 150 g weight require = $\frac{3000}{150}$ = 20.

30. **(b)** Each fence post = 5 inches
    Total fence post = 8
    width of fence post
    = 8 × 5 = 40 inches

31. **(b)** Only one 5 is immediately preceded and immediately followed by an odd number.

    2 3 [5] 7 1 4 6 8 5 0 2 1 5 4 6 8 9 7 6 5 4 3 2 1 5 2 8 9

Answers and Explanations

Level-2

1. **(d)** According to the question,
   •>>©>
   So,
   •> is correct.
   •>© is correct.
   > is correct.
   But,
   >• is wrong.

2. **(c)** Here, ½ cantaloupes weighs
   = 9 apples
   Then, 1 cantaloupes weighs
   = 9 × 2 = 18 apples
   So, 2 cantaloupes weighs
   = 18 × 2 = 36 apples.

3. **(b)** Round the first factor to the nearest ten and the second factor to the nearest thousand.
   41 × 5,799 = ?
   ↓   ↓
   40 × 6,000 = 2,40,000.

4. **(d)** Here,
   1 box = 2 toffees
   Then, 3 boxes = 2 × 3 = 6 toffees
   1 container = 5 ice-creams
   Then, 4 containers = 4 × 5 = 20 containers
   And, Balvinder brought 3 boxes and 4 containers.
   So, 20 − 6 = 14
   Hence, he buys 14 less toffees than ice-creams.

5. **(c)** From the given information,
   @ > % > & > # > $
   $ > @ is wrong.
   & > % is wrong.
   # > % is wrong.
   But , % > $ is true.

6. **(a)** Here,
   1,489 ÷ 2 ? 145
   ↓   ↓
   1,400 ÷ 2 ? 145

Now divide:

1,400 ÷ 2 ? 145

700 ? 145 = 700 > 145

So, 700 is greater than 145. The '>' sign makes the statement true.

7. **(d)** Pizza (49 /-), Amul Tonned Milk (40/-), Mc puff (30/-), Terta pack Juice (20/-) is the correct order.

8. **(d)** When she found a purse lying in the garden, she will call the guard.

9. **(b)** Here,

   1 bucket = 3 juices

   Then, 5 buckets

   = 5 × 3 = 15 juices

   1 jug = 6 pastries

   Then, 2 jugs

   = 6 × 2 = 12 pastries

   So, 15 – 12 = 3

   Therefore, Shalu buys 3 more juices than pastries.

SOLUTIONS (Qs. 10-15) : Here total number of balls 5 + 8 + 7 + 4 = 24

10. **(b)** Red balls = 8 / 24 = 1 / 3

    So, 1/3 is the probability of choosing red.

11. **(c)** Green balls = 4 /24 = 1/6

    So, 1/6 is the probability of choosing green.

12. **(a)** Either red + Or white

    = 5 + 8 = 13 / 24

    So, 13/24 is the probability of choosing either red or white.

13. **(d)** Neither white + nor green

    = 8 + 7 = 15 /24 = 5/8

    So, 5/8 is the probability of choosing neither white nor green.

14. **(a)** Other than yellow is

    5 + 8 + 4 = 17 /24

    So, 17/24 is the probability of choosing other than yellow.

15. **(b)** There is no black ball. So, there is 0 probability of choosing black ball.

16. **(b)** Here,

    15 = 5 ◯

    1 ◯ = 15/5   Then, 1 ◯ = 3

    Now, 3 + 3 + ◆ = 12

    = 12 – 6   Then, ◆ = 6

    So, the value of

    = 6 + 6 + 6 = 18.

17. **(d)** Here,

    ■ = 10

    ◯ + 10 = 14

    ◯ = 14 – 10 = 4

    And, the value of ▽ = 4/2 = 2

SOLUTIONS (Qs. 18-20)

18. **(b)** Number of ways a score of 3 can appear = 1 + 2 and 2 + 1.

19. **(c)** Number of ways a score 6 can appear = 1 + 5, 2 + 4 , 3 + 3 , 4 + 2 , 5 + 1.

20. **(d)** Sum less than 5 means-

    Sum of 2 → 1 way (1 + 1)

    Sum of 3 → 2 ways (1 + 2,2 + 1)

    Sum of 4 → 3 ways (1 + 3,2 + 2, 3 + 1)

    So, 6 ways in all.

21. **(c)** Here,

    4 ice-creams = 52

    1 ice-cream = 52/4 = 13

    Now, 1 glass = 1 ice-cream – ₹ 1

    i.e. 1 glass = 13 – 1 = 12

Therefore, 12 + 12 + 12 + 12 + 12 = 60.

22. (b) Here,

2 [🍎] = 3 [2 + 2 + 2] + 6

2 [🍎] = 3 [6] + 6

2 [🍎] = 18 + 6

2 [🍎] = 24

🍎 = 24/2 = 12.

23. (c) There are 4 possible outcomes:
heads on both coins
tails on both coins
heads on first coin, tails on second coin
tails on first coin, heads on second coin

There is 1 favorable outcome: tails on both coins.

The probability is 1 out of 4, or $\frac{1}{4}$

Now find $\frac{1}{4}$ of 8.

$\frac{1}{4} \times 8 = 2$

So, the best prediction possible is 2 out of 8 times.

You pick a marble at random.

24. (a) Here,
6 ducks = 54
1 ducks = 54/6 = 9

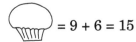 = 9 + 6 = 15

Therefore, 15 + 15 − 15 = 15

25. (d) If ☐ = 6

Then = 6 × 6 + 6 = 42

2 + ◇ + ◇ = 42

2 + 20 + 20 = 42

◇ = 20

26. (c) Container B has 300 L oil less than container A.

27. (d) A bucket can hold about 5 liters of water.

28. (c) Here,
4 × 4 = 16 g (dimes) + 6 × 7
= 42 g (nickles) + 5 × 8
= 40 g (pennies)
Total = 98 grams.

29. (c) 1st step,

5 ◇ = 210

◇ = 210 / 5   Then, ◇ = 42

Now, 2nd step,

Put the value of '◇'

42 ÷ 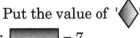 = 7

▬ = 42 / 7

Then, ▬ = 6

3rd step,

◇ + ▬ + ▬

= 42 + 6 + 6 = 54

30. (a) 3 cubes = 1 cylinder = 2 spheres
Hence, 3 cubes = 2 spheres

31. (b) 3rd Monday of 20XX starts from 15th. So, total 15 days she go to office in that month, if every Sunday is a holiday.

CHAPTER 12

Geometrical Shapes

OBJECTIVES

- To identify different objects which represent some kind of geometrical shapes which we are coming across in our day to day life. (Both 2D and 3D)
- To recognise different parts of various geometrical shapes such as vertex and sides of a particular geometrical pattern.
- Use of different geometrical shapes for creating Tangrams.
- Knowledge of line of symmetry. (horizontal and vertical)

GEOMETRIC SHAPE

Geometric Shape is defined as a set of points or vertices and sides connecting to the point to form a closed entry. There are various kinds of geometrical shapes. They are identified based upon the number of vertices and sides.

2D Geometrical Shapes

Shape	Properties
Triangle	• Triangle has three sides. • It has three vertices.
Square	• Squares have 4 equal sides and 4 right angles. • They have 4 lines of symmetry. • All squares belong to the rectangle family. • All squares belong to the rhombus family. • All squares are also parallelograms.
Rectangle	• Rectangles have 4 sides and 4 right angles. • They all have 2 lines of symmetry (4 lines, if they are also a square.) • All rectangles belong to the parallelogram family.

Rhombus		Rhombuses (rhombii) have 4 equal sides.
	•	Both pairs of opposite sides are parallel.
	•	They all have 2 lines of symmetry (4 lines, if they are a square.)
	•	All rhombuses belong to the parallelogram family.
Parallelogram	•	Parallelograms have 2 pairs of parallel sides.
	•	Some parallelograms have lines of symmetry (depending on whether they are also squares, rectangles or rhombuses), but most do not.
Circle	•	Circles have a point in the centre from which each point on the diameter is equidistant.
	•	They have infinite lines of symmetry.
Ellipse	•	Ellipses are like circles which have been squashed or stretched.
	•	They have 2 lines of symmetry.
	•	They are also a special type of oval.
	•	The longest and shortest diameters of the ellipses are called the major and minor axes. These axes are also the lines of symmetry.
Crescent	•	Crescent shapes are made when two circles overlap, or when one circle is removed from another circle.
	•	The perimeter of crescents made from two circular arcs. They have one line of symmetry.
	•	Our moon forms crescent shapes during its phases.
	•	
Pentagon	•	5 sided polygon
Hexagon	•	6 sided polyon

Heptagon	• 7 sided polygon
Octagon	• 8 sided polygon

3D Geometrical Shapes

Cube	• Cubes have 6 faces, 12 edges and 8 vertices. • All sides on a cube are equal length. • All faces are square in shape. • A cube is a type of cuboid.
Cuboid	• Cuboids have 6 faces, 12 edges and 8 vertices. • All the faces on a cuboid are rectangular.
Sphere	• Spheres have either 0 or 1 faces, 0 edges and 0 vertices.
Cylinder	• Cylinders have either 2 or 3 faces, 0 or 2 edges, and 0 vertices.
Cone	• Cones have either 1 or 2 faces, 0 or 1 edges, and 1 apex (which is described by some mathematicians as a vertex).

REGULAR GEOMETRIC SHAPE

The geometric shapes whose all sides are equal sides and equal interior angles are known as regular geometric shape.

IRREGULAR GEOMETRIC SHAPES

The geometric shapes which have sides and angles of any length and size.

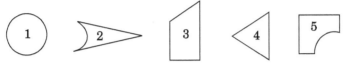

DIRECTION (Examples 1 & 2): Answer the questions based on given figure (X).

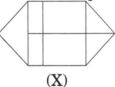

(X)

Example 1:

How many rectangles are three in the given figure (X)?
 (a) 10 (b) 9 (c) 8 (d) 7

(1-2) The figure may be labelled as shown.

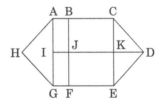

Ans. (b)

The simplest rectangles are ABJI, BCKJ, IJFG and JKEF i.e. 4 in number.

The rectangles composed of two components each are ACKI, BCEF, IKEG and ABFG i.e. 4 in number.

The only rectangle composed of four components is ACEG.

Thus, there are 4 + 4 + 1 = 9 rectangles in the given figure.

Example 2:

How many triangles are there in the given figure (X).
 (a) 1 (b) 2 (c) 3 (d) 4

Ans. (d)

Triangles are :
 △ AHG, △CKD, △KED and △CDE i.e. 4 in number.

Example 3:

Which of the following shapes is regular shape.

Ans. (d)

Explanation : The pentagon has regular shape.

TANGRAMS

These are the dissection puzzles which have seven different pieces of three geometrical shapes placed in specific numbers. The pieces are arranged in such manner that it reflects various features of real life objects/things like houses, people, animals, fruits etc. They are made in such a way that they are easily identifiable.

Here three tangram images are given below. Identify each one of them.

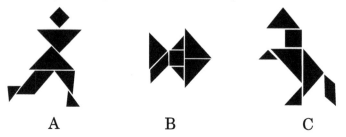

A   B   C

The three images, serially are
(A) A person in a running posture   (B) A fish
(C) A horse

Example 4:

Which of the three images given above is having square in place of its head?

(a) A   (b) B   (c) C   (d) None of these

Ans. (a)

The man in running posture in image A is having a square in place of its head.

SYMMETRY

When an object is cut from the middle, it gives two equal parts of the main item. This is known as symmetrical object. On the other hand, when the sub divided parts are not at all equal to each other, then the object is called an asymmetric object.

There are some symmetrical objects which are given below:

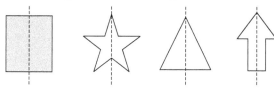

The line from which the image is cut into two equal parts is known as Line of symmetry which can be further divided into horizontal line of symmetry and vertical line of symmetry.

HORIZONTAL LINE OF SYMMETRY

When a line divides an object in such a way that both the upper and lower parts of the image will be equally opposite to each other, it is known as horizontal line of symmetry.

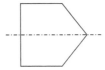

Horizontal Line of Symmetry

VERTICAL LINE OF SYMMETRY

When a line divides an object in such a way that the image on the right hand side is equally opposite to the image of the left hand side, it is known as vertical line of symmetry.

Vertical Line of Symmetry

Example 5:

How many elements given below have at least one line of symmetry?

(a) 3 (b) 4 (c) 5 (d) 2

Ans. (a)

Explanation : Dotted lines are lines of symmetry.

LEVEL-1

1. Which of the following figures below does not have a line of symmetry?

   (a) 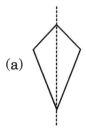   (b) 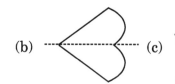   (c) 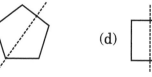   (d) (square with dashed vertical line)

2. How many triangles are there altogether in the given figure?

   (a) 14
   (b) 12
   (c) 10
   (d) 8

3. Which of the following figures below have a line of symmetry?

   (a) 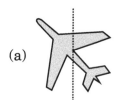   (b)    (c)   (d)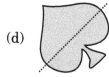

4.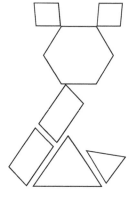

   Carefully observe the picture given above and count how may quadrilateral surround the only hexagon in the image.

   (a) 3   (b) 4   (c) 5   (d) 6

5. Shivam used a crayon to draw a shape on a piece of paper. The shape has 6 angles which shape could Shivam have drawn?

   (a) △   (b) ○   (c) ⬠   (d) ⬡

6.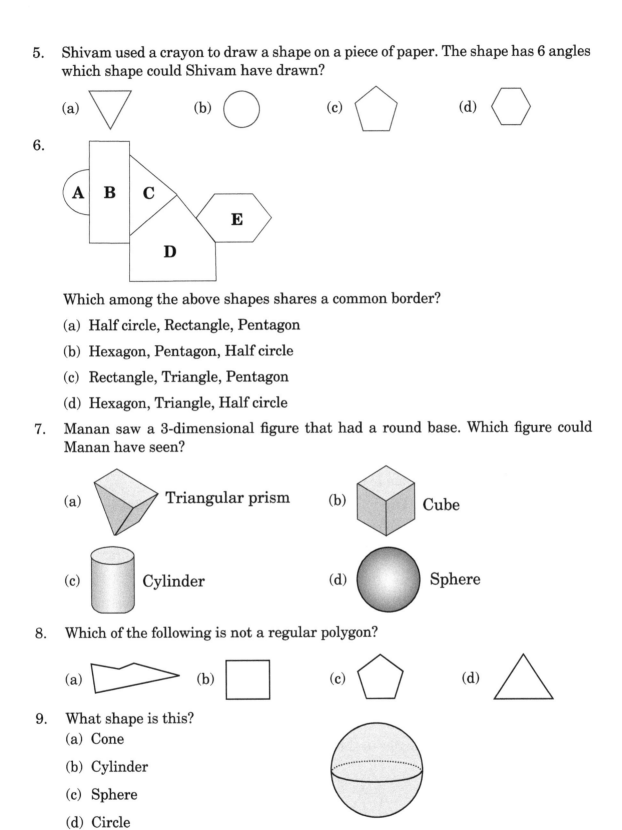

   Which among the above shapes shares a common border?
   (a) Half circle, Rectangle, Pentagon
   (b) Hexagon, Pentagon, Half circle
   (c) Rectangle, Triangle, Pentagon
   (d) Hexagon, Triangle, Half circle

7. Manan saw a 3-dimensional figure that had a round base. Which figure could Manan have seen?

   (a) Triangular prism   (b) Cube
   (c) Cylinder   (d) Sphere

8. Which of the following is not a regular polygon?

   (a)   (b) □   (c) ⬠   (d) △

9. What shape is this?
   (a) Cone
   (b) Cylinder
   (c) Sphere
   (d) Circle

207

Direction (Qs. 10–14): Given below some tangrams which represent some animals. Now carefully observe each one of them and give answer to the following questions.

(a)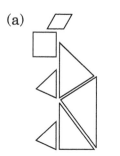
Rabbit

(b)
Dog

(c)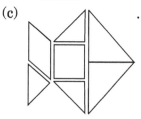
Fish

(d)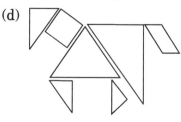
Horse

10. In which of the above figure, is the square surrounded by the triangles and parallelogram?
    (a) Rabbit   (b) Dog   (c) Fish   (d) Horse

11. Which animal has a tail made up of only a parallelogram?
    (a) Rabbit   (b) Dog   (c) Fish   (d) Horse

12. Which animal has an ear in the shape of triangle?
    (a) Rabbit   (b) Dog   (c) Fish   (d) Horse

13. Whose face is made up of 2 triangles?
    (a) Rabbit   (b) Dog   (c) Fish   (d) Horse

14. Which of the following statements is correct?
    (a) Fish has 2 triangles in its tail
    (b) Horse has 2 squares in its legs
    (c) All animals are made us of seven tangrams
    (d) All are correct.

15. Find the number of triangles in the given figure.
    (a) 12
    (b) 24
    (c) 26
    (d) 18

16. Which of the following is a regular shape?

(a)   (b)   (c)   (d)

17. How many lines of symmetry does the letter H have?

    (a) 1
    (b) 2
    (c) 3
    (d) 0

18. Which shape can be depicted from the following figure?

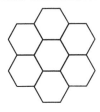

    (a) Square   (b) Pentagon   (c) Square   (d) Hexagon

19. Which shape is depicted by the figure (X)?

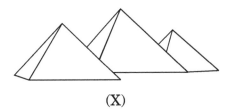

(X)

    (a) Triangle   (b) Rectangle   (c) Square   (d) Circle

20. Which of the following figures correctly shows a line of symmetry?

    (a) 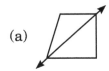   (b) 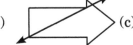   (c)   (d)

21. Find the minimum number of straight lines required to make the given figure.

    (a) 13
    (b) 15
    (c) 17
    (d) 19

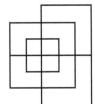

22. How many lines of symmetry does this shape have? 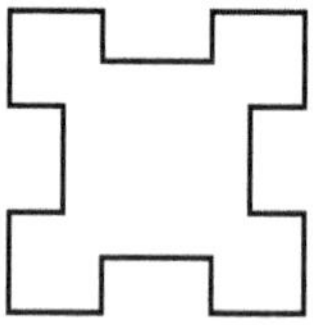
    (a) 2
    (b) 3
    (c) 4
    (d) 5

23. How many lines of symmetry does the parallelogram have? 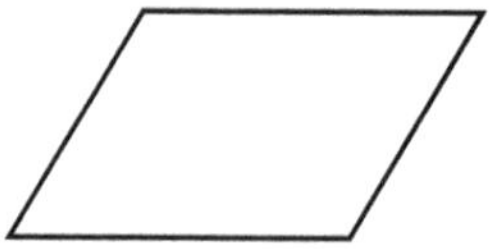
    (a) 1
    (b) 2
    (c) 4
    (d) None

24. If the quadrilateral will be cut along AB then which shape would have more area 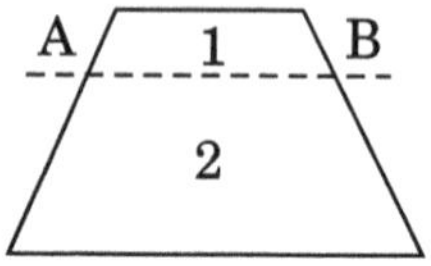
    (a) 1
    (b) 2
    (c) Both will be equal
    (d) None of these

25.

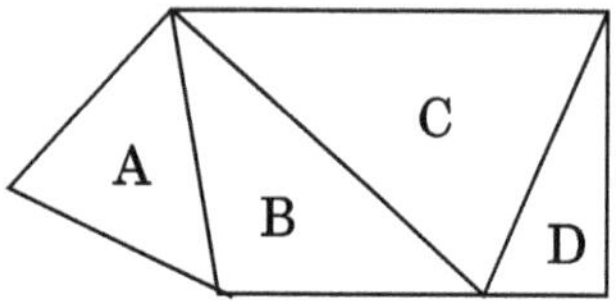

    Which of the above triangles has the largest area?
    (a) B
    (b) C
    (c) A
    (d) D

26. How many vertical lines are there in the figure below?

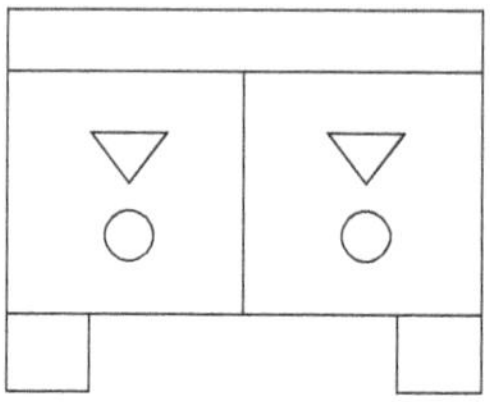

    (a) 4
    (b) 5
    (c) 6
    (d) 7

27. Which figure has only one base and one vertex?
    (a) 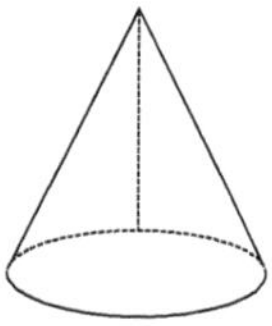
    (b) 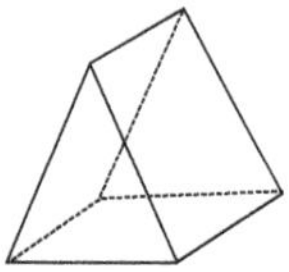
    (c) 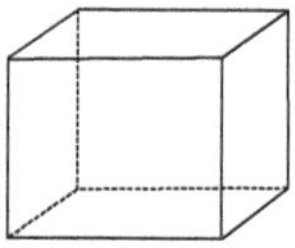
    (d)

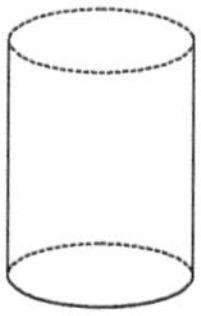

28. What is the intermediate shape of the given image (X)?

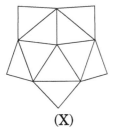
(X)

(a)   (b)  (c)   (d)

29. Which shapes have Point Symmetry?

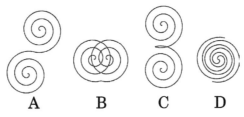
A B C D

(a) Only A (b) Only D (c) A and D only (d) All of them

30. The three shapes shown can be used to make the faces of which of the following solids?

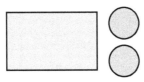

(a) A Cone
(c) A Cube
(b) A Cylinder
(d) A Square Pyramid

31. How many triangles are there in the figure given below? (2022)

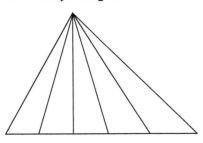

(a) 10
(c) More than 14
B. Less than 10
D. Between 11 to 14

LEVEL-2

1. How many lines of symmetry does this star have?

    (a) 4
    (b) 5
    (c) 6
    (d) 2

2. Which of the following has point symmetry about the origin?

    (a)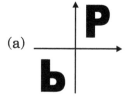
    (b)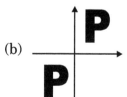

    (c)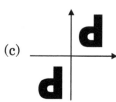
    (d)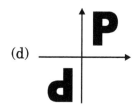

3. Which part of the given shape has a minimum number of squares?

    (a) D
    (b) A
    (c) B
    (d) E

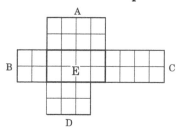

4. Which two shapes could be placed together to form the rectangle?

    (a)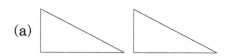
    (b)

    (c)
    (d)

5. How many minimum number of circles have to be separated so as to free all the circles?

    (a) 5
    (b) 3
    (c) 2
    (d) 9

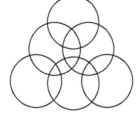

6. Sunita was making a border across her notebook paper. She used one shape and kept flipping it over a vertical axis (reflecting the shape). What did her border look like?

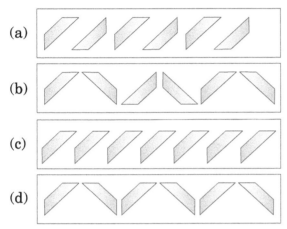

7. Which of the following picture has rotational symmetry?

    (a)   (b)    (c)   (d)

8. Count the number of squares in the given figure.

    (a) 10
    (b) 12
    (c) 18
    (d) 15

9. How many triangles are there in the given figure?
    (a) 8
    (b) 10
    (c) 12
    (d) 14

10. How many different shapes can be derived if the figure(X) is cut along the dotted line?
    (a) 4
    (b) 6
    (c) 5
    (d) 3

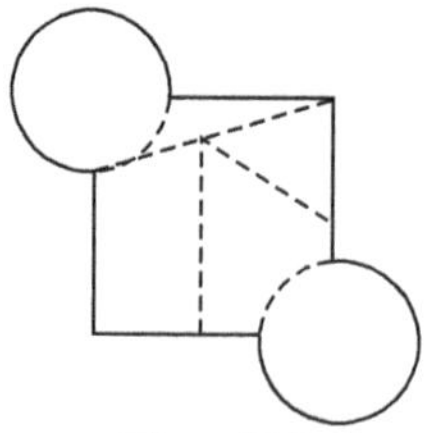

    Fig. (X)

11. In the figure (X), which of the following shapes are identical?
    (a) A and C
    (b) B and D
    (c) D and A
    (d) C and D

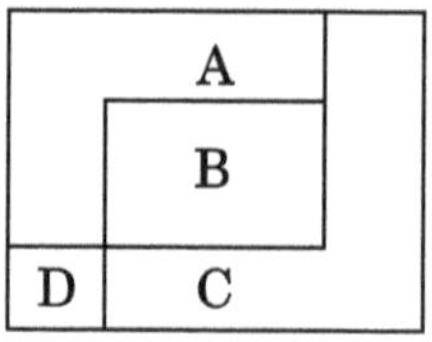

    Fig. (X)

12. Which among the following shapes doesn't intersect each other?
    (a) A and C
    (b) C and D
    (c) C and E
    (d) A and D

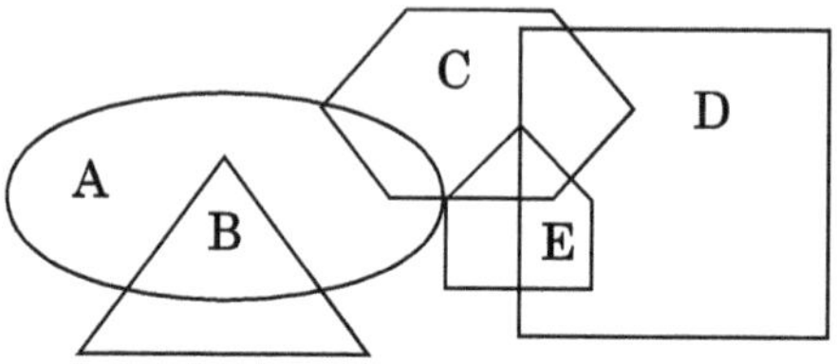

13. The diagram shows the outline of a British 50p coin. How many lines of symmetry does it have?

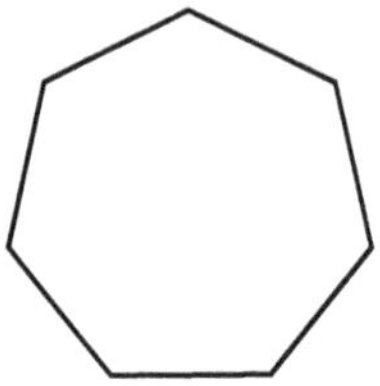

    (a) 4   (b) 5   (c) 6   (d) 7

14. Liya saw a 3-dimensional figure. It had 4 vertices and 6 edges. Which figure could Liya have seen?

    (a) 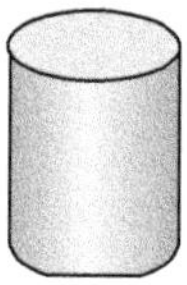 Cylinder
    (b) Sphere
    (c) 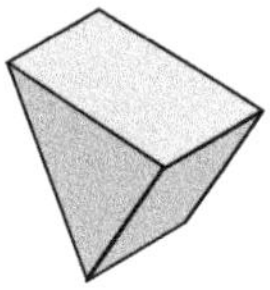 Triangular prism
    (d) 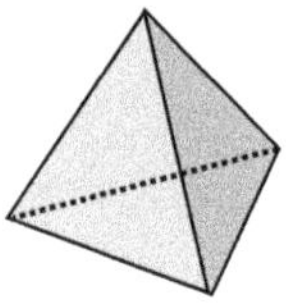 Triangular pyramid

15. What is the minimum number of straight lines that is needed to construct the figure?

    (a) 11
    (b) 13
    (c) 15
    (d) 21

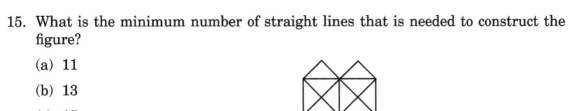

16. How many more triangles than squares are there in the figure (X)?

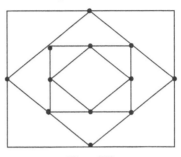

Fig. (X)

    (a) 4   (b) 8   (c) 7   (d) 12

17. How many squares are there in Figure (X)?

    (a) 1
    (b) 2
    (c) 3
    (d) There are no squares in Figure (X).

Fig. (X)

18. Name the shape which is hidden.

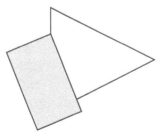

    (a) Circle   (b) Triangle   (c) Hexagon   (d) Octagon

19. The letter A is symmetrical. A symmetrical figure can be folded in half and have both sides match exactly. Of the 26 capital letters of the alphabet, how many are symmetrical (vertical or horizontal)?

    (a) 12   (b) 13   (c) 13   (d) 15

20. A sculptor cuts a corner of a cube. How many edges does the new shape have?

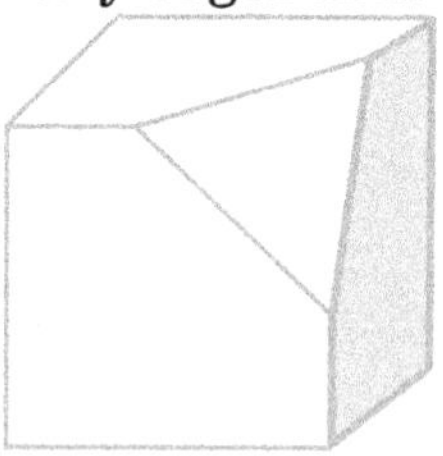

   (a) 11

   (b) 12

   (c) 15

   (d) 18

21. Minimum number of straight lines required to make the given figure is _____.

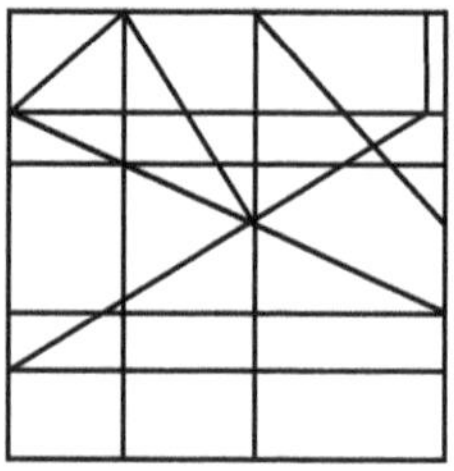

   (a) 12

   (b) 14

   (c) 16

   (d) 17

   (Olympiad)

22. How many triangles are there in the given figure?

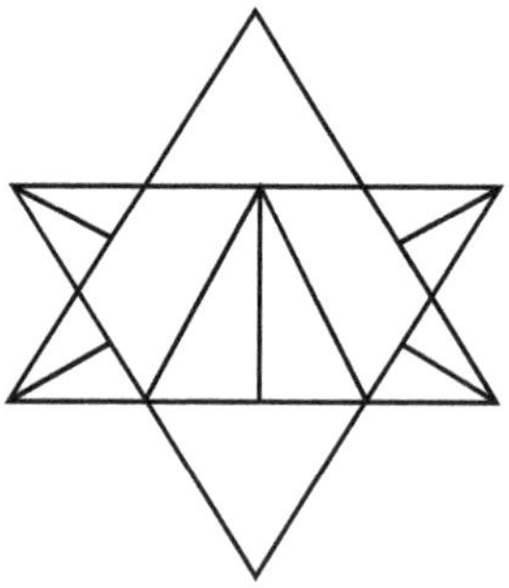

   (a) 19

   (b) 21

   (c) 18

   (d) 20

   (Olympiad)

23. The model of a tower shown here is made up of unit cubes stacked on top of each other. How many unit cubes in all are used to form the tower?

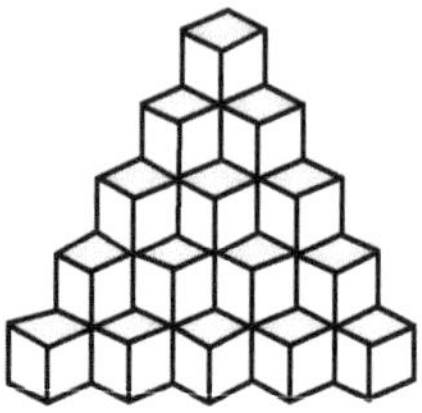

   (a) 35

   (b) 36

   (c) 37

   (d) 38

   (Olympiad)

24. If _____ square is removed from the given figure, the perimeter of the figure will be decreased.

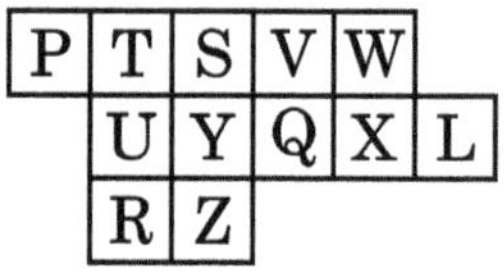

   (a) P

   (b) Q

   (c) R

   (d) S

P	T	S	V	W	
U	Y	Q	X	L	
R	Z				

   (Olympiad)

25. _____ figures have atleast one line of symmetry.

    (a) 2
    (b) 1
    (c) 3
    (d) 4

    (Olympiad)

26. Given below is the net of a cube. If it is folded, then _____ is opposite to the face marked ✦.

    (a) ✚
    (b) ♥
    (c) ■
    (d) ▲

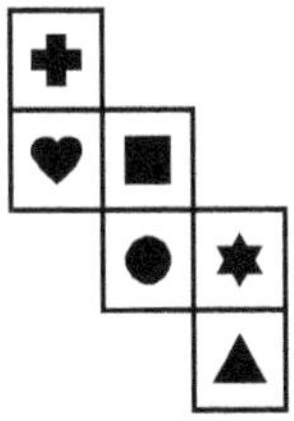

    (Olympiad)

27. How many lines of symmetry does the given figure have?

    (a) 0
    (b) 1
    (c) 2
    (d) 3

    (Olympiad)

28. Count the number of cubes in the given figure.

    (a) 23
    (b) 22
    (c) 20
    (d) 24

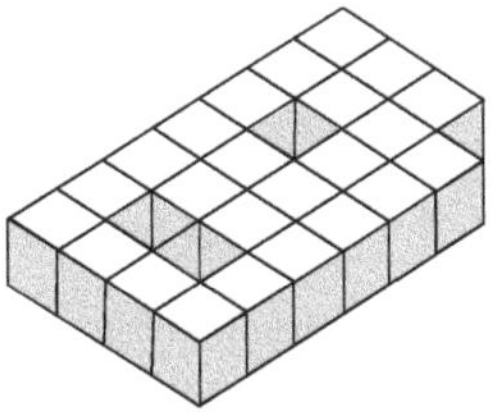

    (Olympiad)

29. The top half of a symmetrical figure is shown below. XY is the line of symmetry. Which of the following options will complete the symmetric figure?

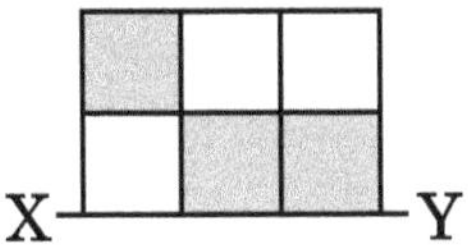

    (a) 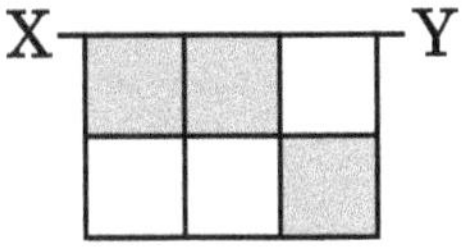
    (b) 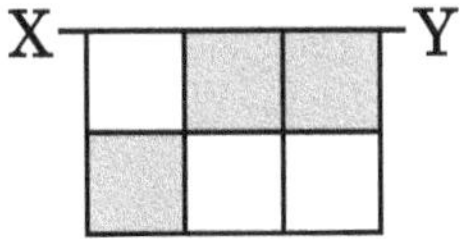
    (c) 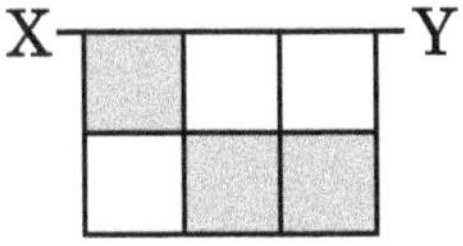
    (d)

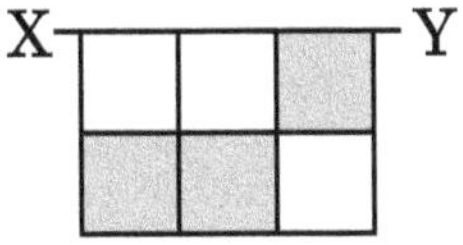

    (Olympiad)

30. Count the number of squares in the given figure.
    (a) 11
    (b) 21
    (c) 18
    (d) 19 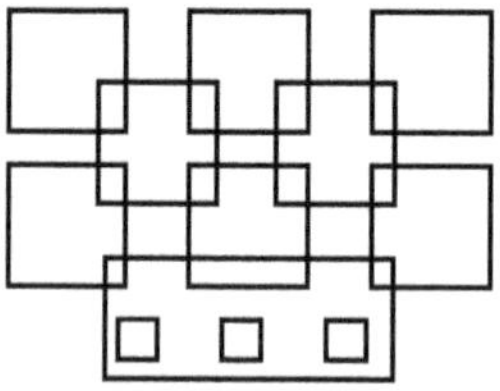
    (Olympiad)

31. Find the minimum number of straight lines required to draw the given figure.
    (2019) 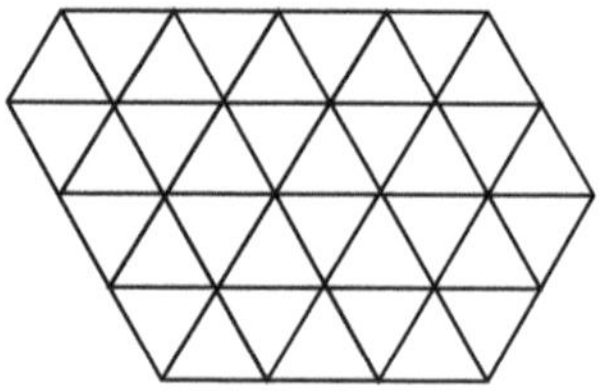
    (a) 18
    (b) 16
    (c) 19
    (d) 21

32. Find the number of triangles formed in the given figure. (2020)
    (a) 9
    (b) 10
    (c) 11
    (d) None of these

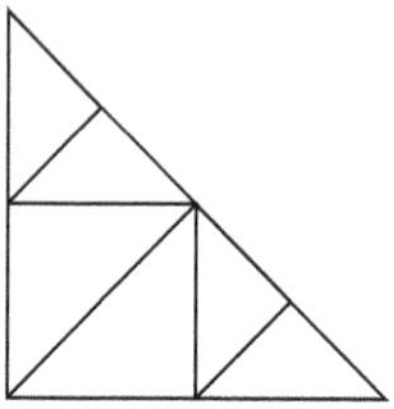

33. Find the number of triangles formed in the given figure. (2020)
    (a) 11
    (b) 12
    (c) 10
    (d) 14

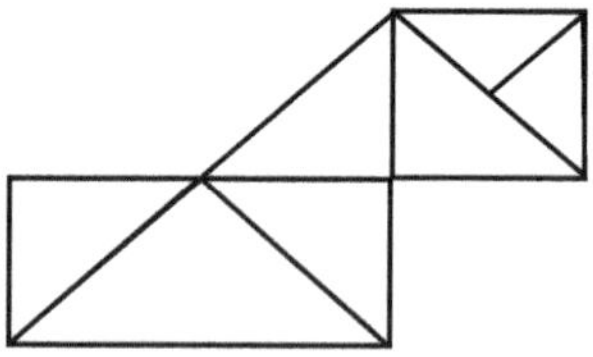

34. Count the number of cubes in the given figure. (2021)
    (a) 16 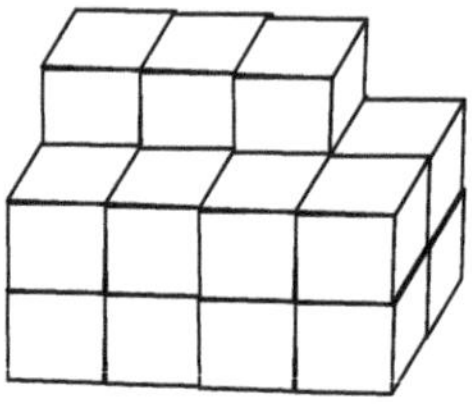
    (b) 17
    (c) 18
    (d) 19

35. Find the number of triangles formed in the given figure. (2021)
    (a) 10
    (b) 18
    (c) 12
    (d) 16

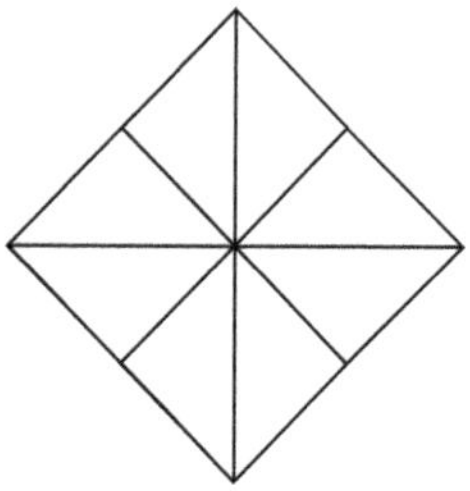

36. How many lines of symmetry are there in the given figure? **(2021)**

    (a) None

    (b) One

    (c) Two

    (d) Three

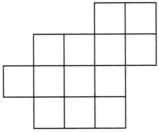

37. How many squares are formed in the given figure? **(2022)**

    (a) 19

    (b) 20

    (c) 18

    (d) 22

38. How many cubes are there in the given figure? **(2022)**

    (a) 24

    (b) 20

    (c) 25

    (d) 28

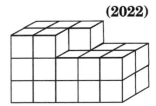

Answers and Explanations

Level-1

1. **(c)** Only (c) does not have a line of symmetry.

2. **(a)** The figure may be labeled as shown.

    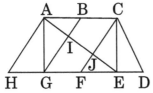

    The simplest triangles are AHG, AIG, AIB, JFE, CJE and CED i.e. 6 in number.

    The triangles composed of two components each are ABG, CFE, ACJ and EGI i.e. 4 in number.

    The triangles composed of three components each are ACE, AGE and CFD i.e. 3 in number.

    There is only one triangle i.e. AHE composed of four components.

    Therefore, there are 6 + 4 + 3 + 1 = 14 triangles in the given figure.

3. **(b)** Only (b) have a line of symmetry.

4. **(a)** 3 quadrilaterals surround the only hexagon in the above image.

    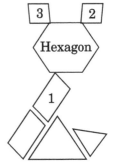

5. **(d)** Shivam has drawn a hexagon.

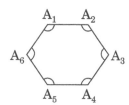

6. **(c)** B, C and D i.e. Rectangle, Triangle and Pentagon share the common boundary.

7. **(c)** Cylinder has a round base. So, Manan could have seen a cylinder.

8. **(a)** Here, A polygon is regular if all of its sides have the same length and all of its angles have the same measure. But, this shape given in option (a) is not a regular polygon. Its sides have different lengths and its angles have different measures.

9. **(c)** The shape is completely round. It has no flat surfaces.

10. **(c)** The fish tangram has a square which is surrounded by triangles and parallelogram.

11. **(d)** Horse has a parallelogram in its tail.

12. **(b)** Dog has a triangle shape of ear.

13. **(c)** The face of fish is made up of two triangles.

14. **(c)** All animals are made up of seven tangrams.

15. **(d)** The figure may be labeled as shown.

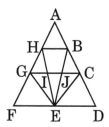

The simplest triangles are AHB, GHI, BJC, GFE, GIE, IJE, CEJ and CDE i.e. 8 in number.

The triangles composed of two components each are HEG, BEC, HBE, JGE and ICE i.e. 5 in number.

The triangles composed of three components each are FHE, GCE and BED i.e. 3 in number.

There is only one triangle i.e. AGC composed of four components.

There is only one triangle i.e. AFD composed of nine components.

Thus, there are 8 + 5 + 3 + 1 + 1 = 18 triangles in the given figure.

16. **(c)** Option (c) is a regular shape.

17. **(b)** Letter 'H' has 2 lines of symmetry.

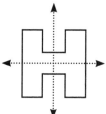

18. **(d)** Hexagon is a six sided polygon.

19. **(a)** Triangle is the shape that is depicted from the figure (X).

20. **(d)**

21. **(a)** The figure may be labelled as shown.

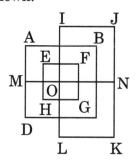

The horizontal lines are IJ, AB, EF, MN, HG, DC and LK i.e. 7 in number.

The vertical lines are AD, EH, IL, FG, BC and JK i.e. 6 in number.

Thus, there are 7 + 6 = 13 straight lines in the figure.

22. (c) The above figure has 4 lines of symmetry.

23. (d) A parallelogram that has no special properties (such as a rectangle or a rhombus) has no lines of symmetry.

24. (b) The figure 2 will be of more area.

25. (b) The triangle C is of largest area.

26. (b)

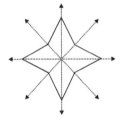

27. (a)

28. (a) The intermediate shape is a pentagon.

29. (c)

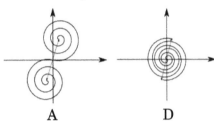

A   D

So, only A and D have point symmetry.

30. (b) A cylinder shape can be used to make the face.

31. (c)

Level-2

1. (a) It has 4 lines of symmetry.

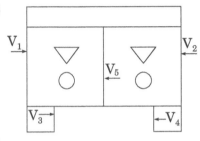

2. (c) Option (c) has the point symmetry about the origin.

3. (c) The section "B" has the least number of squares i.e. 5.

4. (a)

5. (b) At least three circles have to be separated so as to free all the circles.

6. (d)

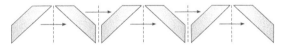

7. (d) If you rotate these picture ½ turn or less, it will not look exactly the same.

So, these pictures do not have rotational symmetry. Only option (d) has rotational symmetry.

8. **(d)** The figure may be labeled as shown.

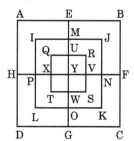

The simplest squares are QUYX, URVY, YVSW and XYWT i.e. 4 in number.

The squares composed of two components each are IMYP, MJNY, YNKO and PYOL i.e. 4 in number.

The squares composed of three components each are AEYH, EBFY, YFCG and HYGD i.e. 4 in number.

There is only one square i.e. QRST composed of four components.
There is only one square i.e. IJKL composed of eight components.
There is only one square i.e. ABCD composed of twelve components.

Total number of squares in the given figure = 4 + 4 + 4 + 1 + 1 + 1 = 15

9. **(d)**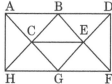

△ABC, △BCE, △BDE, △DEF, △EGF, △CHG, △CEG, △ACH, △ABH, △DBF, △HAG, △FDG, △ADG, △BHF

10. **(c)** 5

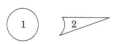

11. **(a)** A and C are identical.

12. **(d)** A and D didn't intersect with each other.

13. **(d)** It is a regular heptagon (7 sided figure) and has 7 lines of symmetry.

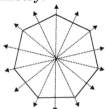

14. **(d)** Triangular Pyramid has 4 vertices and 6 edges. So, Liya could have seen a triangular pyramid.

15. **(b)** The figure may be labeled as shown.

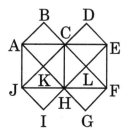

The horizontal lines are AE and JF i.e. 2 in number. The vertical lines are AJ, CH and EF i.e. 3 in number.

The slanting lines are AG, BF, JD, IE, AB, DE, JI and FG i.e. 8 in number.

Total number of straight lines needed to construct the figure = 2 + 3 + 8 = 13.

16. **(b)** Squares = 4

Triangles = 12

There are 12 − 4 = 8 more triangles than squares.

17. **(d)** A square has four right angles.

18. **(b)** Hidden part of the shape is triangle.

19. (d) 15 letters are symmetrical, either along the vertical axis or along the horizontal axis.

Letters are:

A B C D E F G H I J K L M
N O P Q R S T U V W X Y Z

20. (c) A cube has 8 vertexes, 6 rectangular faces, and 12 edges.

There are 3 additional edges.
12 + 3 = 15.

21. (c) Number of straight lines required to make the given figure is 16.

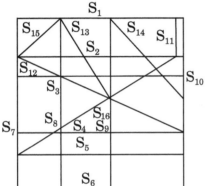

S_1, S_2, S_3, S_4, S_5, S_6, S_7, S_8, S_9, S_{10}, S_{11}, S_{12}, S_{13}, S_{14}, S_{14}, S_{15}, and S_{16},

22. (b) The figure may be labeled as shown:

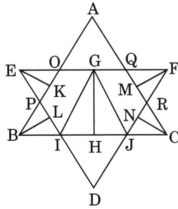

The simplest triangles are: AOQ, DIJ, EPK, EKO, PLB, LBI, JCN, CNR, RFM, FMQ, IGH, HJG i.e. 12 in number.

The triangles composed of two triangles such as: EOP, PBI, FQR, RJC, IGJ, EIG and FGJ i.e. 7 in number.

The largest triangles are ABC and DEF i.e. 2 in number. Thus, there are 12 + 7 + 2 = 21 triangles in the given figure.

23. (a) 35 unit cubes in all are used to form the tower.

24. (a) If 'P' square is removed from the given figure, the perimeter of the figure will be decreased.

25. (a) '2' figures have atleast one line of symmetry.

26. (b) '♥' is opposite to the face marked ★.

27. (c) 2 lines of symmetry does the given figure have.

28. (d) The number of cubes in the given figure is 24.

29. (b) Option (b) will complete the symmetric figure.

30. (a) The figure may be labeled as shown:

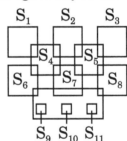

The member of squares in the figure are S_1, S_2, S_3, S_4, S_5, S_6, S_7, S_8, S_9, S_{10} and S_{11}.

31. (a) 18 lines are needed to draw this figure.

32. (c) 11   **33. (a)** 11

34. (d) Total number of cubes
= (4 × 2) + (4 × 2) + 3
= 8 + 8 + 3 = 19

35. (d) 16   **36. (a)** None

37. (a) 19

38. (c) Total number of cubes
= (5 × 2) + (5 × 2) + 5 = 10 + 10 + 5 = 25

CHAPTER 13

Mirror and Water Image

OBJECTIVE
- Students will learn how different objects are seen when they get reflected both in Mirror and in Water.

INTRODUCTION

The reflection of object into the mirror is called its mirror image. It is obtained by inverting an object laterally. If we combine the original figure and mirror image together they form symmetry.

MIRROR IMAGES

Mirror Images of Capital letters

A	A	H	H	O	O	V	V
B	ꓭ	I	I	P	ꟼ	W	W
C	Ɔ	J	ꓡ	Q	Ϙ	X	X
D	ꓷ	K	ꓘ	R	ꓤ	Y	Y
E	ꓱ	L	ꓶ	S	ꙅ	Z	Z
F	ꓞ	M	M	T	T		
G	ꓨ	N	И	U	U		

- The capital letters which have the same mirror images are:

   A, H, I, M, O, T, U, V, W, X, Y

Mirror Images of Small letters

a	ɒ	n	п
b	d	o	o

c	ɔ	p	q
d	b	q	p
e	ǝ	r	ɿ
f	ʇ	s	ƨ
g	ǵ	t	ƚ
h	ɓ	u	ʊ
i	i	v	v
j	ĺ	w	w
k	ʞ	x	x
l	l	y	ʏ
m	m	z	ƺ

- The small letters which have the same mirror images are:

  i, l, o, v, w, x

Mirror Images of Numbers

0 1 2 3 4 5 6 7 8 9 10 11 12 13 14 15
0 Ɩ S Ɛ ߄ ܒ ϱ ⦜ 8 ϱ 0Ɩ ƖƖ SƖ ƐƖ ߄Ɩ ܒƖ

- 0 and 8 numbers have the same mirror images.

Mirror Image of Clock Time

For mirror image of clock time, the given time shall be subtracted from 12.00 or 11.60.

Example 1:

What will be the mirror image of clock time 3:40?

Explanation:

By using simple trick

```
  11 : 60
   3 : 40
  -------
   8 : 20
```

WATER IMAGES

INTRODUCTION

The reflection of an object into the water is called its water image. It is obtained by inverting an object vertically.0

Technical Definition
In water image (horizontal), the LOWER and UPPER parts interchange positions and the LEFT and RIGHT parts remain constant.

Water Images of Capital Letters

A B C D E F G H I J K L M N O P Q R S T U V W X Y Z
∀ B C D E F G H I J K L M N O P Q R S T U V W X Y Z

Water Images of Small Letters

a	b	c	d	e	f	g	h
ɐ	p	c	q	ɘ	ţ	&.	ᖯ
i	j	k	l	m	n	o	p
!	ͰͰ	ʞ	J	ɯ	ᴜ	o	b
q	r	s	t	u	v	w	x
d	ɪ	ƨ	ƒ	ᴖ	ʌ	ʍ	x
y	z						
ʎ	ƨ						

Water Images of Numbers

1	2	3	4	5	6	7	8	9
I	ƨ	3	ᒣ	ᒐ	e	⊥	8	ə

Water Images of Clock Time

For water image of clock time, the given time shall be subtracted from 18 : 30.

Example 2:

What will be the water image of clock time 4 : 20?

Explanation:

By using simple trick

```
    18 : 30
     4 : 20
    ───────
    14 : 10
```

14 : 10 means 2 : 10

Points to be Remembered

There is a short trick which can be applied while doing this exercise.

- Certain alphabets in capital form have the mirror image as well as the water image are the same.
  They are

  H   I   O   X

- Some alphabets have similar water reflection i.e.

  C   D   E   H   I   O   X

- Two numbers 0 and 8 have their water images exactly the same.
- The mirror image of number 6 is the same as the water image of number 9.

Example 1:

Choose the mirror image of the following combination of alphabets from the four alternatives given mirror below.

ULTRA

(a) ARTLU   (b) ∩ΓTRA   (c) AЯTJU   (d) A ЯL JU

Ans. (c)

Explanation: The correct mirror image is as shown below:

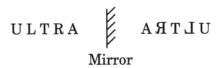

Example 2:

Choose the correct mirror image for the given image.

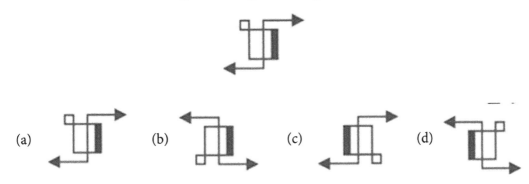

Ans. (d)

Explanation: The correct mirror image of the given image is as shown below:

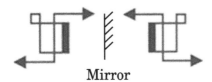

Example 3:

Given below is a set of alphabets along with its four alternatives. Now, identify the correct option which resembles the exact water image of the given combination.

pynkrai
―――――
water

(a) uqkreʎ (b) pynkrai (c) ıɐɹʞuʎd (d) pynreiu

Ans. (b)

Explanation:

pynkrai
―――――
pynkrai

Example 4:

In the question given below, choose the correct option for the water image from the four given alternatives

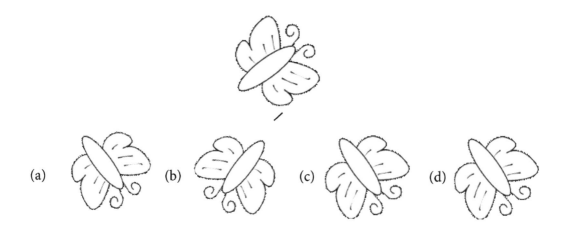

Ans. (c)

Explanation:

Example 5:

In the question there is a combination of small letter alphabets and numbers. Choose the correct mirror image of the following combination.

(a) 2qɔɘabɿ   (b) bsɘɿɔqa   (c) apɘSobɿ   (d) sqɘSbɿɔ

Ans. (b)

Explanation:

The mirror image will be

LEVEL-1

DIRECTIONS (Qs. 1-5): Find the mirror image of each of given figure (X).

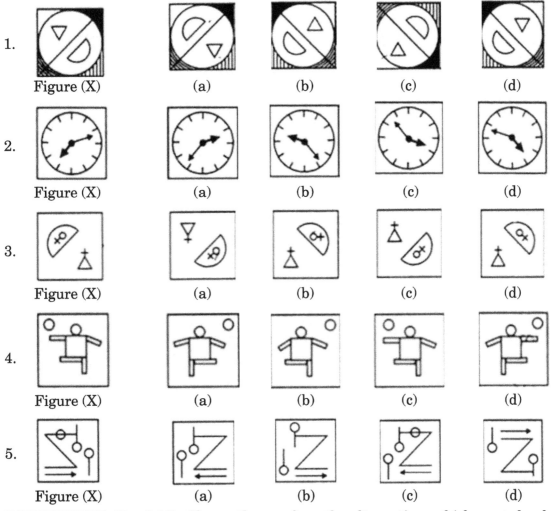

DIRECTIONS (Qs. 6-10): Choose the one from the alternatives which most closely resembles the mirror image.

6. PROVE
   (a) ƎVOЯꟼ (b) ꟼVOЯE (c) ꟼROVE (d) OƎVЯꟼ

7. BATTLE
   (a) ƎJTTAB (b) ꓭATTLE (c) BATTLE (d) ƎTTAƎJ

8. UNION
   (a) NIONU (upside down) (b) UNION (upside down) (c) IONNU (upside down) (d) UNION (upside down)

9. 5239
   (a) 5236 (upside down) (b) 5259 (upside down) (c) 5239 (upside down) (d) 6325 (upside down)

10. %9≠☆
    (a) ≠%9☆ (b) ☆9%≠ (c) ☆≠9% (d) ☆≠9%

DIRECTIONS (Qs. 11-15): Find the water image of each of the figure (X).

11. Figure (X) (a) (b) (c) (d)

12. Figure (X) (a) (b) (c) (d)

13. Figure (X) (a) (b) (c) (d)

14. Figure (X) (a) (b) (c) (d)

15. Figure (X) (a) (b) (c) (d)

DIRECTIONS (Qs. 16-18): Choose the option from the alternatives that closely resembles the water image.

16. PEACE
    (a) PEACE (upside down) (b) PEACE (upside down) (c) PEACE (upside down) (d) ECAEP (upside down)

17. INFER
    (a) REFNI (upside down) (b) IFENR (upside down) (c) INFER (upside down) (d) IEFNI (upside down)

18. 275%1
    (a) 1%572 (upside down) (b) 1%5752 (upside down) (c) %5∆51 (upside down) (d) 1%5∆5 (upside down)

DIRECTIONS (Qs. 19-21): Find the mirror image each of the given figure (X), if mirror is placed along dotted line.

19. **STROKE** | ƨTROKƧ EKORTS ROKETS ƎKORTƧ
    Figure (X)   (a)   (b)   (c)   (d)

20. **QUALITY** | ɄИAᒉITY YTIJAUQ YTIJAUQ YTIJAUꝖ
    Figure (X)   (a)   (b)   (c)   (d)

21. K2B3M4R | M4RƐBSK ꓤㄣMƐBSK ꓤㄣMK2B3 ꓤㄣMƐBSK
    Figure (X)   (a)   (b)   (c)   (d)

DIRECTIONS (Qs. 22-24): Choose the one from the alternatives which most closely resembles the mirror image.

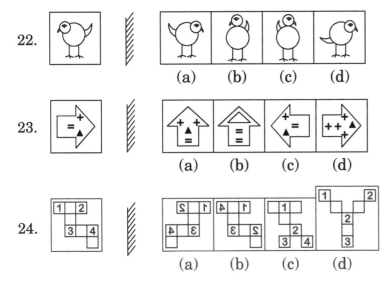

22. (a) (b) (c) (d)

23. (a) (b) (c) (d)

24. (a) (b) (c) (d)

DIRECTIONS (Qs. 25-28): Choose the one from the alternatives which most closely resembles the water reflection of the image given below.

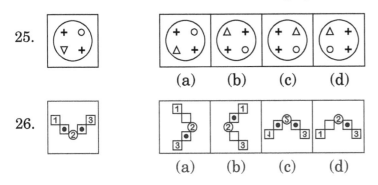

25. (a) (b) (c) (d)

26. (a) (b) (c) (d)

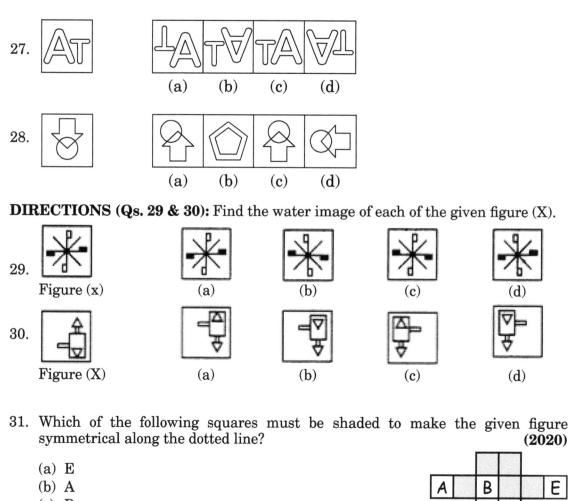

DIRECTIONS (Qs. 29 & 30): Find the water image of each of the given figure (X).

31. Which of the following squares must be shaded to make the given figure symmetrical along the dotted line? **(2020)**

    (a) E
    (b) A
    (c) B
    (d) C

32. Select the correct mirror image of the given word **(2021)**

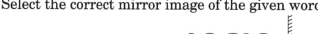

Mirror

LEVEL-2

DIRECTIONS (Qs. 1-3) : Find the mirror image of each of given figure (X).

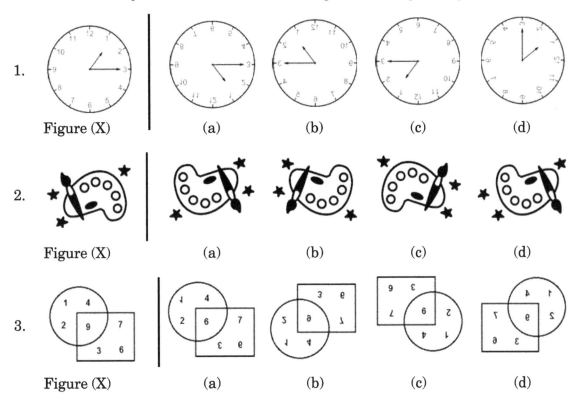

DIRECTIONS (Qs. 4-6): Choose the one from the alternatives which most closely resembles the mirror image of the given combination

4. BENIGN

NƎIGƎB	NGINƎB	BƎGINE	BEGINE
(a)	(b)	(c)	(d)

5. CURRENT

TNƎRRUƆ	TNƎRRUƆ	ƆURRƎNT	ƆURRƎNT
(a)	(b)	(c)	(d)

6. GULF

ꟻLUG	ƆULꟻ	LGUꟻ	ƆUFI
(a)	(b)	(c)	(d)

DIRECTIONS (Qs. 7-9): In each of the questions there is a picture which is followed by four alternatives (a), (b), (c), (d). Identify the option which most closely resembles the mirror reflection of the given image.

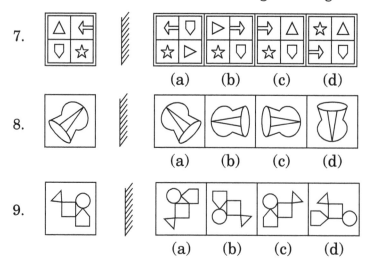

DIRECTIONS (Qs. 10-12): Find the water image of each given figure (X).

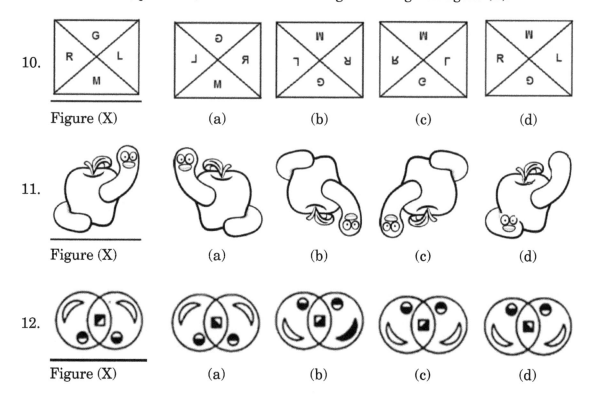

DIRECTIONS (Qs. 13-15): Choose the one from the alternatives which most closely resembles the water image of the given combination.

13. TULIP	PULIT	ꟼIJUT	TUJIꟼ	ᒐႶᒐIꟼ
	(a)	(b)	(c)	(d)

14. PARKING	ꟼVRKIИG	ꟼVRING	PVRKIИG	ꟼVRKING
	(a)	(b)	(c)	(d)

15. LUMINOUS	TUMINOUS	SИOИIWꞀ	ꞀႶWIИOႶS	ꙄႶꞀႶWIИO
	(a)	(b)	(c)	(d)

DIRECTIONS (Qs. 16-18): Choose the one from the alternatives which most closely resembles the water image of the given image.

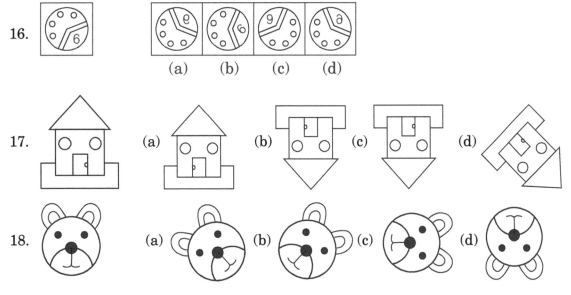

19. Find the mirror image of the given Fig.(X), if the mirror is placed along MN.

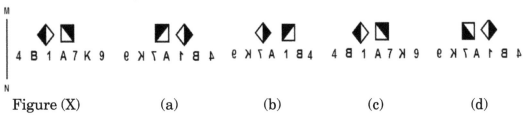

20. Find the water image of the given Fig.(X).

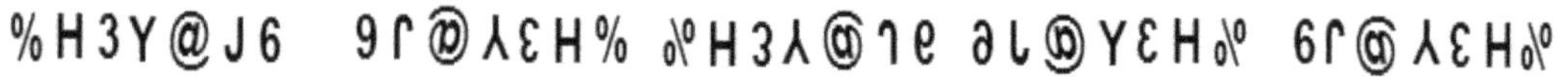

Figure (X) (a) (b) (c) (d)

DIRECTIONS (Qs. 21 & 22): In each of the questions there is a picture which is followed by alternatives (a), (b), (c), (d). Identify the option which most closely resembles the mirror reflection of the given image.

21. 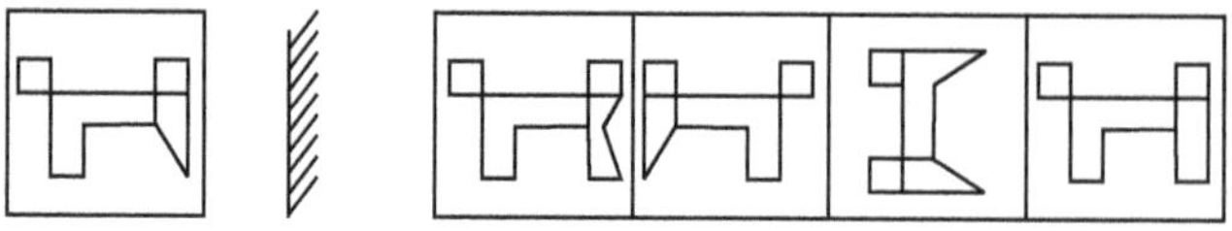

(a) (b) (c) (d)

22. 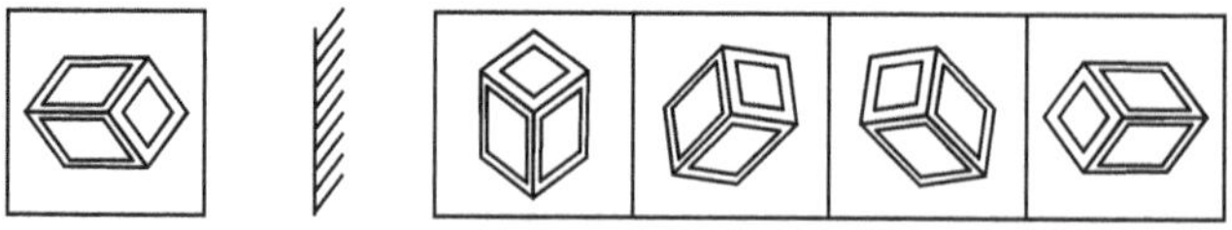

(a) (b) (c) (d)

23. Which of the following options is the mirror image of figure (X)?

Figure (X) Mirror

(Olympiad)

(a)  (b) 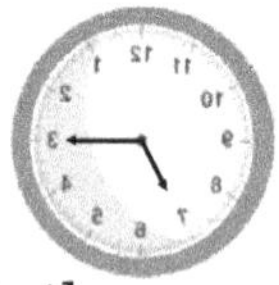 (c)  (d) 

24. Which of the following is the correct mirror image of given word, if the mirror is placed vertically left?

V T 5 6 B 2 L

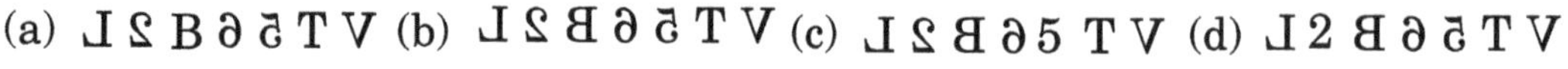

(Olympiad)

25. Find the mirror image of the given Fig. (X), if the mirror is placed along MN.

(a) 

(b) 

(c) 

(d) 

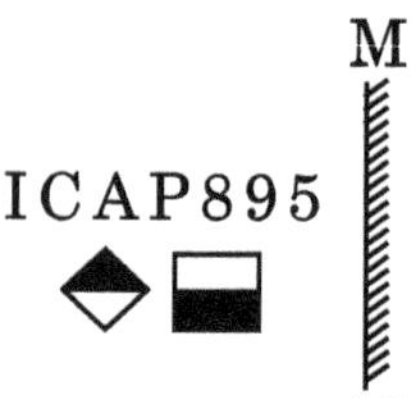

Figure (X)

(Olympiad)

26. Select the mirror image of Fig (X), if the mirror is placed along MN.

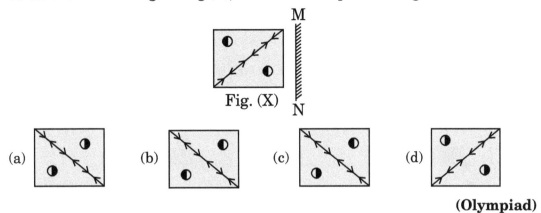

(Olympiad)

27. Select the correct mirror image of Figure (X), if the mirror is placed along MN.

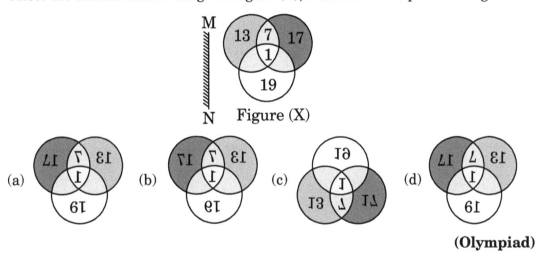

(Olympiad)

28. Select the correct mirror image, if the mirror is placed vertically to the left.

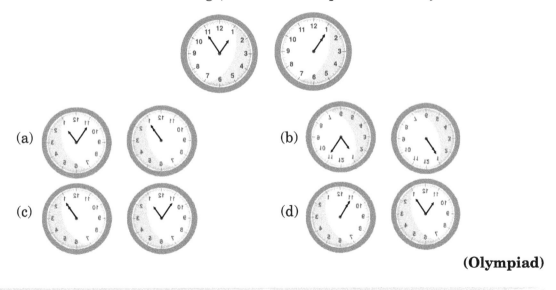

(Olympiad)

29. Select the correct mirror image of the given Fig. (X).

(a)    (b)

(c)    (d)    **(Olympiad)**

30. Select the correct mirror image of Fig (X).

IMO2014

Mirror **(Olympiad)**

(a)  ꟻIOƧOMI   (b)  IMOƧOIꟻ   (c)  ꟻIOƧOWI   (d)  ꙄIOƧOMI

31. Select the correct mirror image of the given figure. **(2018)**

(a) 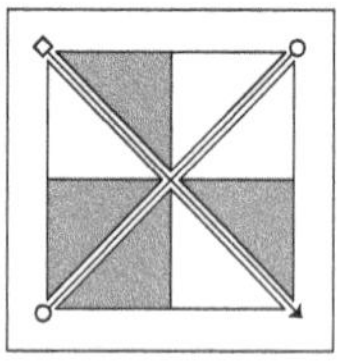   (b)

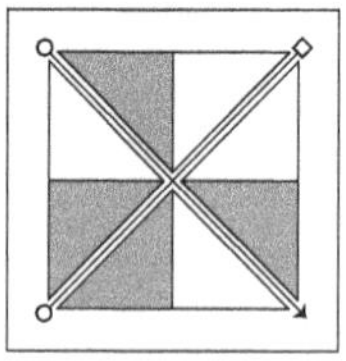

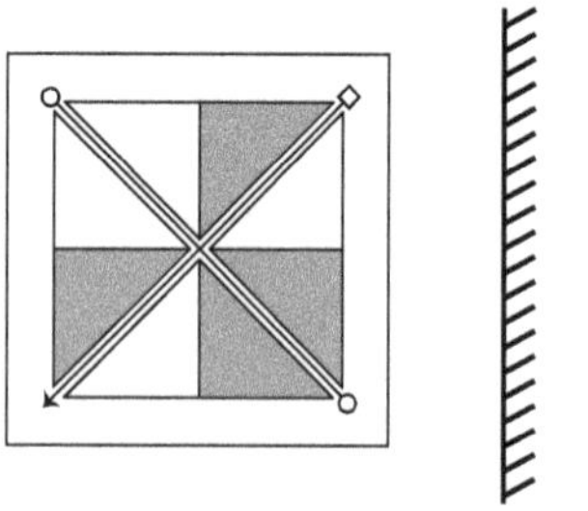

(c) 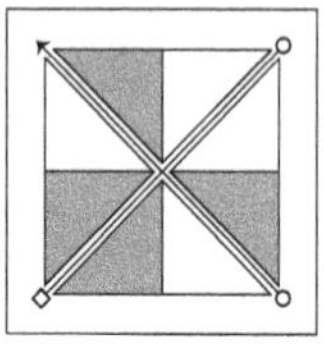   (d)

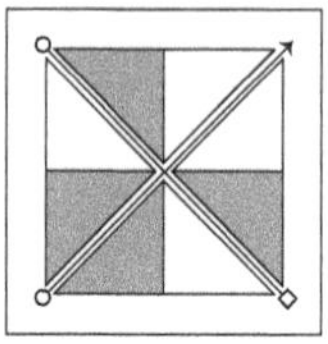

32. Which of the following Venn diagrams best represents the relationship amongst, "Tailor, Female and Father"? **(2019)**

(a) 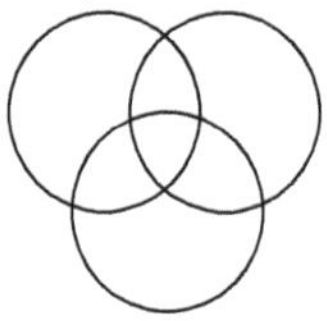   (b)

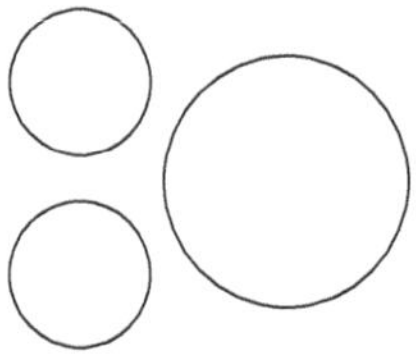

(c) 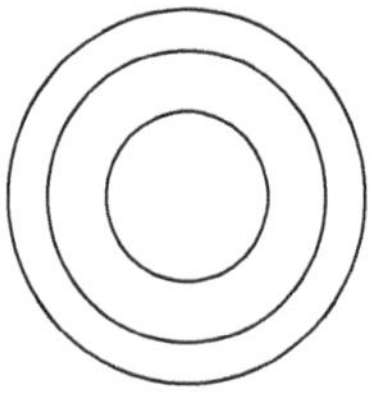   (d)

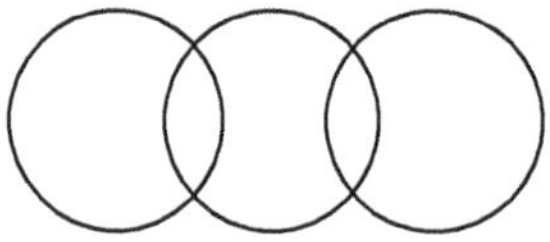

33. Find the correct mirror image of the given figure. **(2019)**

34. Find the correct water image of the given word **(2020)**

QUIET

(a) UQIET   (b) ⊥ƎIUꝊ   (c) ꝊNIE⊥   (d) ⊥ƎIUꝊ

35. Select the correct water image of the given figure **(2020)**

36. Find the correct water image of the given figure. **(2021)**

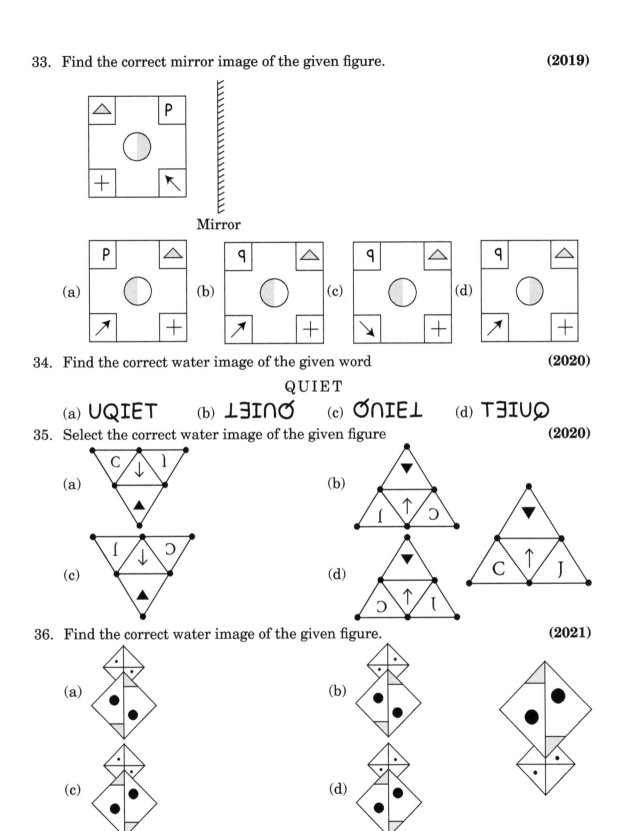

37. Find the correct mirror image of the given combination of letters and numbers, if the mirror is placed vertically to the right. **(2022)**

T4RE3NID

(a)    (b)    (c)    (d)

38. Find the water image of the given figure. **(2022)**

(a) 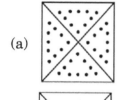   (b)

(c) 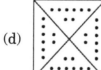   (d)

39. A piece of paper is folded and cut as shown below in the question figures. From the given answer figures, indicate how it will appear when opened. **(2022)**

(a)   (b)

(c)   (d)

Answers and Explanations

Level-1

1. (d)   2. (d)   3. (b)   4. (d)
5. (c)
6. (a) PROVE | PROVE
7. (a) BATTLE | BATTLE
8. (b) UNION | UNION
9. (c) 5239 | 5239
10. (d) % 9 ≠ ☆ | ☆ ≠ 9 %
11. (c) Object / Water / Image
12. (c)   13. (b)   14. (a)   15. (d)
16. (a) PEACE / PEACE

17. (c) INFER / INFER (mirror)

18. (b) 275%1 / 275%1 (mirror)

19. (d) **STROKE** | **STROKE** (mirror)
   Object | Image
   Mirror

20. (c) **QUALITY** | **QUALITY** (mirror)
   Object | Image
   Mirror

21. (b) K 2 B 3 M 4 R | R 4 M 3 B 2 K (mirror)
   Object | Image
   Mirror

22. (a) 23. (c) 24. (a) 25. (b)
26. (c) 27. (d) 28. (c) 29. (b)
30. (a)
31. (c)

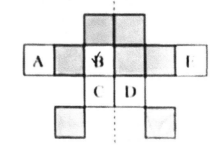

32. (d)

Level-2

SOLUTIONS (Qs. 1-3)

1. (b)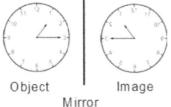

2. (c)

3. (d)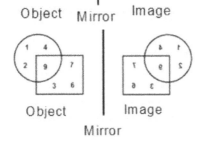

4. (b)   5. (a)   6. (a)

7. (c)

8. (a)

9. (c)

10. (c)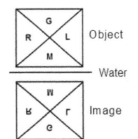

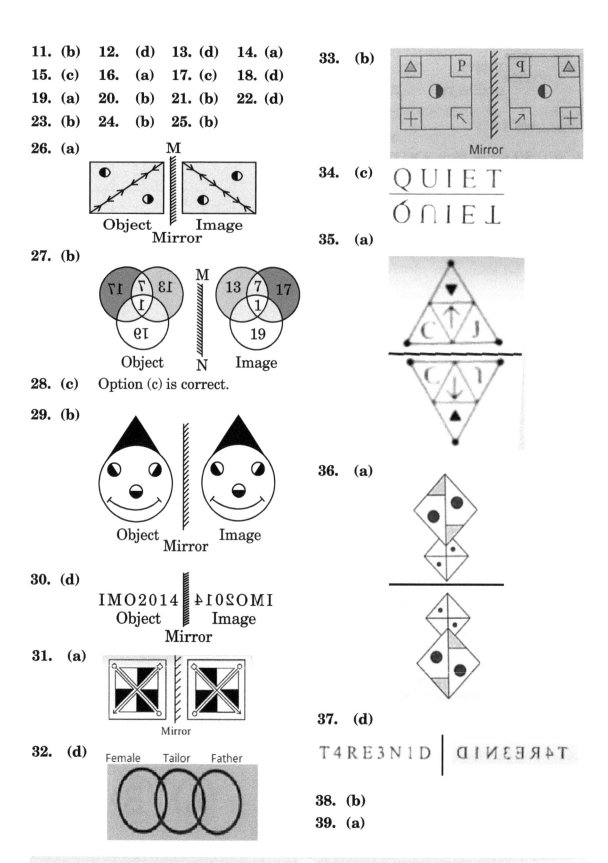

CHAPTER
14

Embedded Figures

OBJECTIVES
- It will measure cognitive functioning and style of students.
- Students will be able to find shapes within the large more complex image.

INTRODUCTION
A figure is said to be embedded in figure (X), if figure (X) contains a part of that figure.

Types of Questions

Type I: Identify the Small Part hidden in given figure:
In such type of problems, a figure (X) is given, followed by four parts, such that one of them is hidden in figure (X), students have to identify that part.

Examples

DIRECTION (Example 1 - 3) : In the following questions, identify which shape is hidden in the figure (X).

1.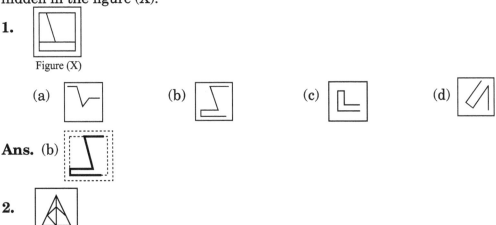

Ans. (b)

2.

(a) (b) (c) (d)

Ans. (d)

3.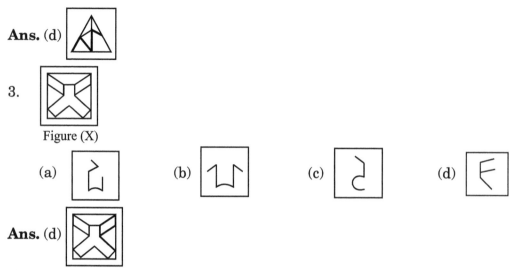

Ans. (d)

Type II: Identify the Figure in Which Given Part is Hidden

In such problems, a figure X is given which is followed by four alternative of complex figures in such a way that figure (X) is hidden or embedded in one and only one of them. The students have to identify that particular figure in which the figure (X) is hidden.

DIRECTIONS (Example 4 & 5) Choose the alternative which contains figure (X) as its part.

4.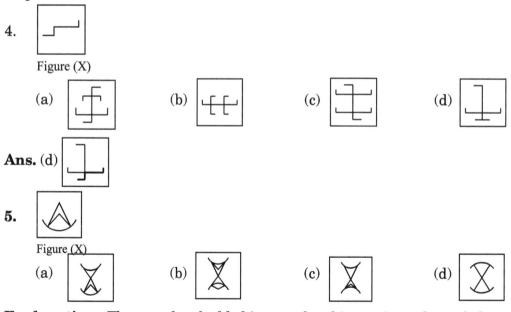

Explanation : The actual embedded image of real image is as shown below:

Ans. (a)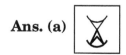

LEVEL-1

DIRECTIONS (Qs. 1-12): One problem figure is followed by four options. In one of the options, the figure similar to the problem figure is embedded / hidden. Find the option.

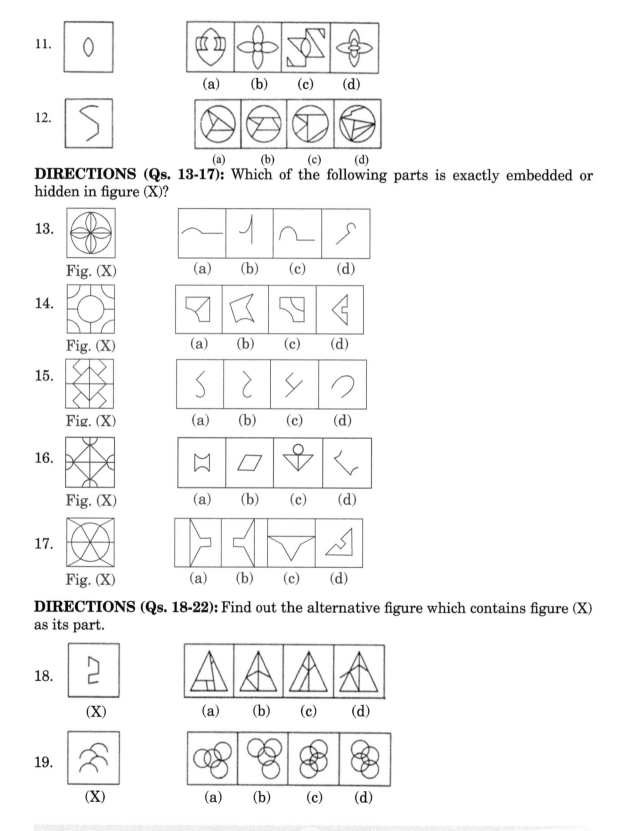

20.
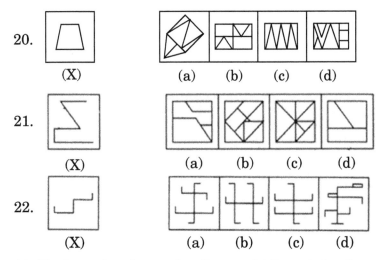

21.

22.

23. Find out the alternative figure which contains figure (X) as its part.

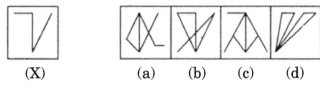

DIRECTIONS (Qs. 24-30): Which of the following options is exactly embedded or hidden in figure (X) ?

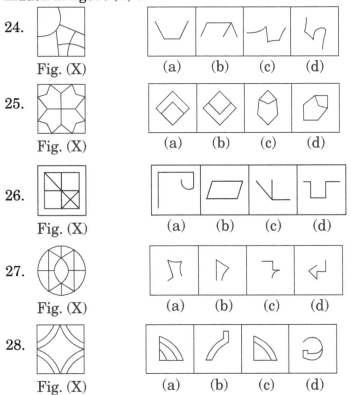

29.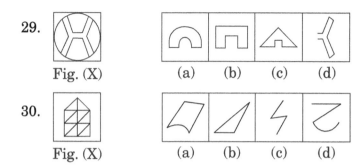

30.

31. Which of the following options will complete the given figure pattern? (2020)

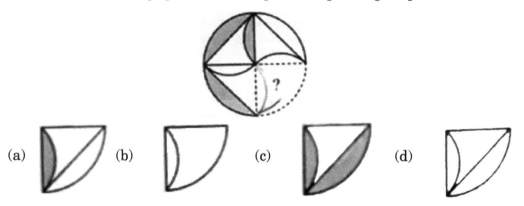

LEVEL-2

DIRECTIONS (Qs. 1-16): One problem figure is followed by four options. In one of the options, the figure similar to the problem figure is embedded / hidden. Find the option.

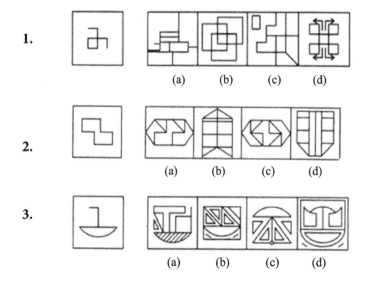

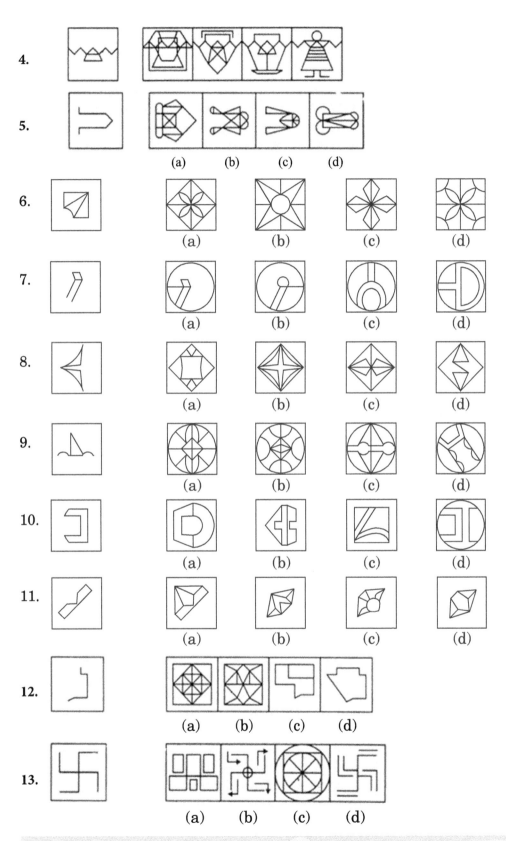

14.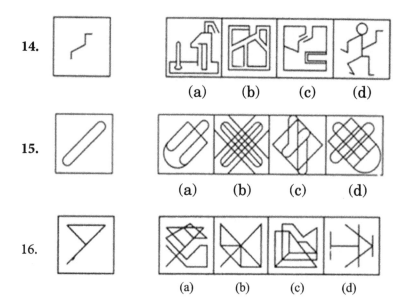

15.

16.

DIRECTIONS (Qs. 17-21): Which of the following parts is exactly embedded or hidden in figure (X)?

17.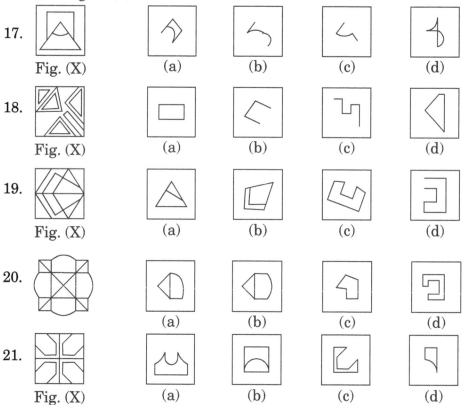

18.

19.

20.

21.

DIRECTIONS (Qs. 22-26): Find out the alternative figure which contains figure (X) as its part.

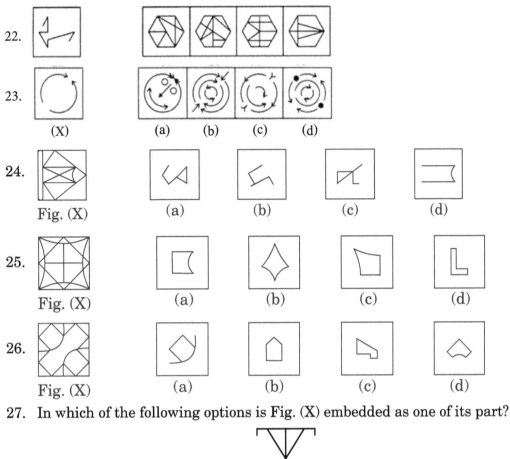

27. In which of the following options is Fig. (X) embedded as one of its part?

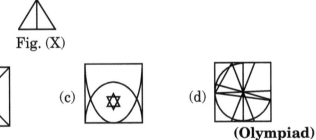

(Olympiad)

28. Select a figure from the given options, in which Fig. (X) is exactly embedded as one of its part.

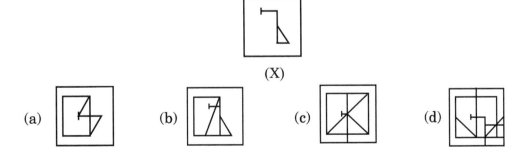

(Olympiad)

29. Select a figure from the options in which figure (X) is exactly embedded as one of its part.

Fig. (X)

(a) (b) (c) (d)

(Olympiad)

30. Which of the following options is exactly embedded or hidden in Figure (X)?

Fig. (X)

(a) (b) (c) (d)

(Olympiad)

31. Select a figure from the options which will replace the (?) to complete the pattern in the given figure. **(2018)**

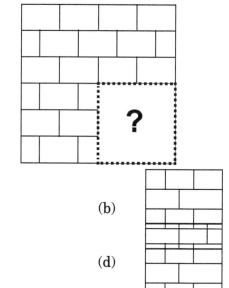

(a) 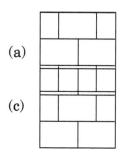 (b)

(c) (d)

32. Select a figure from the options which will replace the '?' in the given figure to complete the pattern. **(2019)**

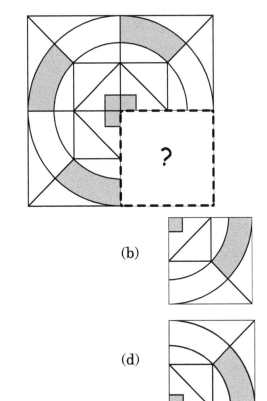

33. Select a figure from the options which is exactly embedded in the given figure as one of its parts. **(2021)**

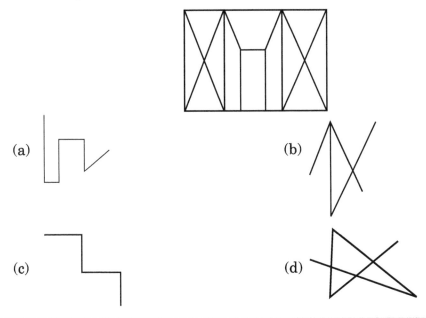

34. Which of the following options will complete the pattern in the given figure?

(2021)

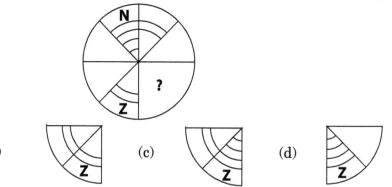

35. Select a figure from the options which is not exactly embedded in the given figure as one of its parts.

(2022)

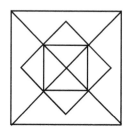

Answers and Explanation

Level-1

Solutions(Qs. 1-3)

1. (d)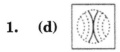

2. (a)

3. (b)

4. (d)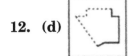

5. (b)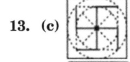

6. (a)

7. (a) 8. (d)
9. (c) 10. (b)
11. (c)

12. (b)

13. (a)

14. (c)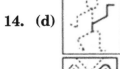

15. (c)

16. (d)

17. (c)

18. (a) 19. (c)
20. (c) 21. (d)
22. (c) 23. (b)

24. (c)

25. (d)

26. (c)

27. (b) 28. (c)
29. (d) 30. (c)
31. (a) Option A will complete the given figure pattern.

Level-2

1. (b) 2. (c) 3. (b)
4. (d) 5. (b) 6. (b)
7. (a) 8. (b) 9. (c)
10. (d) 11. (a)

12. (d)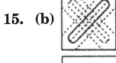

13. (c)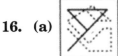

14. (d)

15. (b)

16. (a)

17. (c) 18. (d)
19. (a) 20. (b)
21. (c)

22. (d)

23. (a)

24. (d)

25. (c)

26. (a) 27. (d)
28. (b) 29. (a)
30. (b)
31. (a) Figure given in option A will complete the pattern.

32. (b) Figure shown in option B will complete the pattern.

33. (b) Figure shown in option B is exactly embedded in the given figure.

34. (a) Option A will complete the pattern in the given figure.

35. (c) Figure shown in option C is not exactly embedded in the given figure.

CHAPTER

15

Visual Reasoning

OBJECTIVES

- To identify relationships, similarities and differences between shapes and patterns.
- To recognise visual sequences and relationships between objects and remembering these.

INTRODUCTION

Visual reasoning is the process of manipulating one's mental image of an object to reach a certain conclusion.

Types of Questions

TYPES OF VISUAL REASONING

1. Paper Folding and Cutting

In these types of questions, there are three or four figures given in one line. Each figure followed a pattern. Each figure consists of a dotted line along which it is to be folded and the arrow shows the side which it is to be folded.

After folding, the paper is cut or punched and then students have to visualize the correct figure that will be produced when the paper is unfolded.

Direction (Example 1) : In the following example, a piece of paper is folded and cut and then unfolded. One of the four options resembles the unfolded paper. Select the correct option.

Example 1.

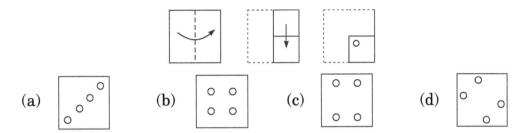

Ans. (b) The punch is made at the corner of the folded paper near the top of the left end. So, the unfolded paper shows equidistance punches.

2. **Merging and Splitting of Images**

Merging of images: In this segment, there are two different images. The student has to visualize the resulting image which will be produced by merging these two images.

Direction (Example 2) : Two different images (x) and (y) are given which will be merged to form an image which appears in one of the options given below. Identify the correct option.

Example 2.

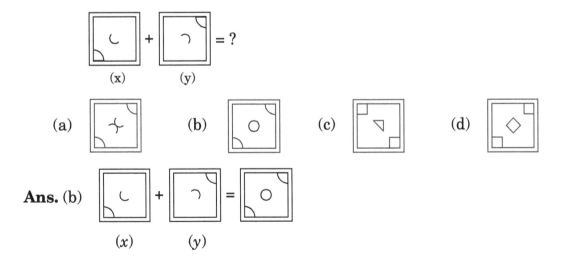

3. Completion of Image

In these types of questions, a particular matrix or a set of figures follows a particular pattern, out of which one part, generally a quarter, is left blank. Now, the student has to identify the missing part out of four alternatives that follow the pattern.

Direction (Example 3) : Complete the given figure.

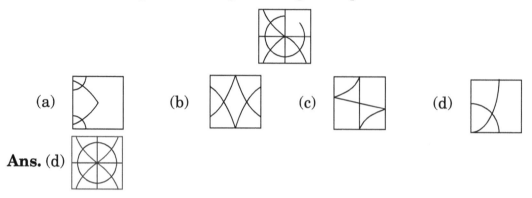

Ans. (d)

Example 4. Complete the given figure.

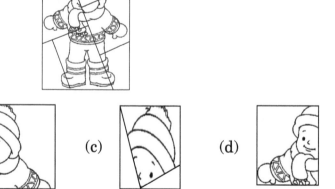

Ans. (c)

Solution: From the given four alternatives, figure (c) will correctly fit into the missing section.

LEVEL-1

DIRECTIONS (Qs. 1-5) : In each of the following questions, group the given figures into three classes using each figure only once.

1.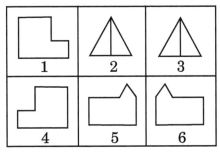

(a) 1,4 ; 2,3 ; 5,6 (b) 1,5 ; 2,6 ; 4,3
(c) 1,6 ; 2,3 ; 4,5 (d) 1,2 ; 3,6 ; 4,5

2.

(a) 1,3,9 ; 2,5,6 ; 4,7,8 (b) 1,3,9 ; 2,7,8 ; 4,5,6
(c) 1,2,4 ; 3,5,7 ; 6,8,9 (d) 1,3,6 ; 2,4,8 ; 5,7,9

3.

(a) 1,5,9 ; 3,6,2 ; 4,7,8 (b) 1,3,5 ; 2,4,6 ; 7,8,9
(c) 1,2,3 ; 4,5,6 ; 7,8,9 (d) 1,9,7 ; 2,8,5 ; 3,4,6

4.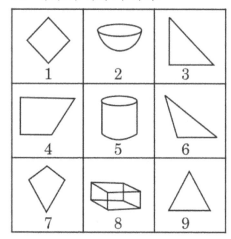

(a) 1,4,7 ; 2,5,9 ; 3,6,7 (b) 1,3,4 ; 2,5,8 ; 6,7,9
(c) 1,2,3 ; 4,5,6 ; 7,8,9 (d) 1,4,7 ; 2,5,8 ; 3,6,9

5.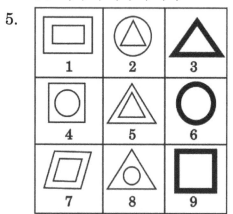

(a) 1,5,7 ; 2,4,6 ; 3,9,8 (b) 1,5,7 ; 2,4,8 ; 3,6,9
(c) 1,4,7 ; 2,5,8 ; 3,6,9 (d) 1,7,9 ; 3,5,8 ; 2,4,6

DIRECTIONS (Qs. 6-10) : Given below are some questions in which two different parts of an image are given. Identify the image after merging the two parts.

6.

(a)   (b)   (c)   (d)

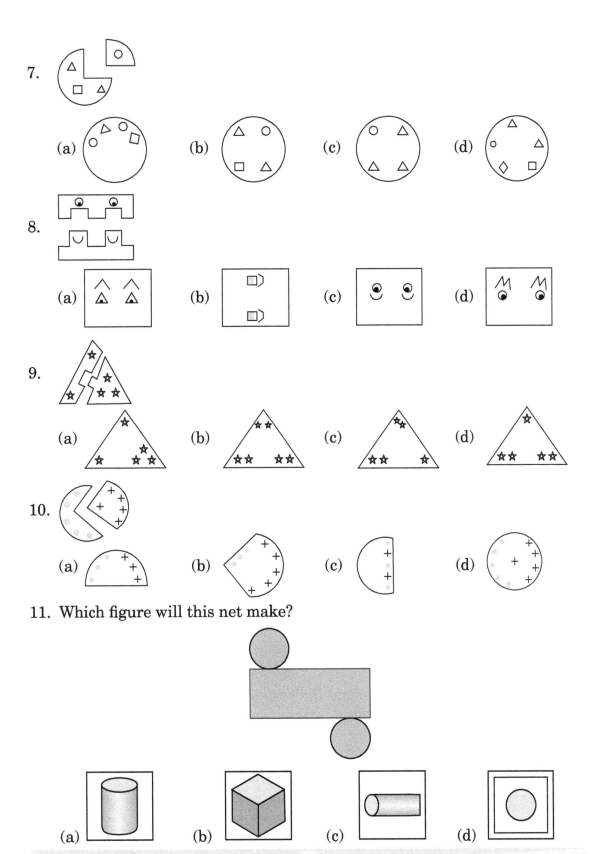

12. Which net will make this figure?

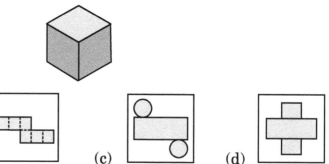

13. Look at the puzzle. Which piece completes the puzzle?

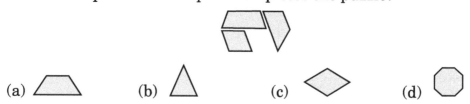

DIRECTIONS (Qs. 14 & 15) : Given below is the folded form of paper. Which of the following shows the correct figure when the paper is unfolded along the dotted line?

14.

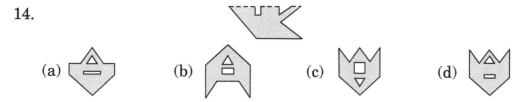

15. Which of the following shows the correct figure when the paper given below is unfolded along the dotted line?

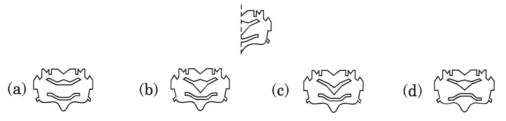

DIRECTIONS (Qs. 16-20) : In the figures shown below, one of the shapes (a-d) is identical to the first figure but has been rotated. Which figure is identical to figure X after rotation?

16.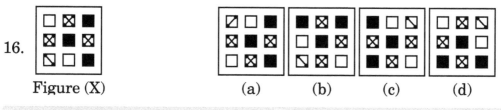

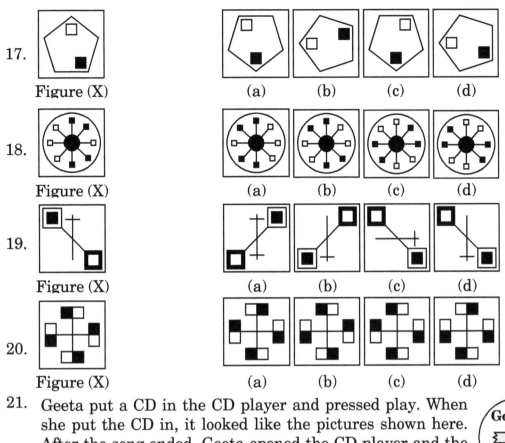

21. Geeta put a CD in the CD player and pressed play. When she put the CD in, it looked like the pictures shown here. After the song ended, Geeta opened the CD player and the CD looked like it had rotated (turned) 90° clockwise. Which figure given below shows the CD after it rotated (turned) 90° clockwise?

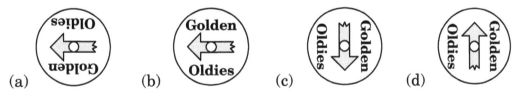

22. Sujith drew the design given.

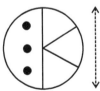

He rotated the design by 180° and then flipped it over the dashed line. Which of the following is Sujith's final design?

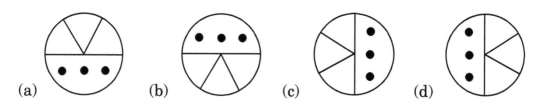

Directions (Qs. 23-27) : In each of the following questions, find out which of the figures (a), (b), (c) and (d) can be formed from the pieces given in figure (X).

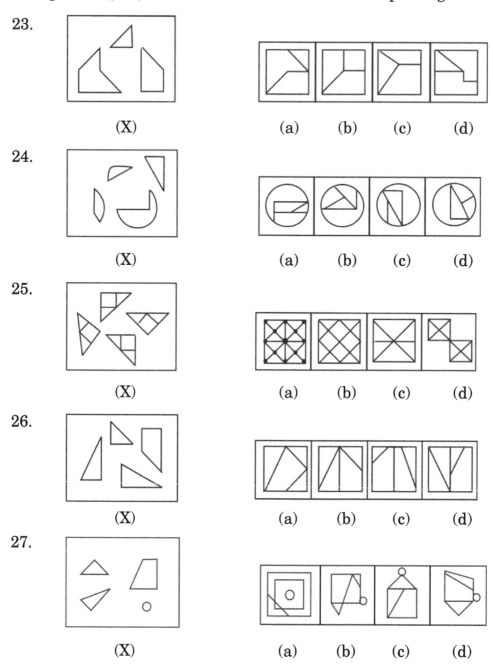

Directions (Qs. 28-30) : In each of the following questions, a key figure marked (X) is given, followed by four other alternative figures marked (a), (b), (c) and (d). It is required to select one figure from the alternatives, which fits exactly into figure (X) to form a complete square.

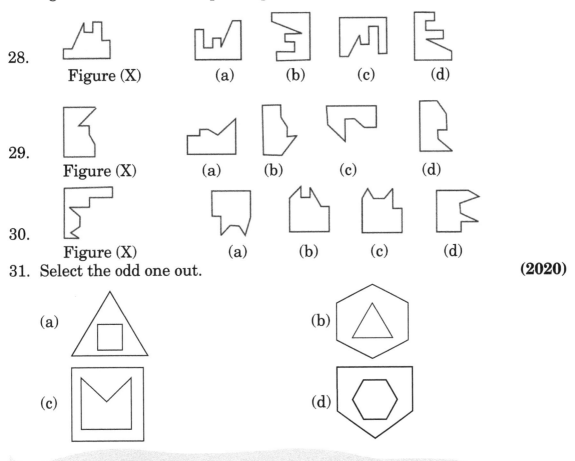

31. Select the odd one out. **(2020)**

LEVEL-2

Directions (Qs. 1-5) : In each of the following questions, a set of five alternative figures 1, 2, 3, 4 and 5 followed by a set of four alternatives (a), (b), (c) and (d) is provided. It is required to select the alternative which represents three out of the five alternative figures which when fitted into each other would form a complete square.

1.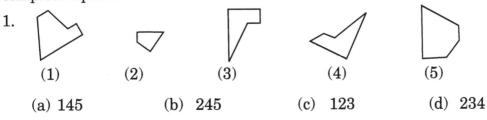

(a) 145   (b) 245   (c) 123   (d) 234

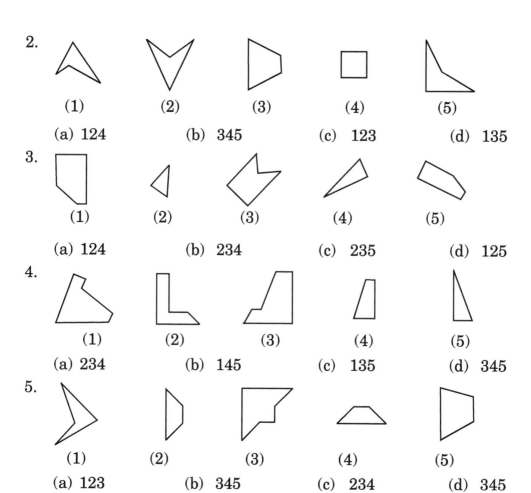

(a) 124 (b) 345 (c) 123 (d) 135

(a) 124 (b) 234 (c) 235 (d) 125

(a) 234 (b) 145 (c) 135 (d) 345

(a) 123 (b) 345 (c) 234 (d) 345

Directions (Qs. 6-10) : In each of the questions given below, there is a box with six sections which are occupied by segments of a complete image. One of the four alternatives is not a part of the complete image. Now, identify which alternative is not a part of the complete image.

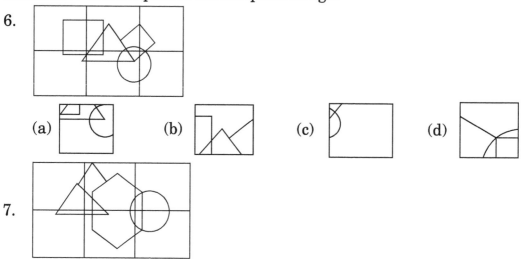

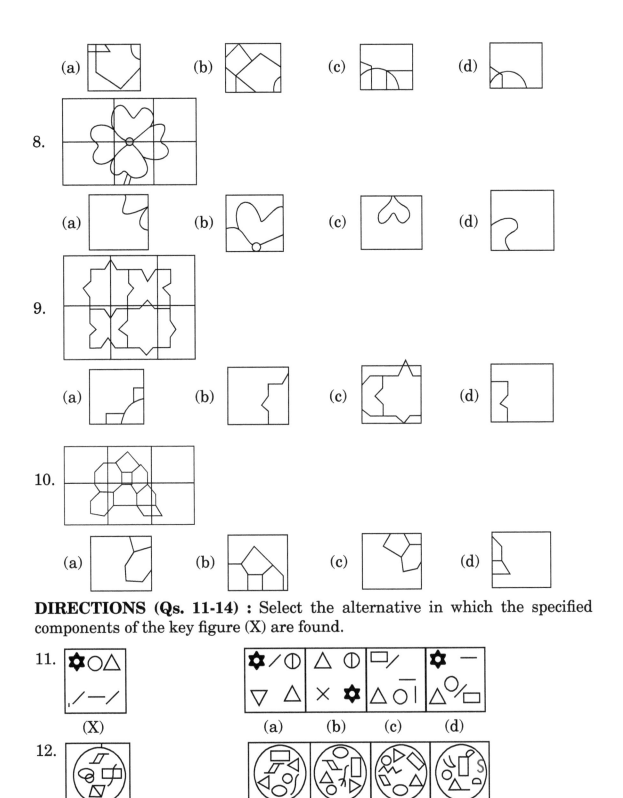

DIRECTIONS (Qs. 11-14): Select the alternative in which the specified components of the key figure (X) are found.

13.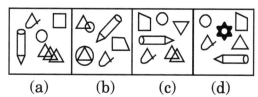
(X) (a) (b) (c) (d)

14.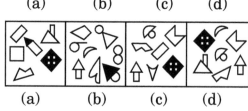
(X) (a) (b) (c) (d)

DIRECTIONS (Qs. 15-19): In each of the following questions, group the given figures into three classes using each figure only once.

15.
  1   2   3   4   5   6

  7   8   9

(a) 1, 4, 8; 3, 5, 7; 2, 6, 9   (b) 1, 6, 9; 2, 4, 3; 5, 7, 8
(c) 2, 5, 6; 1, 3, 7; 4, 8, 9   (d) 1, 3, 5; 2, 4, 6; 7, 8, 9

16.
  1   2   3   4   5   6

  7   8   9

(a) 1, 2, 4; 5, 7, 9; 3, 6, 8   (b) 1, 3, 5; 2, 6, 8; 4, 7, 9

(c) 1, 2, 7; 3, 8, 9; 4, 5, 6   (d) 1, 5, 7; 4, 6, 9; 2, 3, 8

17.
  1   2   3   4   5   6

  7   8   9

(a) 1, 2, 9; 6, 7, 8; 3, 4, 5 (b) 1, 6, 9; 3, 5, 7; 2, 4, 8
(c) 2, 7, 9; 4, 5, 6; 1, 2, 3 (d) 1, 5, 9; 3, 6, 8; 2, 4, 7

18.

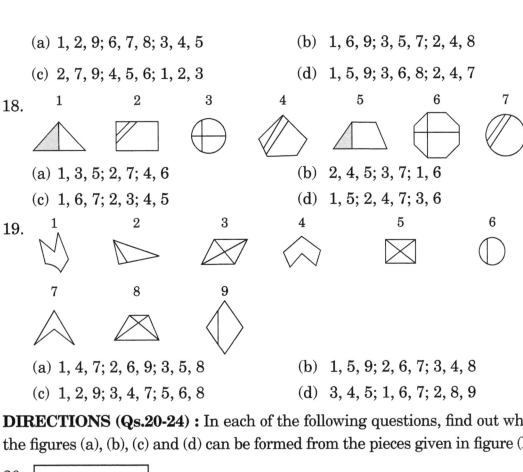

(a) 1, 3, 5; 2, 7; 4, 6 (b) 2, 4, 5; 3, 7; 1, 6
(c) 1, 6, 7; 2, 3; 4, 5 (d) 1, 5; 2, 4, 7; 3, 6

19.

(a) 1, 4, 7; 2, 6, 9; 3, 5, 8 (b) 1, 5, 9; 2, 6, 7; 3, 4, 8
(c) 1, 2, 9; 3, 4, 7; 5, 6, 8 (d) 3, 4, 5; 1, 6, 7; 2, 8, 9

DIRECTIONS (Qs.20-24) : In each of the following questions, find out which of the figures (a), (b), (c) and (d) can be formed from the pieces given in figure (X).

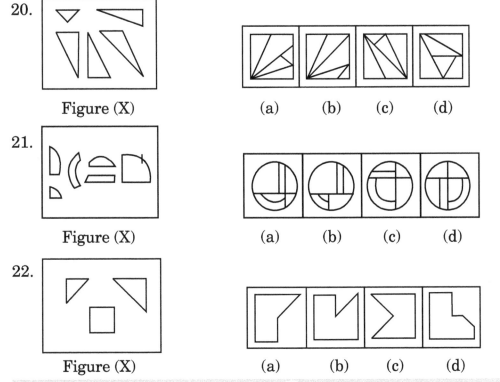

23.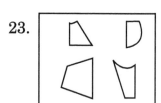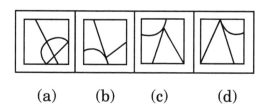

Figure (X)   (a)   (b)   (c)   (d)

24.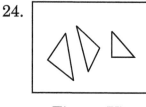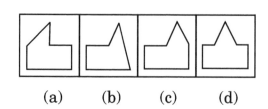

Figure (X)   (a)   (b)   (c)   (d)

25. How many cubes must be added to solid A so that it becomes solid B?

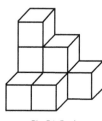

Solid A   Solid B

(a) 8
(b) 19
(c) 11
(d) 27

(Olympiad)

26. Which of the following options is exactly same as that of Fig. (X)?

Fig. (X)

(a)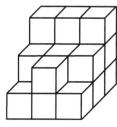

(b)

(c)

(d)

(Olympiad)

27. Which of the following figures is the top view of the solid?

(a)

(b)

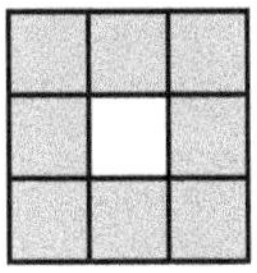

(c)

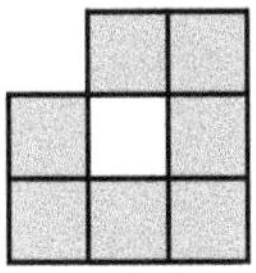

(d)

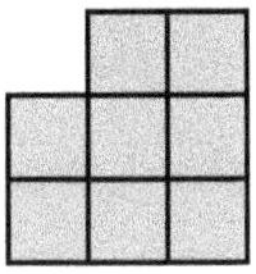

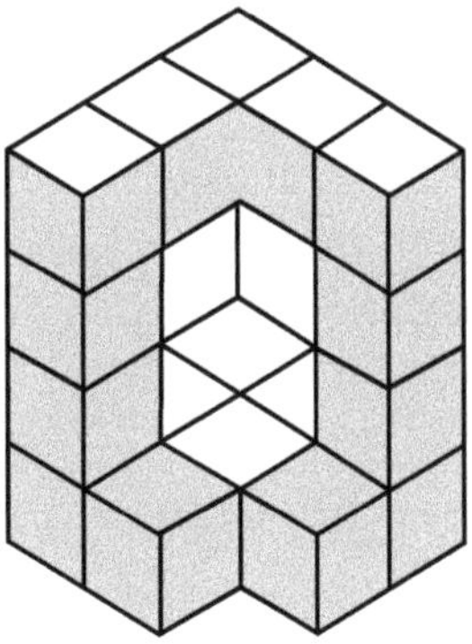

(Olympiad)

28. How many minimum squares must be shaded to make the given figure symmetric?

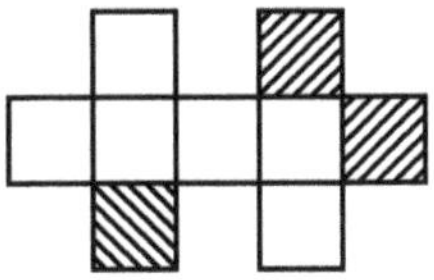

(a) 1   (b) 2
(c) 3   (d) 4   **(Olympiad)**

29. Identify the two figures which are out of position place and requires interchanging of position to put the entire series in order.

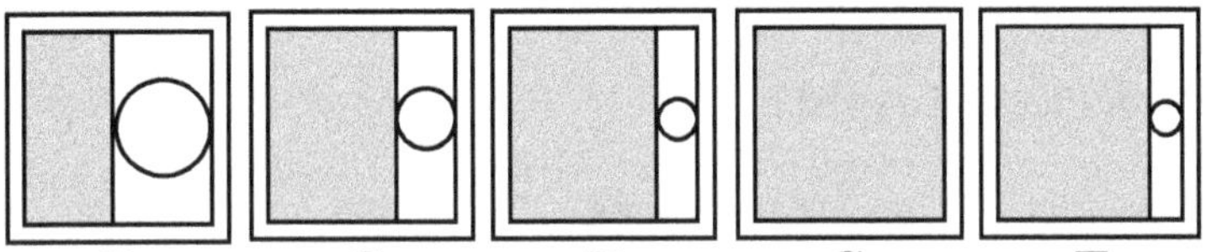

P   Q   R   S   T

(a) Q and R   (b) S and T   (c) R and P   (d) P and S
(Olympiad)

30. Consider the figures X and Y showing a sheet of paper folded and punched in figure Z. Select the figure. Which will most closely resemble the unfolded form of figure Z.

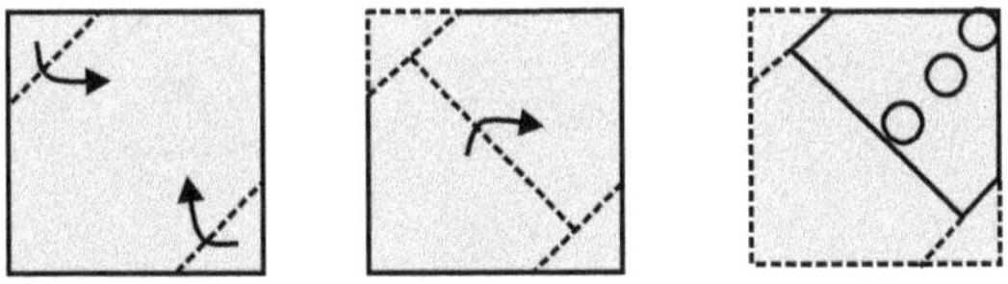

X   Y   Z

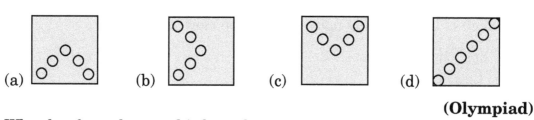

(a) (b) (c) (d)

(Olympiad)

31. What has been done to this letter?

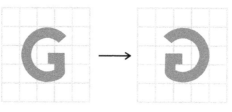

(a) flip (b) turn (c) slide (d) None of these

(Olympiad)

32. Which of the following squares must be shaded to make the given figure symmetrical along the dotted line? **(2020)**

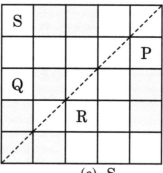

(a) Q (b) P (c) S (d) R

33. Which of the following options will be obtained after rotating the given figure $4\frac{1}{4}$ turns to the right? **(2022)**

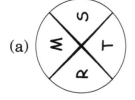 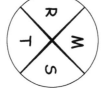 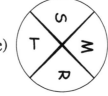 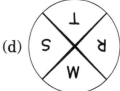

(a) (b) (c) (d)

Answers and Explanation

Level-1

1. **(a)** (1, 4), (2, 3) and (5, 6) are three different pairs of identical figures.

2. **(a)** 1, 3, 9 have one element placed inside a different element.
   2, 5, 6 contain two mutually perpendicular lines dividing the figure into four parts.
   4, 7, 8 have two similar elements (unequal in size) attached to each other.

3. **(c)** 1, 2, 3 are figures composed of two straight lines.
   4, 5, 6 are figures composed of three straight lines.
   7, 8, 9 are figures composed of four straight lines.

4. **(d)** 1, 4, 7 are all (two-dimensional) quadrilaterals.
   2, 5, 8 are all three-dimensional figures.
   3, 6, 9 are all (two-dimensional) triangles.

5. **(b)** 1, 5, 7 have two similar elements, one inside the other.
   2, 4, 8 have one element placed inside a different element.
   3, 6, 9 have two similar elements, one inside the other and the area between the two elements is shaded.

6. (a)   7. (b)   8. (c)
9. (a)   10. (d)

11. **(a)** Imagine folding this net so that two edges of the rectangle each wrap around a circle.

    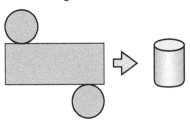

    This net makes a cylinder.

12. **(b)** Fold this net along the dotted lines. This net makes a cube. This is the correct net.

    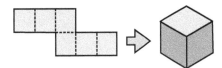

13. **(c)**

14. (d)   15. (b)   16. (c)
17. (b)   18. (a)   19. (d)
20. (b)   21. (c)
22. **(d)** Design after 180° rotation.

    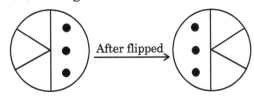

23. (a)   24. (c)   25. (b)
26. (b)   27. (c)
28. **(c)**

    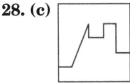

29. (b)

30. (c)

31. **(b)** Number of sides in inner figure = Number of sides in outer figure + 1

Level-2

1. (b)

2. (d)

3. (d)

4. (d)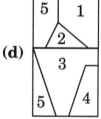

5. (c)

6. (d) 7. (c) 8. (c)
9. (a) 10. (c) 11. (b)
12. (a) 13. (c) 14. (d)
15. (a) 1, 4, 8; 3, 5, 7; 2, 6, 9
16. (c) 1, 2, 7; 3, 8, 9; 4, 5, 6
17. (b) 1, 6, 9; 3, 5, 7; 2, 4, 8
18. (d) 1, 5; 2, 4, 7; 3, 6
19. (a) 1, 4, 7; 2, 6, 9; 3, 5, 8

20. (c) 21. (a) 22. (a)
23. (b) 24. (b) 25. (c)
26. (c) 27. (d) 28. (a)
29. (b) 30. (d)

31. **(a)** This is a flip. Flip the letter over the dotted line.

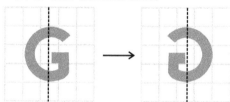

32. **(d)** R

33. **(b)** Total rotation = $4\frac{1}{4} = 4 + \frac{1}{4}$

1 rotation = 360°

¼ rotation = $360° \times \frac{1}{4} = 90°$

On rotating the figure 4 ¼ turns to the right, we get the figure given in option B.

Milton Keynes UK
Ingram Content Group UK Ltd.
UKHW030634051024
449102UK00007B/50